10/11

The Apple Lover's Cookbook

Pork and Apple Pie with Cheddar-Sage Crust
(page 129)

The Apple Lover's Cookbook

AMY TRAVERSO

photographs by Squire Fox

W. W. Norton & Company

New York • London

For information about permission to reproduce selections from this book,
write to Permissions, W. W. Norton & Company, Inc.,
500 Fifth Avenue, New York, NY 10110

For information about special discounts for bulk purchases, please contact
W. W. Norton Special Sales at specialsales@wwnorton.com or 800-233-4830

Manufacturing by Toppan Printing Co.
Book design by Jan Derevjanik
Production manager: Devon Zahn

Library of Congress Cataloging-in-Publication Data

Traverso, Amy.
The apple lover's cookbook / Amy Traverso ; photographs by Squire Fox. — 1st ed.
p. cm.
Includes bibliographical references and index.
ISBN 978-0-393-06599-2 (hardcover)
1. Cooking (Apples) 2. Cookbooks. I. Title.
TX813.A6T73 2011
641.6'411—dc23

2011016560

W. W. Norton & Company, Inc.
500 Fifth Avenue, New York, N.Y. 10110
www.wwnorton.com

W. W. Norton & Company Ltd.
Castle House, 75/76 Wells Street, London W1T 3QT

1 2 3 4 5 6 7 8 9 0

· For Scott, Max, and Eva ·

CONTENTS

Recipe Index ~ 8

Acknowledgments ~ 11

• chapter one •
INTRODUCTION
Why an Apple Book? ~ 14

A Brief History of the Apple ~ 17

The Wild World of Apple Genetics ~ 24

How to Use This Book ~ 26

• chapter two •
APPLE VARIETIES: A PRIMER
How to Match the Apple to the Recipe ~ 28

Apple Varieties: The Cheat Sheet ~ 30

59 Great Apple Varieties: An In-Depth Guide ~ 31

How to Tell If an Apple Is Fresh ~ 61

Do Apples Express *Terroir*? ~ 62

• chapter three •
COOKING TIPS AND PANTRY NOTES
Tips and Techniques ~ 64

Ingredient Notes ~ 69

Tools of the Trade ~ 71

• chapter four •
SOUPS AND STARTERS
The Fruit of the Future: Inside the Cornell Apple Breeding Program ~ 74

• chapter five •
VEGETABLE ENTREES, SIDES, AND SALADS
The Gift of Graft: A Visit to Red Apple Farm in Phillipston, Massachusetts ~ 90

• chapter six •

POULTRY, MEAT, AND FISH ENTREES

Fruit from the Desert: New Mexico's Hidden Apple Country ~ 120

• chapter seven •

PANCAKES, DONUTS, BISCUITS, AND BREADS

On Heirlooms and Cider: A Visit to Poverty Lane Orchards in Lebanon, New Hampshire ~ 150

• chapter eight •

PIES, CRISPS, COBBLERS, BUCKLES, AND BETTIES

The Business of Apples: A Tour of Washington's Wenatchee Valley, "Apple Capital of the World" ~ 182
The Best Apples for Pie ~ 196

• chapter nine •

DUMPLINGS, BAKES, CAKES, AND PUDDINGS

Rediscovering Forgotten Fruits: The Preservation Orchards of Palermo, Maine ~ 224

• chapter ten •

CONDIMENTS AND COCKTAILS

267

• chapter eleven •

BEYOND BAKING: APPLE FESTIVALS, PRODUCTS, AND PAIRINGS

A Select List of American Apple Festivals ~ 280
Where to Buy Fresh Apples by Mail ~ 282
Favorite Apple Products, from Cider Donuts to Vinegar ~ 283
Cider: Twenty Favorite Labels, with Tasting Notes ~ 286
Pairing Cider and Cheese ~ 290

Bibliography ~ 291
Index ~ 293

RECIPE INDEX

SOUPS AND STARTERS

Bacon-Wrapped Dates with Curried Apple Hash ~ 78

Chicken Liver Pâté with Apple ~ 81

Apple, Cheddar, and Caramelized Onion Pastry Puffs ~ 83

Apple Chips with Spiced Yogurt Dip ~ 84

Sweet Potato, Apple, and Ginger Soup ~ 85

Chestnut Soup with Spiced Apple-Cranberry Compote ~ 87

VEGETABLE ENTREES, SIDES, AND SALADS

Endive Salad with Apples, Walnuts, and Gorgonzola ~ 92

Autumn "Coleslaw" with Dates, Apples, and Pecans ~ 93

Apple, Pistachio, Persimmon, and Pomegranate Salad ~ 95

Chicken Waldorf Salad ~ 96

Spinach, Apple, Pickled Onion, and Bacon Salad with Cider Vinaigrette ~ 98

Cider-Glazed Root Vegetables ~ 99

Squash and Apple Gratin ~ 101

Parsnip-Apple Puree ~ 103

Apple Risotto (Risotto alle Melle) ~ 104

Apple and Mustard Grilled Cheese Sandwiches ~ 107

Welsh Rarebit with Apples ~ 109

Pumpkin and Apple Custard ~ 111

Acorn Squash Stuffed with Kasha and Apple ~ 112

Squash Stuffed with Apples, Pancetta, and Walnuts ~ 114

Sweet Potato–Apple Latkes ~ 117

POULTRY, MEAT, AND FISH ENTREES

Apple Cider–Brined Turkey with Applejack-Sage Gravy ~ 123

Braised Brisket with Apples and Hard Cider ~ 126

Pork and Apple Pie with Cheddar-Sage Crust ~ 129

Tennessee Cornbread Dressing with Sausage and Apple ~ 132

Sausage and Red Onion Sandwich ~ 135

Sausage with Braised Cabbage and Apples ~ 137

Duck Panzanella with Apples and Thyme ~ 138

Cider-Braised Pork with Calvados and Prunes ~ 140

Cider-Brined Pork Chops with Mustard Pan Sauce ~ 142

Apple and Chestnut–Stuffed Pork Loin with Cider Sauce ~ 145

Pan-Seared Salmon with Cider-Glazed Onions ~ 148

PANCAKES, DONUTS, BISCUITS, AND BREADS

Vermont Apple Cider Donuts ~ 153

Baked Apple French Toast with Hazelnut Crumb Topping ~ 156

Dutch Baby ~ 159

Oatmeal-Apple Pancakes ~ 161

Baked Apple Oatmeal Pudding ~ 163

Apple-Stuffed Biscuit Buns ~ 164

Apple Cranberry Scones ~ 167

Apple-Studded Brown Butter Streusel Coffee Cake ~ 169

Apple-Apricot Kuchen ~ 171

Apple Pumpkin Walnut Muffins ~ 173

Morning Glory Muffins ~ 174

Sausage, Apple, and Cheddar Strata ~ 175

Irish Soda Bread with Apples and Currants ~ 177

Holiday Apple-Raisin Challah ~ 179

PIES, CRISPS, COBBLERS, BUCKLES, AND BETTIES

Grandma's Apple Crisp ~ 185

Oatmeal-Topped Apple Crisp ~ 187

Swedish Apple Pie ~ 189

Double-Crust Apple Pie ~ 190

Blue Ribbon Deep-Dish Apple Pie ~ 193

Apple Pie with Crumb Topping ~ 197

Skillet Apple Pie ~ 199

Marlborough Pie ~ 201

Tarte Tatin ~ 203

Gravenstein Apple-Raspberry Tart ~ 205

Free-Form Apple-Pear-Cranberry Tart ~ 208

Rustic Apple Brown Betty ~ 211

Apple-Pear Cobbler with Lemon-Cornmeal Biscuits ~ 212

Buttermilk Apple Buckle ~ 214

Williamsburg Wrapples ~ 217

Apple Empanadas ~ 219

Apple Pandowdy ~ 221

DUMPLINGS, BAKES, CAKES, AND PUDDINGS

Cider-Baked Apples ~ 228

Baked Apples with Frangipane Filling ~ 229

Apple Dumplings with Cider-Rum Sauce ~ 231

Apple Bread Pudding with Salted Caramel Sauce ~ 233

Cinnamon Rice Pudding with Spiced Apple-Cranberry Compote ~ 235

Spiced Apple-Cranberry Compote ~ 236

Apple Clafoutis ~ 237

Apple Brownies ~ 238

Simple Apple Nut Cake ~ 239

Apple Tea Cake with Lemon Glaze ~ 240

Crêpes Filled with Caramelized Apples and Served with Maple Crème Fraîche ~ 245

Caramelized Apples ~ 247

Kentucky Apple Stack Cake—Modern Version ~ 248

Kentucky Apple Stack Cake—Traditional Version ~ 251

Apple Gingerbread Upside-Down Cake ~ 253

Applesauce-Pistachio Bundt Cake with Cider Glaze ~ 255

Lowfat Gingerbread Applesauce Cake ~ 257

Spiced Apple Cupcakes with Cinnamon Cream Cheese Frosting ~ 259

Salted Caramel Apples with Cinnamon Graham Cracker Crumbs ~ 262

Apple-Gingersnap Ice Cream ~ 264

Green Apple Sauvignon Blanc Sorbet ~ 266

CONDIMENTS AND COCKTAILS

Classic Applesauce ~ 268

Orange-Scented Spiced Applesauce ~ 269

Quick Bread-and-Butter Apple Pickles ~ 270

Apple, Date, and Almond Charoset ~ 273

Apple, Cucumber, Lime, and Mint Salsa ~ 274

Overnight Apple Butter ~ 275

Mulled Apple Cider ~ 276

Jack Rose ~ 277

Coming-in-from-the-Cold Cocktail ~ 278

ACKNOWLEDGMENTS

I am grateful to many people who made this book possible. First, to my husband, Scott, thank you for your patience, good humor, cheerleading, and willingness to taste just about anything. Nothing in life would be as good as it is without you. Thank you to Max for being our joy. And endless gratitude to Maria Guarnaschelli, my editor, for believing in this book, sticking with it, and making it so much better than it would have been otherwise.

Thanks to Melanie Tortoroli for her kindness, hard work, and wise counsel; to Susan Sanfrey for her careful eye; to the late Michael Carlton for giving me my start as a food writer; and to my agent and friend Joy Tutela for believing that I had a book in me.

I learned much about apples and their history, genetics, and diversity from Dr. Susan Brown, Christie Higginbottom, John Bunker, Stephen Wood, and Ben Watson.

For their help with recipe development and testing, thanks to Adeena Sussman, Meredith Rogers, Jessica Battilana, Molly Watson, Will Gilson, Dena Ehrlich, and the Twitter foodie community. And thanks to the Mullane and Rose families and to Roger Pepperl for your help with the essays.

The beautiful photos in this book are thanks to the talents of Squire Fox, Peter Thompson, Michael Pederson, Tracy Keshani, Charan Devereaux, and Beth Flatley. The design is the work of the talented Jan Derevjanik, the meticulous Devon Zahn, and the creative Ingsu Liu.

For their excellent fruit (and for their willingness to do rush deliveries), thanks to Randy Kiyokawa, Mike Zingler, Tim Bates, and Gene Calvi.

Lastly, thanks to friends and family whose support meant everything: In particular, Henry and Elaine Traverso; Rose Traverso, Joan Traverso, Madeline Zanardi, and Mary Quagliaroli; Jill, Fred, Abbie, and Will Vogel; Nancy Kirsner; Harry, Brenda, Ashley, and Shira Kirsner; Ashley Adler and Katelyn Bhatti; Bridget Samburg; Richard Jacobs; Gil Martinez (the logo was the beginning of it all!); and many friends who offered their help and ideas along the way.

CHAPTER ONE

INTRODUCTION

Calville Blanc d'Hiver

Why an Apple Book?

"So . . . you must like apples." Tell a stranger at a cocktail party that you're a food writer working on an apple cookbook, and that's the response you'll likely get. And, of course, one would hope that the answer is yes, I do, very much. In fact, the more I've eaten them, cooked with them, learned their history, and studied their intricacies, the more passionate I've become.

Sometimes the conversation ends there—not everyone finds fruit so fascinating. But if it continues, the topic usually turns to favorite varieties—mine (Pink Pearl and Calville Blanc d'Hiver) and theirs (Honeycrisp is popular, as is Gala, with a few still holding fast to Red Delicious)—which almost always sparks memories of a favorite childhood recipe. "Oh," they say, "My mom used to make the *best* apple crisp . . ."

I enjoy these conversations because it's nice to know that I'm not alone in my enthusiasm. In the years I've spent working on this book, I've discovered that apples are not only tasty, but infinitely varied and intrinsically connected to human history. They're the world's third most widely grown fruit (bananas are first, grapes second). In this country, they're grown commercially in thirty-five states, and home orchards can be found from Alaska to Florida, where the variety Tropic Sweet was developed at the state university. Apples have been a window through which my knowledge of food has deepened. I hope that the more time you spend with this book, the more passionate you'll become as well.

I wasn't always such an apple enthusiast. I grew up in Connecticut, enjoying the fruit in the way of most children. I snacked on a McIntosh or Red Delicious when there weren't any Oreos on offer. I looked forward to fall, when my mother made my grandmother's apple crisp (page 185). We made an annual apple-picking trek to nearby Glastonbury, where a handful of family-run orchards still continues to resist suburban development.

And somewhere in that very conventional introduction, apples took root in my imagination. I saw the lush beauty of an orchard at full fruit, and understood why so much early literature, from the Bible to Greek and Scandinavian mythology, equates the orchard with Paradise itself. To me, an apple farm in September or October represents everything that is inspiring in nature—its abundance and sweetness—and strikes me as a spiritual setting as much as any church or temple. Setting aside the centuries of decidedly human effort that gave rise to these highly selected fruits—and forgetting that orchards don't exactly plant themselves—walking among these trees gives the most pleasing vision of nature, in which sweet fruit is given in abundance as if by some universal benevolence.

After I left home and began exploring food and cooking as a serious hobby, and later as a food editor and recipe developer, I experimented with apple varieties outside my narrow circle of McIntosh, Macoun, Granny Smith, and Golden Delicious, and found breeds that seemed almost exotic—the sweet yellow Winter Banana, the tart and rough-skinned Roxbury Russet. Here was a fruit that thrived in my northern home state—where remnants of former orchards can be found in most cities and suburban towns. In fact, I often snack from several scraggly survivors in my urban Brookline, Massachusetts, neighborhood.

Apples are so adaptable and grow in so many places that they provide an easy way to eat locally and in season, and to support nearby farms instead of relying only on fruit shipped in from far away. All worthy goals, with more and more popular appeal—just look at the farmers' markets sprouting up all over the country. For those of us who live in regions with short growing seasons, locally grown apples aren't just delicious, they're politically correct!

Even far from any orchard, the average shopper has access to an incredible diversity of apple varieties—something rare on a mass scale. Consider the typical supermarket's produce section: you can buy plain "raspberries," "nectarines," or "lemons." For all the tons of strawberries grown year-round in California and Florida, the fruits are still known only by their generic names. Head over to the apple section, however, and you can choose from Granny Smith, Pink Lady, Fuji, and Gala, among others. Only apples have earned such specific interest.

Why? Because in addition to being highly available, apples are delicious, with the sort of tart-sweet balance that delights the palate. They keep well—in my refrigerator's produce drawer, I've successfully stored Newtown Pippin and Northern Spy well into spring (for best results, put them in a paper bag or a plastic bag into which you've punched a few holes). And they're easy to cook with, shining in preparations sweet and savory, fresh and baked.

My own love affair with this fruit hit new highs (and perhaps went overboard) when, on October 2, 2004, I married my husband, Scott, in the apple orchard of Arrows Restaurant in Ogunquit, Maine. As our guests arrived, we served them cider made from the fruit of the trees around us. At the reception, we set small wedding cakes on each table and scattered tiny Lady Apples around them as an edible centerpiece. My bridesmaids wore shades of red and rose, like the blush on the fruit, and Scott and his groomsmen sported apple-green ties. My friend Gil even designed an apple tree logo for the invitations and programs. The wedding favors?

Caramel apples. Really, it was a harvest festival disguised as a wedding. And naturally, when our son, Max, began talking, he called every fruit an "apple."

My passion for apples has shaped my work life as well. As a food writer and editor, I've seen how popular apples are with readers. Every fall, at magazines from California to New England, my job has been to develop great apple recipes. All of these experiences have brought me to this cookbook. I love this fruit. I love how it represents home and autumn and big slabs of pie, and I love cooking with it.

Chances are, apples have a place in your own food memories. I can't think of another fruit that comes as close to the heart of the American table. We save an apple for the teacher. We eat an apple a day. We are "as American as apple pie" (an ironic statement, if you think about it, given that apple pie really is very British), and we call our greatest city the Big Apple. Some combination of those phrases and a thousand servings of apple cider donuts and mulled cider, combined with my New England roots or your Virginia or Sonoma or Yakima Valley childhood, and all those rounds of the Johnny Appleseed song (*"Oh, the Lord is good to me . . ."*), all add up to such strong associations with apples and America that I half expected to hear that the Pilgrims found rows of Baldwin and McIntosh when they first stepped ashore at Plymouth.

In reality, the sweet apple we associate with home and country had to travel through time and across the world before it could become a homegrown favorite. Let's go back to the beginning and find out how we got here . . .

A Brief History of the Apple

America's first apple trees were planted from seeds, cuttings, and small plants brought by the Jamestown settlers to the New World in the early 1600s. The Pilgrims planted their orchards soon after. But going back much farther, before recorded human history, we find the origin of the modern domesticated apple, *Malus domestica*, deep in the southeastern corner of Kazakhstan, along the Tien Shan mountain range, which borders Kazakhstan, China, and Kyrgystan. The Tien Shan's forests are still filled with ancient groves of wild apple and other fruit trees. They grow as high as fifty feet, with fruit ranging in size from tiny walnut-shaped fruitlets to enormous globes, and in every color from yellow to deep violet.

It was here and in another nearby mountain range, the Dzungarian range, that the ancestors of today's sweet table apples first appeared about 4.5 million years ago—the result of an evolutionary dance between the native wild apple trees—botanical name *Malus sieversii*— and the mountain birds and animals who favored the fleshiest, most honeyed fruits on offer, and then distributed the seeds far and wide. It was natural selection at its finest, allowing the fruits with the highest sugar levels to come to dominate their habitat.

Of course, the apple genus, *Malus*, is a large one, and there were other, less palatable types of apples growing in the world at this time. More than thirty other native species can be found in every corner of the globe: the small, bitter crab apples of Europe, Chinese crabs, native American crabs. These apples have all been known and used by humans throughout history, but it is the large, honeyed *Malus sieversii* that most resemble today's orchard apples. So how did they become today's McIntosh and Gala? How did they get from there to here?

The simplest answer is that the Tien Shan forests happened to lie in the path of ancient trade routes. Travelers encountered the fruit on their journey and, like the bears and birds before them, carried apples out beyond their home turf. Imagine how wonderful an apple might have seemed to those early travelers, who were hard-wired like all humans to crave sweet things, and lived in a world before cane sugar or high-fructose corn syrup. Here was a sweet food that was portable and could be stored for relatively long periods.

Apples are also extremely adaptive plants. Different varieties easily hybridize with each other, and sweet apples can also exchange DNA with crab apple species. As apples from the East moved west and mingled with the native crabs, their offspring could fold in genes from each new habitat, allowing them to cope with cold weather, heat, drought—any number of threats. This adaptability allowed apples to thrive in an incredible range of environments—a wide area of the planet's temperate zones with the right balance of warm and cold weather.

It's no surprise, then, that as humans began mastering the basics of agriculture, they began cultivating orchards. By 2000 BC, the ancient Hittites, who lived in the lands that now comprise Turkey, were growing apples. And by about 500 BC, apples had found a place of honor in Persian culture and cuisine.

The apples themselves were improving. By 300 BC, Greek farmers were practicing the technique of grafting (see page 90), branches (scions) onto hearty trunks (rootstock). Now they could select a favorite apple and clone it directly, rather than relying on the more random process of planting a tree from seed and waiting a few years to see what kind of fruit came up.

Soon, sweet apples were spreading all over the lands we now call southern Europe, and then farther north as the Roman Empire grew. They were prized by wealthy landowners and featured in the cuisine of the time. They were woven into some of the most famous Greek and Roman myths—even playing a role in the start of the Trojan War. In that story, Eris, the Greek goddess of discord, was denied an invitation to a wedding on Mount Olympus and retaliated by lobbing a golden apple inscribed with the words "To the fairest" into the middle of the party. This caused a ruckus among the proud and beautiful goddesses Hera, Athena, and Aphrodite. Paris of Troy stepped in as mediator and Aphrodite won the contest by bribing him with the hand of Helen of Sparta. And the rest was mythic history.

The association of apples with romance, beauty, temptation, immortality, and sensuality is a theme in cultures all over the globe. In Norse, Icelandic, Babylonian, Celtic, and Roman myths, we see gods eating apples to preserve their immortality, and suitors using apples to achieve a conquest, women conceiving with the help of magical apples, and heroes falling from grace because they couldn't resist the temptation of a perfect fruit.

Which brings us to Adam and Eve. In the original Hebrew text of Genesis, the specific fruit that led to man's downfall isn't actually named. Greek and Latin translations used the word *melon* or *malum*, respectively, which could refer to either "fruit" in general or "apples" specifically. Considering the geography of the region where the story is set, a fig, apricot, or pomegranate would seem the most likely culprit. But over time, the apple was chosen, perhaps because it was a well-known fruit of the northern monks who later translated the Bible into Latin. Perhaps it was the time-honored practice of interweaving ancient myths with "new" religions to create a story that the locals could accept. Or maybe it was the perfect pentagram shape formed by apple seeds when sliced horizontally (slice the apple from stem to flower end, and the shape resembles a womb). In any case, the apple was implicated and has remained the symbol for temptation ever since. In 1470, when Flemish artist Hugo van der Goes painted his famous *Fall of Man*, in which Adam and Eve consort with the devil under an apple tree, the popular association of the apple with the original Tree of the Fruit of Knowledge was fixed in oil.

Despite this stain on its reputation, the apple's fortunes improved in northern Europe, where it thrived in its cooler climate. And as the Renaissance ushered in a period of scientific discovery, the field of botany emerged. That effort to systematize and categorize the natural world spurred further attempts to identify exceptional apple varieties and propagate them. During this time, French varieties such as the Pomme d'Api, the Reinette, and, my favorite, the Calville Blanc d'Hiver, became popular—and are still in demand today. Likewise, in England, with the Rennet, the Pippin, the Pearmain, and the Costard. The British Puritans of the sixteenth and seventeenth centuries held fast to the virtues of thrift and self-sufficiency, so orchard-keeping became a common practice. And when they left England for America, they took apples with them.

In Jamestown, in 1629, Captain John Smith wrote of peaches, apples, apricots, and figs that "prosper[ed] exceedingly" in the coastal climate. Around the same time, the first new American apple variety was given the name Blaxton's Yellow Sweeting. It came from a Boston orchard around 1625, a product of the Beacon Hill estate of William Blaxton, the first British settler in Boston. He was chaplain to the 1623 Gorges expedition, which preceded the Puritans to that particular spot by several years. And as he was not a Puritan, he soon suffered repeated skirmishes with his newly arrived fundamentalist neighbors before relocating to more tolerant Rhode Island. Today, at the corner of Beacon and Spruce streets, you can find a plaque marking Blaxton's old homestead.

Not long after his success, someone—it's not clear who—discovered a sweet russeted green apple growing in a field in Roxbury, south of Boston, and liked it well enough to propagate it. This became the Roxbury Russet apple, which is still in active production today.

For early colonists, apples weren't just a sweet table fruit. They were the source of cider vinegar, which was used in preserving. They provided hard apple cider to drink, and from cider came distilled ciderjack, which was used as a spirit, a preservative, and an anesthetic. By 1775, 10 percent of farms in New England boasted a cider mill. Soon there were orchards lining the Eastern Seaboard, as far south as northern Georgia. And as apples began to grow abundantly, they became a staple of American cooking.

With American independence in 1776, the westward migration began, and apples traveled right along with the early settlers. Homesteading laws required that they plant fifty apple or pear trees in order to take title to the land. It was a good way to ensure that people stayed put long enough to see those trees bear fruit.

And so, in the early 1800s, a young missionary named John Chapman left Massachusetts and headed west by canoe into the nascent territories of Pennsylvania, Ohio, West Virginia, Illinois, and Indiana to preach the Good Word and spread the gospel of apples. He planted trees everywhere he went, eventually earning the nickname Johnny Appleseed.

In the popular depiction of Appleseed, familiar to most schoolchildren or fans of the 1948 Disney short *Johnny Appleseed* (watch it on YouTube—it's terrific), he's presented as our country's crazy great-great-great-uncle: a lovable eccentric who spent his happiest childhood days in his father's orchard learning how to cultivate the fruit. When he hit the trail, he traveled barefoot and clad in a coffee sack, fearing that shoes would dull his sensitivity to the nature all around him. He was a vegetarian proto-Transcendentalist and Swedenborgian missionary, who, in the tradition of his church, believed that nature was a manifestation of God himself. Therefore, time spent communing with nature was in essence a form of worship.

But Chapman wasn't one to pass his days meditating under a Baldwin tree. He had a plan: to travel a bit ahead of the settlers and clear plots of land for planting orchards. He'd build fences around them, then persuade a neighbor to tend to the land in exchange for a cut of his sales. He knew that once his trees matured and the hordes arrived, they'd need those trees for their own plots. Of course, he often sold them on credit and was never repaid—he seemed more interested in the planting than in actually making a profit. But by claiming land in this way, Chapman had such vast holdings by the time he died, that he was, at least on paper, a very wealthy man.

Interestingly, Chapman generally held a firm anti-grafting line, considering such human interference an affront to God's natural order. Though grafting had been practiced since the country's founding, the thousands of American acres Chapman covered with apple orchards were grown from seeds that he collected from cider mills along his route. He knew that most of the apples they'd produce would prove wholly unappetizing as eaters. But they would make a decent cider, which was, after all, the most widely consumed beverage of that period. The settlers who planted their three or five or twenty acres of apples were guaranteed, in time, ample sources of mildly boozy refreshment and, they hoped, a few seedlings that would turn up pie-worthy fruit. And they sometimes did. From the hundreds of thousands of seedlings planted during the nineteenth century, many thousand edible hybrids emerged: the Jonathan, the Grimes Golden, the King David, the Maiden Blush, the Blue Pearmain, the Ben Davis, to name just a handful. Other varieties from that time were produced by industrious farmers who had the skill to cross hybrids under controlled conditions. But random chance accounted for most of the breeds, the best of which were given the poetic names that indicate just how prized they were.

Interest in apples ran so high during the nineteenth century that the era had many of the traits of the Gold Rush. Discovering a particularly appealing apple variety could bring sudden riches to an enterprising farmer able to market and distribute the scion, and people scoured rural orchards in search of the next Baldwin or Newtown Pippin. During this period, Thoreau wrote, "Every wild-apple shrub excites our expectation thus, somewhat as every wild child. It is, perhaps, a prince in disguise. What a lesson to man!"

All this planting gave the apple a tremendous opportunity to express itself in all its genetic diversity. According to the nurseryman and apple historian Tim Hensley in the book *The Best Apples to Buy and Grow*, the United States Department of Agriculture produced a catalog in 1905 of all the known apple varieties grown domestically during the previous century. Their total: 14,000. It's an incredible number, especially when you remember that there were no domesticated apples being grown on our soil in 1607, when the Jamestown settlers arrived.

Over the course of the nineteenth century, large-scale apple production expanded from New England, New York, and Ohio to Washington and Oregon. The first apples were planted in that region in the mid-1820s, when a British officer for the Hudson Bay Company named Aemilius Simpson brought apple seeds to Fort Vancouver in Washington. When covered wagons traveled over the Oregon Trail westward in the mid-1800s, they carried apple trees and scion wood for grafting as part of their cargo. With ample irrigation from western rivers, the dry, sunny climate of inland California and central and eastern Oregon and Washington proved excellent for growing vast stores of apples.

But in a blow to apple diversity, the cider era came to an end in this country in the latter half of the nineteenth century, thanks to the double blow of the Temperance Movement with its wholesale rejection of cider and other alcohol, and the arrival of German immigrants who brought with them improved methods for making beers and ales. No longer reliant on apples to produce their drink of choice, Americans who did consume alcohol were less eager to maintain orchards. Today, the word "cider" has come to describe nonalcoholic apple juice, while "hard" cider has become a specialty beverage made by a small (though growing) number of cideries, mostly in the Northeast, upper Midwest, and Northwest. Meanwhile, as the apple-growing industry grew and centralized, it began to focus its efforts on a smaller number of sweet, productive, transportable apple varieties and many homelier or less hardy types were forgotten.

Today, Washington is by far the top apple-growing state, accounting for 58 percent of the country's harvest (see page 182). But the apple industry is a global one, with growers and botanists—most notably those in the United States, Japan, Australia, and New Zealand—continuing to create new blockbuster breeds like the Jazz and Pink Lady, mostly by crossing choice varieties to produce new hybrids. Attempts to improve apples through genetic engineering—by, say, splicing genes from a fungus-resistant crab apple into a domesticated fruit—are still in the relatively early stages (see page 24). Chance seedlings are also still discovered on occasion—one example: the Ambrosia from British Columbia (see page 31)—but in the global apple economy, very little is left to chance.

In the early 1990s, China overtook the United States in apple production, and it now grows about 35 percent of the world's crop (most of the fruit that enters the United States does so in the form of apple juice concentrate). Thousands of years after the first sweet apples made their way along ancient eastern trade routes to satisfy the world's hunger, that same hunger has spawned a thriving new industry back at their source.

Two Black Oxford apples, one large, one small, from John Bunker's orchard in Palermo, Maine. This firm-sweet variety is a Maine native, and its singularity inspired Bunker to devote his career to preserving heirlooms like this. For more on Bunker and his work, see page 224.

THE WILD WORLD OF APPLE GENETICS

Before I began researching this book, I thought that if you wanted to grow a Granny Smith tree, you could simply take a seed from a supermarket apple and plant it. Easy!

Only . . . not so easy. Apple trees don't produce little seedling clones. Instead, like humans, they produce offspring whose DNA is a unique combination of parental genes. This means that just as my son is not an exact replica of me or his father, any seed I might plant from the Granny Smith will produce a seedling quite distinct from the parent tree. Actually, that seedling will be even *more* distinct than a human child because apple genetics are mind-bogglingly complex—so much so that, according to the science writer Sue Hubbell in her book *Shrinking the Cat: Genetic Engineering Before We Knew About Genes*, early botanists who studied apple reproduction "suggested that they did not obey the rules of Mendelian genetics."

It's easy to understand why they were baffled. Consider the matter of pollen. With few exceptions, apple trees can't fertilize themselves, so they must be fertilized by another tree. In a typical orchard setting during the apple blossom season (spring in the Northern Hemisphere, fall in the Southern Hemisphere), the pollen might travel by honeybee or on the wind, but regardless of how it arrives, it will land on a flower, attach to the sticky stigmas, and travel down the five antenna-like styles to reach the five ovules, each of which will eventually produce seeds.

Now, in an orchard filled with many varieties of apple, there's a lot of different pollen floating around. It's possible that on any particular apple blossom, each stigma could receive pollen from a different source. Therefore, each seed in the very same apple could have a different "father," and thus, a unique genetic makeup.

"There's a tremendous amount of genetic recombination in apples," says Dr. Susan Brown, Professor of Horticultural Sciences at Cornell's College of Agriculture and Life Science. Recombination is the process by which strands of DNA can break apart, mix and mingle with other strands, and combine to form new chromosomes. "There are also hidden and recessive genes in apples, which may or may not express themselves in different conditions," Brown says. "There are just many more variables than there are with humans."

Think of an apple tree in a large orchard, loaded with fruit, each globe possessed of multiple seeds. Between the recessive genes and the recombining genes and the multiple pollen sources, every single apple seed on that tree—and in creation—could represent its own individual hybrid. A whole new kind of apple. See? Mind-boggling.

This is all to the dismay of apple farmers through the centuries. Apples have a very long evolutionary history, and they carry within their genetic code more instructions for survival traits (cold tolerance, disease resistance, etc.) than for sweetness and satiny red skin. As with slot machines, most pulls of the genetic lever result in what is, from our perspective, a dud: bitter, mealy flesh; leathery skin, tiny size. It's extremely rare for an apple tree grown from seed to produce fruit with a narrow band of human-approved traits. So in order to keep propagating the luscious, sweet Spitzenburg and Gala, humans have had to master the art of grafting—fusing branches from, say, a McIntosh tree onto the trunk of another tree, called the rootstock, which is chosen for its hardiness and disease resistance (for more on grafting, see page 90). Botanists also continue to develop new breeds by making controlled crosses—hand-transferring pollen from a prized apple variety like a Cox's Orange Pippin to the blossoms of, say, a Golden Delicious tree to try to produce offspring that bear the best qualities of both parents.

Recently, apples have entered the world of genetic engineering, in which desirable genes can be identified, retrieved, and introduced to an existing apple plant to make it more productive, hardier, or more disease-resistant. And those genes can come from some unbelievable sources. For example, in one study described in *Shrinking the Cat*, scientist isolated a gene that produces a bacteria-fighting protein in the silkmoth *Bombyx mori* and then added the gene to the DNA of apple rootstocks. They found that the apples that were later grafted onto those stocks were resistant to a very destructive bacterial disease called fireblight—one that can wipe out entire orchards unless controlled with pesticides.

It remains to be seen whether or not consumers will accept genetically modified apples. But as the popularity of new hybrids like Jazz and SweeTango prove, there's a thriving market for varieties produced by old-fashioned controlled breeding. And there are still so many potential crosses to make, so many new varieties on the horizon. We've only just begun to explore the apple.

How to Use This Book

In these pages, I'll take you to some of my favorite orchards and country fairs and cideries—all the places where people celebrate this beautiful, ancient fruit. Then we head back to the kitchen armed with dozens of recipes, from apple–sweet potato soup, to apple skillet pie, to a simple, delicious apple nut cake. I promise you'll eat well.

The recipes come from my imagination, from ideas inspired by chefs, friends, and family, and from my growing collection of old American cookbooks. Some are adaptations of recipes I developed in years past, some were handed down on worn slips of paper from my great-aunt Madeline, a talented cook and young widow who lived with my grandparents in Windsor Locks, Connecticut, and was the designated baker for our weekly Sunday dinners. They cover ground both sweet and savory, designed to complement, say, the vegetal notes of a tart green Pippin apple (see Apple, Cucumber, Lime, and Mint Salsa on page 274) or the milder Golden Delicious or Jazz varieties that hold up well in pies (pages 189–202). Apples are so diverse, with such different flavor profiles, it was easy to develop recipes that spanned breakfast to dinner.

To ensure your success with these recipes, I've come up with a simple way to guarantee that you're always using the best apple for any particular dish. Based on my own cooking and research, I've grouped 59 popular varieties into four categories based on how they perform in cooking: **Firm-Tart** apples such as Granny Smith, which work in rich desserts that need some acidity; **Firm-Sweet**, such as Golden Delicious, best for more delicate cakes and savory baked dishes; **Tender-Tart** such as McIntosh, best for sauces and for eating fresh; and **Tender-Sweet**, such as Gala, which are generally eaten fresh or used in quick-cooking dishes such as pancakes. Now, instead of looking for a single variety for your pie, you can choose from many compatible ones in the same category. I hope this will encourage you to try new varieties and experiment in your cooking. Each variety of apple brings something new and delicious to the mix: a bit more spice here, extra tartness there.

Recipes begin on page 78 with some soups and starters, such as Bacon-Wrapped Dates with Curried Apple Hash (page 78) and Sweet Potato, Apple, and Ginger Soup (page 85). But first, let's take an in-depth look at some wonderful apple varieties and learn about how to use them.

CHAPTER TWO

APPLE VARIETIES:
A PRIMER

Braeburn

How to Match the Apple to the Recipe

Apple varieties are as individual as people, with their own quirky flavors and textures and strengths and behavioral issues. Some perform best in desserts, others in salads. Some are just meant to be eaten out of hand. You can't tell by simply looking at them, of course, and they don't come with a label.

I've taken some of the guesswork out of this process by organizing fifty-nine popular and worthy varieties into four simple categories, which correspond to their best use in the kitchen. I did this based on my own cooking and research and advice from the growers and experts I've met over the years. Apples can vary tremendously depending on where they're grown, and under what conditions. Too much rain one year can dilute flavor, extra sun can enhance sweetness. As apples age, they tend to break down more when cooked. However, if you buy fresh apples from a reputable grower or grocer, you'll have good results.

Most of the recipes in this book will guide you to a category, rather than a specific variety. The categories are:

Firm-Tart, such as Granny Smith, Rhode Island Greening, Northern Spy, or Roxbury Russet. These apples, which hold their shape when cooked, are best in sweet baked desserts like pies or cakes—anything that benefits from a bit of acidity and bright flavor.

Firm-Sweet, such as Golden Delicious, Braeburn, Ginger Gold, or Pink Lady. These work best in sweet and savory baked dishes that need a firm apple with more sweetness than sourness.

Tender-Tart, such as McIntosh, Cortland, and Macoun. These apples break down easily during cooking, which makes them best for cooked soups and sauces. If you like a tart apple, you'll also enjoy these eaten out of hand.

Tender-Sweet, such as Gala and Fuji. I use some of these in salads, dessert sauces and the occasional quick-cooked dish, but mostly enjoy them right out of hand.

There are just a couple of exceptions to my category system: the Gravenstein Apple-Raspberry Tart on page 205, and the Apple, Cucumber, Lime, and Mint Salsa on page 274—in those cases, the dishes really do work best with the specified fruits. I'm also specific about which apples are best for baking whole (Jazz, Pink Lady, recipes pages 228 and 229); these varieties hold their rosy hue, though other firm-sweet apples are fine.

In all other cases, you can refer to the Cheat Sheet on page 30 when planning your shopping list. Apples do vary quite a bit, even within categories, and choosing a Bramley's Seedling over a Northern Spy will give you a different flavor. But you can't go wrong with any choice—you might just have more lemony notes with one, or spicy notes with another. Some tart apples have a hint of honey on the finish while others are more strictly tart. But these guidelines will still keep you in the proper range and assure the texture you want.

One last note: You'll notice that Red Delicious doesn't appear in any of the following categories. Over the past 120 years, as growers bred the fruit more for uniform good looks than flavor, the apple lost the succulence that first merited its name. I honestly can't think of a single good use for it. But if it were to fit in a category, it would be Tender-Sweet (or, in my opinion, Mush-Sweet).

Apple Varieties: The Cheat Sheet

FIRM-TART	FIRM-SWEET	TENDER-TART
BEST FOR RICHER BAKED DESSERTS	**BEST FOR LIGHTER BAKED DESSERTS**	**BEST FOR FRESH PREPARATIONS, SAUCES, AND EATING OUT OF HAND**
Arkansas Black	Baldwin	Black Twig
Ashmead's Kernel	Black Oxford	Cortland*
Bramley's Seedling	Blue Pearmain	Empire*
Calville Blanc d'Hiver	Braeburn	Jonathan
Esopus Spitzenburg	Cameo	Lady Apple
Goldrush*	Ginger Gold*	Macoun
Granny Smith	Golden Delicious*	McIntosh
Hidden Rose	Golden Russet	Westfield Seek-No-Further
Idared	Gravenstein	
Newtown Pippin	Grimes Golden	**TENDER-SWEET**
Northern Spy	Honeycrisp	**ALSO GOOD FOR FRESH PREPARATIONS, SAUCES, AND EATING OUT OF HAND**
Pink Pearl	Jazz	
Rhode Island Greening	Jonagold	Ambrosia
Ribston Pippin	Keepsake	Cox's Orange Pippin
Rome	Melrose	Fameuse
Roxbury Russet	Mutsu	Fuji*
Sierra Beauty	Opalescent	Gala*
Stayman Winesap*	Piñata*	Hudson's Golden Gem
Suncrisp*	Pink Lady	Pomme Gris
	Reine des Reinette	Spencer
	Spigold	
	SweeTango	
	Winter Banana	
	Zabergau Reinette	

* Apple variety that doesn't brown quickly when sliced; a good choice for salads.

59 Great Apple Varieties: An In-Depth Guide

AMBROSIA

CATEGORY: Tender-sweet.

BEST USE: This apple is lovely fresh, in salads, or served with cheese. The flesh keeps its shape reasonably well, but it doesn't have enough acidity to work well in pies or tarts.

ORIGIN: In 1989, Wilfried and Sally Mennell discovered the first Ambrosia tree growing in their Jonagold orchard in the Similkameen Valley of British Columbia. The exact parentage isn't certain, but Ambrosia likely came from a cross between Jonagold and Golden Delicious—another apple that was growing nearby.

AVAILABILITY: The Ambrosia is now grown in New Zealand, Chile, North America, and Europe, where it is particularly popular in Piedmont, Italy. With such wide distribution, it has become a common supermarket variety.

SEASON: In the Northern Hemisphere, the Ambrosia ripens in late September and early October and can be kept in a home refrigerator for up to three months. Southern Hemisphere fruit starts appearing in stores in early spring.

APPEARANCE: The skin is yellow and smooth, with a bright-pink flush. The flesh is creamy white. Its conical shape resembles its (likely) Golden Delicious parent.

TASTE: The Ambrosia has a distinctively honeyed flavor and very little acidity, bringing to mind a slightly more intense Golden Delicious fruit. The aromas are strongly floral.

TEXTURE: Firm, fine, and crisp when fresh, but it softens quickly, so store Ambrosia in your fruit drawer.

ARKANSAS BLACK

CATEGORY: Firm-tart.

BEST USE: The favored pie apple of many Southern cooks, the Arkansas Black also makes a great cider.

ORIGIN: First grown in Benton County, Arkansas, in the mid-1800s, it's thought to be a chance seedling from a Winesap.

AVAILABILITY: This tree thrives in warmer climates, from the southern states to the Southwest and California, and is popular at pick-your-own orchards. When I lived in San Francisco, this apple was a regular at the Ferry Plaza farmers' market.

SEASON: Ripens in October and November, but keeps well through the winter. The flesh turns sweeter in storage, so if the recipe calls for firm-tart fruit, use only Arkansas Black apples that have been picked within the past month.

APPEARANCE: Medium-sized and nicely round, with stunning deep red skin that turns purple-black the longer it stays in storage. The flesh has a yellow tinge.

TASTE: Aromatic like a Gala, but with enough acidity to keep it lively, and a cherry-spice finish.

TEXTURE: Quite hard when harvested. Crisp and moderately juicy, with a fine-grained flesh.

ASHMEAD'S KERNEL

CATEGORY: Firm-tart.

BEST USE: Unlike most of the other apples in this category, the Ashmead isn't favored mostly for baking, though it does hold up well under heat. True connoisseurs let the apple age in storage for a month or two and enjoy it fresh, or press it into extraordinary juice. It's also a popular hard cider apple.

ORIGIN: Grown from seed around the turn of the eighteenth century by a physician named Dr. Ashmead in Gloucester, England.

AVAILABILITY: The Ashmead has earned a following among heirloom apple aficionados. Look for it in farmers' markets near apple-growing regions—I've seen it in California, Washington, Vermont, and Virginia, and it's popular in Pennsylvania, New York, Oregon, Ohio, Minnesota, and Michigan as well.

SEASON: Ripens from late September to November; keeps well into spring.

APPEARANCE: Medium-sized, oblate, and somewhat lumpy, with green-gold skin, patches of russeting, and a rusty blush.

TASTE: Extremely tart when first picked, with a flavor reminiscent of citric acid, green grapes, or Champagne combined with nutty notes from the skin. It becomes much sweeter after a few weeks of storage.

TEXTURE: Very crisp and juicy.

BALDWIN

CATEGORY: Firm-sweet.

BEST USE: I like to combine this New England native with firm-tart apples in old-fashioned desserts like pies, crisps, and pandowdies. It's also delicious when eaten fresh.

ORIGIN: Discovered in 1740 on the farm of John Ball in Wilmington, Massachusetts. It was originally called a Woodpecker because of the birds who frequented the original tree, but was renamed in the early nineteenth century. It is named after Colonel Loammi Baldwin, who took an interest in the apple and propagated it around the Northeast.

AVAILABILITY: This was for many years the dominant commercial variety in New York and New England, but it lost ground to the Jonathan and McIntosh in the early twentieth century due to its vulnerability to hard frosts and its tendency to bear fruit every other year.

SEASON: Generally ripens in late September through October, keeps until February.

APPEARANCE: Medium-large in size, it has yellow-orange skin with red stripes. Apples that grow in full sun turn more uniformly red.

TASTE: More tart than the others in this category, but the sweetness dominates. It's quite aromatic, with flavors of spice and ripe apricots.

TEXTURE: Juicy and tender when eaten fresh, but able to hold its shape when cooked.

BLACK OXFORD

CATEGORY: Firm-sweet.

BEST USE: The Black Oxford makes a gorgeous pink applesauce when cooked with its skin on, but it also performs well in crisps and other baked desserts. As an eating apple, it's best in the winter—like other long-storing fruit, it gets sweeter with time.

ORIGIN: Its parentage is unknown, but this seedling first appeared on the Valentine farm in Paris, Maine, around 1790. In nearby Hallowell, a two-hundred-year-old Black Oxford is still bearing crops to this day.

AVAILABILITY: This cold-tolerant apple is most popular in its native Maine, but it is also grown in Vermont, New Hampshire, and as far south as Virginia.

SEASON: Harvested in November, it keeps well through late spring.

APPEARANCE: This stunner is such a deep and rich purple color that it looks more like a plum than an apple. It can be nearly black in patches, with a red blush peeking through. It's round in shape and usually medium in size.

TASTE: There's a pure apple flavor here that's more subtle than you'll find in modern fruit bombs like the Jazz or Honeycrisp. Fresh off the tree, it tends to be semi-tart, but the acidity fades relatively quickly.

TEXTURE: Hard, dense, and moderately juicy.

BLACK TWIG
(also known as Mammoth Blacktwig)

CATEGORY: Tender-tart.

BEST USE: This apple is primarily used as a dessert and cider apple, which is why I categorized it here. But some cooks consider it an all-purpose fruit, so feel free to experiment with it in, say, an apple crisp or other rich baked dessert.

ORIGIN: Most likely a native Tennessean, it is thought to have been discovered in the early nineteenth century as a chance seedling on the farm of Major Rankin Toole near Fayetteville. It was introduced commercially around 1830, and was reportedly Andrew Jackson's favorite apple.

AVAILABILITY: Southerners have the best shot at finding this apple, though it is also grown commercially in New York and California.

SEASON: It generally ripens in October, and can store very well through the spring.

APPEARANCE: The yellow-green skin is washed with a rose-red and purple blush and has pale lenticels (essentially "pores" on the skin, which appear as little spots). The flesh is yellow.

TASTE: Tart-sweet, spicy, and aromatic, with a healthy dose of tannins to lend complexity.

TEXTURE: Crisp, juicy, and breaking when fresh, softer in storage.

BLUE PEARMAIN

CATEGORY: Firm-sweet.

BEST USE: Cider is its first use, eating fresh is second, but the Blue Pearmain also holds up pretty well when baked whole.

ORIGIN: Its origins are uncertain, but it is a New England native, probably from the late eighteenth or early nineteenth century.

AVAILABILITY: A very hardy apple and a cider-maker's favorite, the Pearmain is best represented in the northern states, particularly New York. Look for it at farmers' markets and pick-your-own orchards.

SEASON: Ripens in October and November and doesn't keep much past January.

APPEARANCE: A dusty, blue natural bloom gives this apple its name. It is medium to large in size and quite heavy, with deep red skin accented with purple. It's not unusual to find a fine lace of russeting over the fruit.

TASTE: Sweet, mild, and very aromatic, with pear, vanilla, and melon notes.

TEXTURE: The skin is quite tough and waxy, and the flesh is dense and crisp, if somewhat dry.

BRAEBURN

CATEGORY: Firm-sweet.

BEST USE: I like to eat the Braeburn fresh, but its more subtle flavor and firm texture can also work well in delicate desserts like cakes and puddings.

ORIGIN: A chance seedling from New Zealand's South Island, it was discovered on the farm of O. Moran in 1952. Its name comes from Braeburn Orchard, where it was first grown commercially.

AVAILABILITY: Sold in supermarkets everywhere.

SEASON: Grown in the warmer apple-growing regions of both hemispheres, the Braeburn is available year-round. Quality tends to peak in June (for Southern Hemisphere fruit) and early November (for Northern).

APPEARANCE: Medium in size and conical in shape, with bi-colored skin (yellow with a rose-red blush and/or abundant stripes).

TASTE: Lots of sweetness and spice, with a hint of pear.

TEXTURE: Very juicy and crisp, quite easy to bite into, and reasonably firm when cooked.

BRAMLEY'S SEEDLING

CATEGORY: Firm-tart.

BEST USE: This is a popular cooking apple in England, and increasingly here in the States. It also makes as fine a sauce as you'll ever find.

ORIGIN: The first tree grew from a pip planted in 1809 by Miss Mary Anne Bailsford of Southwell, Nottinghamshire. A butcher named Matthew Bramley bought Miss Bailsford's property in 1846 and the variety was named after him. Bramley's Seedling was introduced commercially in 1865 and in the 1900s became England's favorite cooking apple, particularly for sauce.

AVAILABILITY: It's not a common apple in the States, but you can find it at some farmers' markets and pick-your-own farms in New England, New York, Michigan, Virginia, and Washington State.

SEASON: Early September in warmer climates, October in colder ones. Stores well.

APPEARANCE: Very large and unevenly round, with pale green skin and stripy rose-red blush.

TASTE: Given the Bramley's bright acidity, it's not surprising that this variety is high in vitamin C.

TEXTURE: Very firm when raw and baked, but fine-grained enough to cook down into a very smooth puree.

CALVILLE BLANC D'HIVER

CATEGORY: Firm-tart.

BEST USE: This is one of the favored cooking apples in France, and a must-have if you want to make an authentic tarte tatin or any other kind of tart.

ORIGIN: France, late sixteenth century.

AVAILABILITY: It's much harder to find in the U.S. though more independent growers are giving it a try. I get mine from Poverty Lane Orchards in Lebanon, New Hampshire (povertylaneorchards.com).

SEASON: Ripens October to early November. For eating fresh, it reaches peak flavor about a month after picking.

APPEARANCE: Quite large and heavy, it's pale green with a red blush in the spots where the sun hits it on the tree. It's round in shape, with wide shoulders at the top and signature ridges running down the sides. In this way, it resembles a beefsteak tomato.

TASTE: Brightly acidic, spicy, and a bit citrusy, with a honey finish. The Calville Blanc has more vitamin C than an orange, and if not allowed to ripen fully, can seem a bit too acidic for eating fresh. Fully ripe, it has a lovely tart-sweet balance.

TEXTURE: Right off the tree, it is dense, firm, crisp, and very juicy—much more so than many apples in its category. In short, I can find no fault with this extraordinary apple! After a few weeks in storage, though, it does lose some of its crispness, but retains good flavor.

CAMEO

CATEGORY: Firm-sweet.

BEST USE: Eating fresh, or in dishes where a sweeter flavor is desired, such as the Sausage with Braised Cabbage and Apples on page 137 or the Baked Apple French Toast on page 156.

ORIGIN: It sounds like an antique, but was actually a chance seedling discovered in a Red Delicious orchard near Wenatchee, Washington, in the 1980s.

AVAILABILITY: With all the Washington apple industry's marketing might behind it, this apple is widely distributed across the country with a good presence in supermarkets.

SEASON: Harvested in September and October; available all the way through summer, thanks to Southern Hemisphere growers.

APPEARANCE: Medium in size and conical, it looks like a paler, more mottled version of the Red Delicious.

TASTE: Yet again with the comparisons: the Cameo's popularity comes in part from being an improvement on the RD. Its flavor is brighter and a bit lemony, but with the familiar pear overtones of its parent.

TEXTURE: Quite tender, but with a pleasant crispness.

CORTLAND

CATEGORY: Tender-tart.

BEST USE: Many cooks swear that the Cortland makes a fantastic pie, but I've had too many mushy results to make that claim. Of course, if you love cooking with the Cortland, by all means do so! This fruit's flesh is pure white and resists browning as well as any apple, which makes it perfect for salads. The thin skin means you don't have to peel it, either.

ORIGIN: This cultivar was bred in 1898 by Professor S. A. Beach, the famed horticulturist at the New York State Agricultural Experiment Station in Geneva, New York. His 1905 book, *The Apples of New York*, is still considered a primary resource for apple growers. The Cortland's parents are Ben Davis and McIntosh.

AVAILABILITY: Very easy to find in the Northeast, Mid-Atlantic, and Midwest; less common in the western U.S.

SEASON: Ripens late September through October; keeps through early winter.

APPEARANCE: This is a McIntosh-type apple, with yellow-green skin accented or even covered with a deep, blue-red blush and rusty stripes.

TASTE: In flavor, the Cortland is like the tart equivalent of the Golden Delicious: pleasant but not particularly complex. The best examples have a rich, almost jammy fruit flavor.

TEXTURE: Very tender, with just enough crispness to keep it from being mealy (at least when fresh).

COX'S ORANGE PIPPIN

CATEGORY: Tender-sweet.

BEST USE: A beloved dessert apple in Britain, the Cox's Orange has tender flesh that's fantastic when eaten fresh. Nevertheless, I've found many British recipes for puddings and crisps that call specifically for Cox's Orange Pippin, so feel free to experiment.

ORIGIN: Cox's Orange originated in 1830, a chance seedling from a Ribston tree that grew at Colnbrook Lawn in Buckinghamshire, and was discovered by Richard Cox.

AVAILABILITY: An apple lover's favorite, this variety has been showing up more and more in farmers' markets, particularly on the East Coast and the Midwest, where British apples have more of a following, but it is also grown in Northern California.

SEASON: In most regions it ripens between late September and mid-October.

APPEARANCE: Not surprisingly, given the name, this Pippin's skin has an orange base accented with bright red patches. It's medium-sized, nicely rounded, and slightly ribbed, with cream-colored flesh.

TASTE: Citrusy and almost tropical-tasting, with pear aromas. It has more tartness than some of the apples in this category, but the balance still falls on the side of sweet.

TEXTURE: Quite juicy, with a nice tenderness.

EMPIRE

CATEGORY: Tender-tart.

BEST USE: Much like its McIntosh parent, the Empire is best eaten fresh or used in applesauce.

ORIGIN: Bred in the 1940s and introduced in 1966, it is a cross between a Red Delicious and a McIntosh, developed at New York's Agricultural Experiment Station in Geneva.

AVAILABILITY: This is among the minor league apples that do show up on supermarket shelves, but not with the regularity of, say, its Red Delicious parent. Though native to the Northeast and most popular in New York, it's sold throughout the country, and if you can't find it at the grocery store, your local farmstand or farmers' market has a good chance of coming through.

SEASON: September to October. This apple keeps better than a McIntosh, but only by a few weeks.

APPEARANCE: Petite and quite perfectly round, with a deep red blush over a pale green background. Many fruits are entirely red. The flesh is bright white and does not bruise easily.

TASTE: A mild tartness and a flavor that brings to mind rosehip tea with honey. Aromas are similar to those of McIntosh.

TEXTURE: Fresh off the tree, it's quite snappy. After a bit of time, it turns grainy; if you can dent the flesh when gently pressing on it, don't buy it.

ESOPUS SPITZENBURG

CATEGORY: Firm-tart

BEST USE: This apple has so many layers of flavor that it really is extraordinary when eaten fresh or when used to make hard or sweet cider. However, it holds up well enough in baking to qualify as a firm apple, and I'd use it in desserts like the Crêpes Filled with Caramelized Apples on page 245, the Dutch Baby on page 159, or the Swedish Apple Pie on page 189.

ORIGIN: Late eighteenth century, from the town of Esopus in Ulster County, New York. Gained fame as one of Thomas Jefferson's favorite dessert apples.

AVAILABILITY: A popular apple among heirloom aficionados, it performs best in cooler climates and can be found at farmers' markets in the Northeast, mid-Atlantic, upper Midwest, and Northern California.

SEASON: Ripens September to October, but can store well through the winter without losing flavor. A wonderful choice for holiday desserts.

APPEARANCE: Medium-large, smooth, and conical, with scarlet stripes on a pale green background.

TASTE: Incredibly aromatic and rich, with bright acidity and lively floral, citrus, tropical fruit, and spice notes.

TEXTURE: Hard and crisp, with lots of juice that seems nearly effervescent.

FAMEUSE
(also known as Snow Apple)

CATEGORY: Tender-sweet.

BEST USE: Eating out of hand, in cider, or in sauce.

ORIGIN: Its exact history is unknown, and there is a debate about whether the first Fameuse was a seedling brought from France or a Canadian native. In any case, it became the favorite variety around northern Vermont and Canada.

AVAILABILITY: The farther north this apple grows, the happier it is. Look for it in the Lake Champlain and St. Lawrence valleys, as well as the upper Midwest.

SEASON: Ripens in October; stores well into early winter.

APPEARANCE: A smaller, roundish, very beautiful apple, the Fameuse is, well, famous for its acute sensitivity to light. Many fruits will display interesting photographic impressions on the skin that mark where surrounding leaves had shaded them. The skin is bright red with purplish streaks and the flesh is pure white.

TASTE: More sweet than tart, with a flavor like spiced apple cider and strawberries.

TEXTURE: Very tender, which makes this apple perfect for eating fresh but not a good baker. The skin is smooth and very thin—no peeling necessary!

FUJI

CATEGORY: Tender-sweet.

BEST USE: Lots of sugar and low acidity make this primarily a dessert apple, though I also like it in delicate cakes.

ORIGIN: A Japanese import, the Fuji was developed in 1939 at the Tohoku Research Station in Fujisaki. It's a cross between the Red Delicious and the Ralls Janet, an eighteenth-century apple from Virginia by way of France.

AVAILABILITY: Sold in nearly every grocery store that sells apples.

SEASON: Fully year-round, thanks to a very long shelf life and the supply from both Northern and Southern Hemisphere growers.

APPEARANCE: Not always the prettiest apple, it's small to medium-sized and generally conical, with yellow skin tinged with red and rust-colored stripes.

TASTE: Sweet, floral, and not overly complex, the flavor reminds me of the apple slices dipped in honey that we eat every year for the Jewish New Year.

TEXTURE: Crisp, firm, juicy, yet tender.

GALA

CATEGORY: Tender-sweet.

BEST USE: While I consider the Gala primarily a fresh-eating apple, it can keep its shape well enough that I recommend it in quick-cooking dishes such as the Oatmeal-Apple Pancakes on page 161.

ORIGIN: A 1920s cultivar developed in New Zealand by J. H. Kidd, who crossed Golden Delicious with his namesake Kidd's Orange Red. The Gala was introduced commercially in the 1960s.

AVAILABILITY: Another ubiquitous supermarket favorite, the Gala is also popular at farmstands.

SEASON: Year-round.

APPEARANCE: The Gala's bright colors are its trademark: vivid yellow striped with rosy-red lines and a scarlet blush. It is generally small to medium-sized and somewhat oval in shape, with creamy white flesh. Avoid pale-colored fruit: the flavor is often correspondingly weak.

TASTE: A true sweet-tart apple with just a hint more honey than acid and a flowery aroma.

TEXTURE: Like so many popular, newer apples, the Gala is marked by crisp flesh and lots of juice.

GINGER GOLD

CATEGORY: Firm-sweet.

BEST USE: Use in cakes and muffins, such as the Apple Brownies on page 238 or the Morning Glory Muffins on page 174. The flesh resists browning, which makes it a good choice for salads, too.

ORIGIN: The Ginger Gold sprouted up around 1969 in a Nelson County, Virginia, orchard that had been cleared by Hurricane Camille a few years earlier. It was named after Frances "Ginger" Harvey, who owned the land with her husband, Clyde. Local botanists put it as a cross between Golden Delicious, Albemarle Pippin, and another, unknown variety. First marketed in the 1980s, it has won favor with large-scale growers because it ripens as early as July.

AVAILABILITY: Now grown widely in the mild apple-growing regions of California, the Pacific Northwest, and the southeastern states, it's available in an increasing number of supermarkets nationwide through the fall.

SEASON: Fruit ripens July to early September. It stays firm for several months, but I've found that it tends to lose much of its flavor by mid-November.

APPEARANCE: Yellow and conical, with a waxy skin. The flesh is cream-colored.

TASTE: Though this fruit is named after a person and not the spice, it does have a lively lemony spice flavor.

TEXTURE: Light and crisp with moderate juiciness.

GOLDEN DELICIOUS

CATEGORY: Firm-sweet.

BEST USE: Use in combination with firm-tart apples in pies, crisps, and the like. The Golden won't knock your socks off with its flavor, but it's easy to find and performs very well when paired with more aromatic varieties.

ORIGIN: Another chance seedling, the first Golden appeared on a hillside in Bomont, West Virginia, around 1890. Originally named Mullins' Yellow Seedling after its finder, Andrew Mullins, it was renamed by the Stark Bro's Nurseries—famed marketers of the original Red Delicious—when they bought the rights in 1914. It has no relation to the latter apple.

AVAILABILITY: One of the most popular apples in the U.S., it thrives in the warmer regions of California, the Pacific Northwest, and the southeastern states. It's also grown in Australia and New Zealand. It's sold in most every supermarket.

SEASON: Ripens mid-September through October and stays firm for several months, but loses acidity relatively quickly. Southern hemisphere fruit is available through spring.

APPEARANCE: Pale yellow, conical, and lightly spotted.

TASTE: Sweet and quite mild with buttery, honey notes.

TEXTURE: Thin skin, moderately juicy flesh, and a nice snap when fresh off the tree.

GOLDEN RUSSET

CATEGORY: Firm-sweet.

BEST USE: One of the great all-time cider apples, the Golden Russet also holds up fairly well when cooked, and the flavor is exceptional. I particularly like it in applesauce, and in lemon-accented desserts like the Marlborough Pie on page 201.

ORIGIN: Its origins weren't well documented, but it's thought to be a chance seedling from mid-nineteenth-century New York. It is similar but not identical to the English Golden Russet.

AVAILABILITY: Another heirloom with a growing fan base, this is becoming increasingly common in farmers' markets in the Northeast, Mid-Atlantic, Midwest, and Pacific Northwest.

SEASON: Begins ripening in the South in September and runs through late October in the North. It is a good keeper.

APPEARANCE: Stout and often oblate, it has a russeted skin with yellow undertones.

TASTE: Just like eating a slice of lemon custard. There's an almond aroma to the skin, and the juice has a wonderfully syrupy quality. There's plenty of sweetness here, but the acidity keeps it from becoming cloying.

TEXTURE: Very dense, coarse, and hard, which puts it at odds with today's tender Gala-style apples.

GOLDRUSH

CATEGORY: Firm-tart.

BEST USE: The Goldrush takes all the great cooking qualities of its Golden Delicious parent and adds loads of bright, citrusy flavor. I especially like it in spiced, baked desserts like the apple crisps in Chapter 8.

ORIGIN: The first seedling was planted in 1973 at the Purdue University Horticultural Research Farm. Goldrush is a complex cultivar that combines traits of Golden Delicious, Melrose, and Rome Beauty, among others.

AVAILABILITY: Look for it at farmers' markets and pick-your-own orchards in the Northeast, Mid-Atlantic, and Midwest. I've also seen it at specialty produce stores.

SEASON: Here's one apple that manages to keep its flavor and texture for six or seven months in storage. It ripens in October and November.

APPEARANCE: Medium to medium-large in size. Greenish yellow to deep yellow skin, sometimes with a bronze blush where the sun lingered. A bit of russeting is common, too.

TASTE: Almost like biting into a sweet, slightly spicy orange. There is a good deal of acidity, which mellows a short time after picking, but it remains fairly tart.

TEXTURE: Firm and moderately coarse, with nice crispness even after a few months in storage.

GRANNY SMITH

CATEGORY: Firm-tart.

BEST USE: When Northern Spy or Calville Blanc isn't available, this is a decent alternative for pies, tarts, and other rich pastry desserts.

ORIGIN: This apple was a chance seedling discovered by a Mrs. Smith (varying reports have her first name as Anne, Mary, and Maria) in New South Wales, Australia, around 1868. The apple's firm flesh, bright acidity, and excellent keeping qualities have made it one of the world's most popular apples.

AVAILABILITY: You'll be sure to find Granny anywhere apples are sold, but it is mostly grown in warmer regions.

SEASON: This variety ripens around mid-October in the Northern Hemisphere, and mid-April in the Southern, and because it stores so well, quality apples are available year-round.

APPEARANCE: Large, uniformly pale green and slightly conical, with greenish-white flesh.

TASTE: Lemony, a bit vegetal, and not terribly complex, but pleasant and tart.

TEXTURE: Dense, firm, and somewhat coarse; moderately juicy when fresh.

GRAVENSTEIN

CATEGORY: Firm-sweet.

BEST USE: A solid pie apple, the Grav is a good pick for the buttery Rustic Apple Brown Betty on page 211. Its raspberry aromas inspired the Gravenstein Apple-Raspberry Tart on page 205.

ORIGIN: It's not clear exactly where this apple originated. Various claims have it first growing in Russia, Italy, or on the German-Danish border. It was introduced to the U.S. in the eighteenth century and reached California in the early nineteenth century. When raised in a cooler climate, this apple tends to be more tart than those raised on the West Coast.

AVAILABILITY: The western Gravenstein (pictured above) is ubiquitous in regional markets, particularly in California. The northern Gravenstein is available at farmers' markets and pick-your-own farms.

SEASON: It ripens from late July in the West through early October in the North and is best used fresh.

APPEARANCE: The western Grav is usually bright gold with ample red and copper stripes. The skin gets waxy soon after ripening. The northern Grav generally has more green than the western. Both are oblong and often uneven in appearance.

TASTE: Sweet-tart with citrus notes and a hint of raspberry.

TEXTURE: Juicy and tender, with a nice thin skin.

GRIMES GOLDEN

CATEGORY: Firm-sweet.

BEST USE: Its high sugar content means the Grimes makes an excellent hard cider, but it's also a good all-purpose cooking apple. I particularly like it in buttery baked goods.

ORIGIN: Here's an apple with an American pedigree: It was a chance seedling discovered in 1804 near a Brooke County, West Virginia, cider mill and orchard that had been established by Johnny Appleseed himself. The finder was Thomas Grimes, and he got to keep the naming rights.

AVAILABILITY: The Grimes can be grown anywhere, but produces the best flavor in milder zones, such as the Mid-Atlantic states and Virginia, and you're likely to find it at local farmers' markets and farmstands. It's effectively the official apple of West Virginia and can be found in abundance there.

SEASON: Ripens from mid-September to mid-October; stores well through January.

APPEARANCE: Medium-sized and slightly oblong, this apple has yellow-green skin and tends to sport some russeting. The flesh is cream-colored.

TASTE: Sweet, rich, and spicy, with a mild aroma of cilantro. If you don't like that flavor, don't let it discourage you, though; it's very subtle.

TEXTURE: Coarse and quite crisp, but yielding to the bite.

HIDDEN ROSE
(also known as Aerlie Red Fleshed)

CATEGORY: Firm-tart. (Uncut apple photo on page 119.)

BEST USE: Because it's so unusual and pretty to look at, the Hidden Rose is often eaten fresh, but it does cook well. It would be a welcome substitution for the Gravenstein in the Gravenstein Apple-Raspberry Tart on page 205.

ORIGIN: An Oregon native, the apple first appeared as a chance seedling on land belonging to Lucky and Audrey Newell in Airlie. Two decades later, an apple grower named Louis Kimzey found the tree and the Hidden Rose was on its way to being marketed as a red-fleshed novelty.

AVAILABILITY: When properly stored, the Hidden Rose can keep for several months. It is most popular in its native Pacific Northwest, but I have seen it being grown in locations as diverse as Indiana, Massachusetts, and England.

SEASON: It ripens in October and is usually available through mid-November.

APPEARANCE: As with the Pink Pearl, a pink-brown exterior belies its bright pink flesh. The skin is smooth and shiny, and the fruit is medium in size and conical.

TASTE: Red-fleshed apples tend to have berry flavors, and this one is no exception. The Hidden Rose I've tasted vary in flavor intensity. Some are vibrant and tart, others somewhat bland. They tend to have candy-apple aromas.

TEXTURE: Fresh apples are crisp and moderately juicy.

HONEYCRISP

CATEGORY: Firm-sweet.

BEST USE: Most people use it only as a dessert apple, but it does keep its shape well when baked. If you like your apples with a satisfying crunch, eat this one fresh.

ORIGIN: Developed at the University of Minnesota Horticultural Research Center in the 1960s. Interestingly, the patent for this cultivar lists Macoun and Honeygold as its parents, but genetic testing in 2004 proved that claim false. Honeycrisp was released commercially in 1991.

AVAILABILITY: The Honeycrisp is most popular in the upper Midwest region where it was developed, but you can also find it being grown at specially licensed orchards in the northeast and in colder parts of Washington. With its popularity on the rise, expect to see it in more supermarkets in the coming years.

SEASON: Ripens mid-September through October; keeps well through the winter.

APPEARANCE: Medium-large to large and oblate, with a bright red and orange flush over a yellow-green background. If given full sun, it can turn completely red.

TASTE: As sweet as its name implies, with just enough acid to keep it from being saccharine. Flavors of honey and pear add complexity.

TEXTURE: Just as you'd expect, this apple is incredibly crisp and so juicy that it seems nearly effervescent.

HUDSON'S GOLDEN GEM

CATEGORY: Tender-sweet.

BEST USE: This fruit is probably best enjoyed as an eating apple, though you could use it in tender cakes and other delicate desserts.

ORIGIN: This seedling variety was discovered in southern Oregon in the early twentieth century and introduced commercially in 1931 by Hudson Wholesale Nurseries.

AVAILABILITY: It may be a western apple, but Hudson's Golden Gem has a growing following in the Northeast (I had my first taste at the Union Square Greenmarket in Manhattan).

SEASON: Harvest ranges from late September to early November. Kept cold, it can be stored well into January.

APPEARANCE: Generally large in size, this apple has fully russeted—though surprisingly smooth—skin and a conical, somewhat lumpy shape. The color is yellow-brown to green-brown and the flesh is quite yellow.

TASTE: Like most russeted apples, Hudson's Golden Gem has pronounced nutty flavors, but it's sweeter than most, with assertive pear notes.

TEXTURE: Juicy, grainy, and crisp; firm at first bite, but quickly yielding.

IDARED

CATEGORY: Firm-tart.

BEST USE: A good cooking apple, the Idared is also a nice option for baking whole and using in pies and tarts. It produces a pretty pink applesauce when you cook it with the skins on. It's also a popular choice for making apple butter, particularly in mountain regions of the South.

ORIGIN: This cross between Jonathan and Wagener was developed at the University of Idaho Agricultural Experiment Station in Moscow, Idaho, and introduced commercially in 1941.

AVAILABILITY: It's not a typical supermarket variety, but the Idared is grown in many parts of the country, so look for it at pick-your-own orchards and farmers' markets. It is also grown in France and Germany.

SEASON: A very good keeper, this apple tends to last well beyond its mid-September to mid-October harvest period, storing even into spring.

APPEARANCE: Medium to large in size and oblate, the Idared is, indeed, bright red, particularly when allowed to ripen fully on the tree. The flesh is bright white.

TASTE: Tart-sweet and spicy, with a healthy dose of tannins to lend complexity.

TEXTURE: This fruit is generally juicy, quite firm, and moderately coarse.

JAZZ

CATEGORY: Firm-sweet.

BEST USE: Like the Honeycrisp, it's terrific to eat out of hand. It's also nice and firm when baked, and like the Pink Lady, it keeps its rosy hue.

ORIGIN: A cross between Gala and Braeburn, the Jazz was developed in New Zealand in the 1980s and released commercially in 2004.

AVAILABILITY: It's a testimony to this apple's exceptional flavor that it has gone from a novelty to a supermarket standard in just about seven years. Don't bother looking at farmers' markets, though. The New Zealand agency that owns the rights to the fruit have tight controls on where it's grown.

SEASON: Until recently, the apple was only available during the Southern Hemisphere spring growing season, but now that some large orchards in Washington have been granted licenses, the Jazz is available for much of the year.

APPEARANCE: Medium-sized and scarlet red, with yellow-green patches.

TASTE: This is, in my view, one of the best of the new apple breeds that are dominating the market: lots of aromatic, vaguely tropical sweetness balanced by bright acidity. Abundant juice makes it very refreshing.

TEXTURE: Fine-grained but surprisingly hard for an apple from the Gala and Braeburn family.

JONAGOLD

CATEGORY: Firm-sweet.

BEST USE: The Jonagold has enough acidity to make it an even better pie apple than the Golden Delicious. I generally like to mix apple varieties in my pies, but an all-Jonagold pie is a nice thing.

ORIGIN: This cross between the Jonathan and Golden Delicious was made at the New York State Agricultural Experiment Station in the 1950s. The apple was released in 1968. It is extremely popular in Europe, Japan, the Pacific Northwest, and British Columbia.

AVAILABILITY: This is a versatile apple that can be grown from the Northeast to the West Coast, to the upper Midwest and southern mountain states. It is, however, sensitive to sunburn. Look for it in a growing number of supermarkets nationwide, as well as farmers' markets.

SEASON: Ripens from mid-September through October, depending on where it's grown; keeps well for a month or two.

APPEARANCE: A large, golden, conical fruit with a bright flush that turns orange in warmer climates and red in cooler ones. The flesh is nearly yellow.

TASTE: Very sweet, with honeyed notes and the same melon aromas of a Golden Delicious.

TEXTURE: The flesh is very tender and juicy, but overlaid with a tough skin.

JONATHAN

CATEGORY: Tender-tart.

BEST USE: In my experience, many Jonathan apples will cook down to a sauce. For this reason, it's categorized as tender-tart, but some bakers swear by Jonathans as baking apples. If you're making a pie, tart, or cobbler, hedge your bets by adding some firm-sweet apples.

ORIGIN: A seedling from an Esopus Spitzenburg tree, it first appeared in the early 1800s on the farm of Phillip Rick in Woodstock, New York. It is named after Jonathan Hasbrouck, who introduced the apple to Judge J. Buel, president of the Albany Horticultural Society around 1826.

AVAILABILITY: The Jonathan is grown commercially in New York, New England, Michigan, Pennsylvania, Ohio, northern California, and Washington. If you live in these regions and can't find the apple at your supermarket, you'll almost certainly find it at the farmers' market.

SEASON: Generally ripens in October and is rarely available past Thanksgiving.

APPEARANCE: Medium-sized and round, with a tapered end. A fully ripe apple often has yellow skin overlaid by a deep red blush and striping.

TASTE: Flavors range from sweet-tart to tart, with a spicy finish. This apple definitely isn't the shy, retiring type.

TEXTURE: The skin is thin but tough; the flesh crisp and tender, with a very fine-grained texture and abundant juice.

KEEPSAKE

CATEGORY: Firm-sweet.

BEST USE: Fans cite this apple's intense aromatics as a reason to simply eat it fresh, but it is also a very good cooking apple for crisps, cakes, puddings, and pies.

ORIGIN: This hybrid from the University of Minnesota's breeding program, a cross of Malinda and Northern Spy, was introduced commercially in 1979. It has since been determined that Keepsake is one of the parents of the far more famous Honeycrisp.

AVAILABILITY: This variety seems to be gaining popularity ever since the Honeycrisp connection was made public in 2004. Look for it mostly at orchards in the Northeast and Midwest.

SEASON: Keepsake ripens from late September to mid-October. As for how long it keeps, the name says it all: this fruit typically stores well into spring. One grower I know says he's eaten very nice eight-month-old Keepsakes from his root cellar in June.

APPEARANCE: Generally medium in size and conic in shape, the Keepsake has yellowish flesh, and red, striped skin.

TASTE: As with many varieties, the Keepsake's flavor is best after about a month in storage. Then, it is all sweetness (I've seen it compared to sugar cane), with enough aromatic spice to keep it interesting.

TEXTURE: This apple is quite hard, with fine, crisp flesh.

LADY APPLE
(also known as Pomme d'Api)

CATEGORY: Tender-tart.

BEST USE: The tiny Lady Apple is a popular decorative element in fruit baskets or flower arrangements (we scattered it over the tables at our wedding) and is delicious when eaten fresh. The flesh becomes quite soft when cooked, but I sometimes like to roast it with pork or chicken dishes.

ORIGIN: Not to be confused with the modern Pink Lady, this storied apple goes back to early seventeenth-century France, where it was first recorded in 1628. Some say it's a direct descendant of the Appia apple prized by the Romans, but that's a difficult thing to prove.

AVAILABILITY: Look for it in gourmet markets and even florist's shops in November and early December.

SEASON: Ripens from October to early November and keeps for two or three months, which accounts for its popularity as a holiday decoration. I've never had much luck finding it past December, though.

APPEARANCE: Petite and oblate in shape, with bright green skin accented by a red blush so vivid it looks almost airbrushed.

TASTE: A bit like apple jam combined with citrus—very vivid and tart-sweet.

TEXTURE: Tender, crisp, and juicy.

MACOUN

CATEGORY: Tender-tart.

BEST USE: I can't think of a better use for the Macoun than as a fresh snacking or sweet cider apple, but it also makes a terrific applesauce. Some people swear that it makes a good pie, but I think the flesh is too soft.

ORIGIN: This cross between McIntosh and Jersey Black was developed at the New York State Agricultural Experiment Station in Geneva, New York, in 1909. It was introduced commercially in 1923 and named after the Canadian fruit breeder, Dr. W. T. Macoun.

AVAILABILITY: The Macoun is a restrained bearer and has short stems, which can cause the fruits to push themselves off the tree as they ripen. This makes the Macoun difficult to find outside the Northeast, but it has a large following there and can be found at many supermarkets and farmstands.

SEASON: Ripens in early October; keeps through December.

APPEARANCE: Similar in size to the McIntosh, with the same oblate shape and a red-on-green palette. However, the blush on the Macoun is darker—almost purple in spots.

TASTE: The Macoun is sweeter than the McIntosh, but still has enough acidity to qualify as tart. The flavor brings to mind ripe strawberries.

TEXTURE: The tough skin yields to a crunchy, white, juicy flesh.

MCINTOSH

CATEGORY: Tender-tart.

BEST USE: The Mac readily cooks down, which makes it a perfect choice for applesauce. In a pie, it provides a mushy base in which firmer slices can be suspended—a texture my grandmother Rose preferred. If eating fresh, make sure the flesh is firm to the touch; Macs get very grainy and unpleasant when overripe.

ORIGIN: John McIntosh discovered this chance seedling on his farm in Matilda, Ontario, and his son Alan introduced it commercially around 1870. Its genes have given rise to varieties such as Cortland, Empire, Macoun, and Spartan.

AVAILABILITY: Thrives in colder climates and is generally easy to find in East Coast supermarkets during apple season. It's rarer in western states, though it does pop up at markets in California and the Pacific Northwest.

SEASON: Ripens September to early October; keeps until December.

APPEARANCE: Shiny skin, sometimes green with a red blush, sometimes fully red. Small to medium in size, with an oblate shape.

TASTE: Tart and quite spicy, with vegetal undertones.

TEXTURE: Compared to the tender, juicy, snow-white flesh, the skin seems thick and tough. It's packed with flavor, though, so I always cook my applesauce with the skin.

MELROSE

CATEGORY: Firm-sweet.

BEST USE: This apple is a bit more tender than some of the other varieties in its category, but it does hold its shape well when sliced and baked. If you like a more delicate apple in your pies, cakes, and crisps, give this fruit a try. Otherwise, it's perfectly delicious when eaten fresh, especially after it sweetens up a bit in storage.

ORIGIN: This cross between Jonathan and Red Delicious is an Ohio native, introduced in 1944 by Freeman Howlett of the Ohio Agricultural Experiment Station.

AVAILABILITY: It's a supermarket staple in Ohio, and is available at many farmstands in mountain zones and in the northern half of the country.

SEASON: Ripens in September and October; keeps well for several months.

APPEARANCE: The Melrose looks like a larger McIntosh, with an oblate shape and yellow-green skin accented (or nearly covered) with deep red.

TASTE: A Melrose can be tart right off the tree, but grows sweet after a short time in storage.

TEXTURE: The juicy flesh is crisp and somewhat coarse, and holds up well to baking.

MUTSU
(also known as Crispin)

CATEGORY: Firm-sweet.

BEST USE: Here's another apple that really shines when eaten fresh but can also be used in baked goods, such as muffins and cakes.

ORIGIN: A cross between Golden Delicious and the Japanese variety called Indo, the Mutsu was developed in the 1930s at the Aomori Experiment Station in Northern Japan.

AVAILABILITY: This very popular dessert apple can be found in most supermarkets.

SEASON: It ripens in October in most northern climes, but thanks to Southern Hemisphere growers you can find these apples year-round.

APPEARANCE: Very large and quite irregular in shape, with a yellow-green background and sometimes an orange-red blush.

TASTE: Definitely sweet-tart, rather than tart-sweet, with a flowery honeysuckle and mild spice flavor.

TEXTURE: Supremely juicy and as crisp as they come.

NEWTOWN PIPPIN
(also known as Albemarle Pippin)

CATEGORY: Firm-tart.

BEST USE: When first picked, the Newtown Pippin is best for rich desserts such as tarts and pies; its acidity plays well against the butter. As the fruit grows yellower and sweeter, which often happens when it's grown in milder climates, it's still a good all-purpose variety for baking.

ORIGIN: Grown from a seedling in what is now Queens, New York, it gained popularity in the mid-eighteenth century and was brought to England by Benjamin Franklin around 1759. In the past few years, it has been embraced by a group of locavore New Yorkers, who have organized to plant trees in community gardens, schools, and parks.

AVAILABILITY: This apple prefers a mild climate—it thrived at Monticello and was a favorite of George Washington—so it is most readily available in the mid-Atlantic states, the Pacific Northwest, and in California, where it's used in Martinelli's famous sparkling cider.

SEASON: It ripens from late September to early November, and keeps well into the spring.

APPEARANCE: Medium in size and often lopsided or conical with smooth yellow-green skin, a rosy blush, and some russeting; creamy flesh.

TASTE: Extremely fragrant, with an orange-banana flavor and slightly piney aroma.

TEXTURE: Firm, crisp, and quite juicy.

NORTHERN SPY

CATEGORY: Firm-tart.

BEST USE: Many cooks call the Northern Spy the best pie apple around, thanks to its bright flavor and ability to stay firm when sliced and baked. If I had to pick a single variety for my own pies (which I don't like to do, knowing how much a little variety improves the filling), I would choose this one.

ORIGIN: Another early nineteenth-century chance seedling, the Northern Spy was discovered in East Bloomfield, New York, but didn't become popular for several decades.

AVAILABILITY: The Spy has been grown all over the country, but prefers the cooler climates of New England, New York, Michigan, and Ontario. There, you can still find the apple in supermarkets, though farmers' markets are your most reliable source.

SEASON: Peak season is late September through October, but it keeps well through the winter.

APPEARANCE: Large, with deep-red sides and a slightly ridged shape; the flesh is cream-colored.

TASTE: Bright and lively, with a hint of strawberry.

TEXTURE: Firm and fine-grained, with a tender, thin skin.

OPALESCENT

CATEGORY: Firm-sweet.

BEST USE: Its rich flavors make it a good choice for eating fresh, but Opalescent also holds up to heat; try it in combination with firm-tart apples in a pie.

ORIGIN: Opalescent was first introduced commercially in the late nineteenth century by the McNary and Gaines Company of Xenia, Ohio.

AVAILABILITY: Generally a northern apple, it can be found at farmers' markets in Ohio, New York, and New England.

SEASON: Ripens from mid-September through early October and can be stored through the fall.

APPEARANCE: Large and round, with clear yellow skin covered with a deep red wash. The flesh is very pale yellow-green.

TASTE: Sweet, rich, and floral, with tropical and berry notes.

TEXTURE: Tough skin gives way to coarse, crunchy, very dense, and moderately juicy flesh.

PIÑATA

CATEGORY: Firm-sweet.

BEST USE: Consider this an all-purpose winner. I especially like it fresh or in savory preparations, such as Pork and Apple Pie on page 129 or Duck Panzanella with Apples and Thyme on page 138. It doesn't brown when sliced—a great choice for salads.

ORIGIN: A modern cultivar from three traditional apples: Cox's Orange Pippin, Duchess of Oldenburg, and Golden Delicious. First developed in Dresden, Germany, and sold under the names Pinova and Sonata, it was brought to the U.S. by Stemilt Growers of Wenatchee, Washington in 2004.

AVAILABILITY: Stemilt has the exclusive U.S. license for Piñata and they've been expanding distribution to cover most of the country. You can sometimes find it under the Sonata or Pinova names at farmers' markets—a few U.S. growers had secured permission before Stemilt came along, and they can grow the apple as long as they use the original European names.

SEASON: Ripens in late September through mid-October, but sold through the spring.

APPEARANCE: Medium to large in size with rosy-red stripes over an orange background.

TASTE: Vibrant, aromatic, and tropical in flavor.

TEXTURE: Exceedingly snappy and crisp with an exciting effervescence to the juice.

PINK LADY
(also known as Cripps Pink)

CATEGORY: Firm-sweet.

BEST USE: It's delicious when fresh, but the Pink Lady, along with the Jazz, is one of my two favorite apples for baking. It keeps its shape and pink color, and it has just the right blend of sweetness and acidity.

ORIGIN: A cross between Golden Delicious and Lady Williams, this cultivar was developed in the 1970s by John Cripps of the Department of Agriculture and Food of western Australia. "Pink Lady" is actually just the brand name of the Cripps Pink.

AVAILABILITY: In the past five years, this variety has become a supermarket standard across the country.

SEASON: Mid-October for Northern Hemisphere apples; April for Southern. Either way, the fruit keeps well for months, so this is a fully year-round apple.

APPEARANCE: This medium- to large-size apple has shiny, rose-colored skin and creamy white flesh.

TASTE: Not as noteworthy as the Piñata or Jazz, and slightly more tart than both, but it still has a nice sweet/acid balance and subtle strawberry and pear notes.

TEXTURE: Fine-grained and firm.

PINK PEARL

CATEGORY: Firm-tart. (Uncut apple photo on page 279.)

BEST USE: If you're lucky enough to get your hands on one, eat it fresh first, just to enjoy those vivid berry flavors. It does hold up well in cooking, though. A good place to start is by substituting this apple for the Gravenstein in the Gravenstein Apple-Raspberry Tart on page 205.

ORIGIN: One of the remarkable pink-fleshed apples developed by a California nurseryman named Albert Etter in Humboldt County, north of Mendocino. It is the result of a 1944 cross between a red-fleshed German apple called Surprise and an unknown variety. Red-fleshed apples are not uncommon in Europe and may be the result of a long-ago cross between a native crab apple and a sweet domestic apple.

AVAILABILITY: It is still most widely grown in Northern California. You can order it by mail from Kiyokawa Family Orchards in Parkdale, Oregon (mthoodfruit.com). I've also seen it grown at orchards in New York, Indiana, and Massachusetts.

SEASON: Early August until mid-September. This is not a good keeper, so once it's gone, it's gone.

APPEARANCE: Very homely on the outside, with dull yellow-brown, faintly blushing skin and a ridged conical shape. Inside, it's positively vampy, with Pepto-pink flesh.

TASTE: Like lemon custard topped with raspberries.

TEXTURE: Firm, coarse flesh; moderately juicy.

POMME GRIS
(also known as Pomme Grise)

CATEGORY: Tender-sweet.

BEST USE: This small apple is best eaten fresh.

ORIGIN: This fruit was likely brought from France or Switzerland to the St. Lawrence valley of Quebec. It is very similar, if not identical, to the Old World Reinette Grise apple, which dates back to Louis XIV's time.

AVAILABILITY: This apple is most popular in eastern Canada but can also be found at heirloom orchards in the eastern United States.

SEASON: Harvest generally runs through September, and the apple doesn't keep much beyond October.

APPEARANCE: This markedly oblate apple is petite, gauzy, and heavily russeted, often with an orange blush.

TASTE: Sweet-tart and nutty, with pear and vanilla aromas.

TEXTURE: The flesh is creamy and tender, though it can seem quite firm when it's fresh off the tree.

REINE DES REINETTE
(also known as King of the Pippins)

CATEGORY: Firm-sweet.

BEST USE: A popular cooking and cider apple in France, this is a good mixer in pies, tarts, and cakes (try it in the Apple Clafoutis on page 237), and a nice choice for eating fresh.

ORIGIN: The history is uncertain, but this variety most likely originated in Holland or France in the late 1700s.

AVAILABILITY: This isn't an easy apple to find in the United States. Farmers' markets and antique apple farms are the most likely sources.

SEASON: Harvest generally runs from mid-September to mid-October, and the apples can be stored with good results into December and sometimes even January.

APPEARANCE: A yellow-green russeted apple often washed bright red, the Reine des Reinette is medium in size and oblate-to-conical in shape.

TASTE: Sweet-tart, nutty, with a clean apple flavor and moderate tannins. It grows sweeter in storage.

TEXTURE: Its primary characteristic is its fine-grained, crisp, and juicy flesh. It feels quite firm in the hand.

RHODE ISLAND GREENING

CATEGORY: Firm-tart.

BEST USE: Rhode Island Greening makes such a great pie apple. You can cook it to your heart's content and know it will hold its shape. Plus, it has more vibrant flavor than the Granny Smith. It also makes a tasty sauce.

ORIGIN: Believed to have first grown from seed in the mid-seventeenth century, probably near Newport, Rhode Island, where a Mr. Green owned a tavern near Green's End.

AVAILABILITY: One of the tart green apples supplanted by the Granny Smith, this unsung beauty was widely available on the East Coast through the 1960s. Today, your best bet is a pick-your-own orchard in New York or New England.

SEASON: Mid-October is peak harvest time, but this good keeper will store well into the winter.

APPEARANCE: Large, nicely round, and sometimes russeted, with green to yellow-green skin, and yellowish flesh.

TASTE: Tartness and vegetal notes are the primary flavors here, with a hint of green grape and lemon.

TEXTURE: The flesh is dense and solid, but pleasingly juicy and tender once you bite in.

RIBSTON PIPPIN

CATEGORY: Firm-tart.

BEST USE: In England, this is a very popular cider and dessert apple; however, the flesh is firm and dense enough to hold its shape in pies, crisps, cobblers, and the like.

ORIGIN: An early eighteenth-century British apple, raised from seed by Sir Henry Goodricke at Ribston Hall near Knaresborough in Yorkshire. It is a likely parent of Cox's Orange Pippin.

AVAILABILITY: The tree is adaptable to a range of climates, but seems to have a larger following on the East Coast. Look for it at farmers' markets.

SEASON: Ripens in late September and October, achieves peak flavor by November, but doesn't keep much beyond January.

APPEARANCE: Generally medium in size, with an oblate shape and yellow-gold skin accented with dull red stripes and some russeted patches.

TASTE: Quite tart and citrusy (it has high levels of Vitamin C), with musky and pearlike notes.

TEXTURE: Very crisp and juicy, with flesh that yields nicely when bitten.

ROME
(also known as Rome Beauty)

CATEGORY: Firm-tart.

BEST USE: This fruit's ability to stay firm when cooked makes it a baker's friend. Its flavor isn't as exciting as, say, the Northern Spy or Esopus Spitzenburg, but it's a good, versatile performer, especially when mixed with other varieties in pies and crisps.

ORIGIN: Named for Rome Township in Ohio, where it was first discovered in the 1820s, the first apples sprouted off a tree that was supposed to serve as rootstock. Instead it produced winning fruit of its own.

AVAILABILITY: A former supermarket staple, this apple can still be found in many large supermarkets and Whole Foods stores across the country, as well as many farmstands.

SEASON: Depending on where it's grown, it ripens late September through late October and keeps through early winter. Beware of soft apples; chances are they're mealy.

APPEARANCE: Red and glossy like a sports car, the Rome has thick skin and greenish flesh.

TASTE: Moderately tart, and not terribly nuanced, but the flavor improves with cooking, which brings out flowery notes.

TEXTURE: Drier than many apples in this category, this is not a great pick for eating fresh.

ROXBURY RUSSET

CATEGORY: Firm-tart.

BEST USE: This is really a baking apple more than a snacking one. Like the Rhode Island Greening, this other New England native is terrific in pies, tarts, and other rich pastries in which the fruit's acidity can balance the richness of the buttery crust.

ORIGIN: One of America's oldest apples, this variety grew from seed in Roxbury, Massachusetts, in the early 1600s.

AVAILABILITY: The Roxbury likes a good chill, so it sticks to northern climes. Its humble looks have mostly limited its popularity to its home region of New England.

SEASON: Trees generally ripen in mid-October, but the fruit can keep well into the winter, even retaining a bit of crispness.

APPEARANCE: Not much of a looker, this medium-sized apple is heavily russeted, with thick skin and yellow-green flesh.

TASTE: Quite tart, but with a rich sweetness, like lemonade made with honey and served with a pineapple garnish.

TEXTURE: Crisp, dense, and rather coarse, this fruit can still retain some snap after a month or two of storage.

SIERRA BEAUTY

CATEGORY: Firm-tart.

BEST USE: Because this fruit comes into season later than other varieties, it's a popular choice for Thanksgiving and Christmas pies and preserves. It also makes a delicious baked apple, and is my favorite pick for the Tennessee Cornbread Dressing with Sausage and Apple on page 132.

ORIGIN: A Northern California native, the Sierra Beauty was discovered in the Sierra Nevada mountains in the 1890s—grown, as one theory goes, from an apple seed discarded by a Gold Rush miner. It is now a favorite apple in the Anderson Valley area.

AVAILABILITY: Sold at farmstands and farmers' markets in Northern California, the apple is versatile and hardy enough that I wouldn't be surprised to see it spread to the other western apple-growing regions.

SEASON: Ripens around late October.

APPEARANCE: A large apple with a somewhat square shape and yellow skin. Apples grown in full sun develop a bright red blush.

TASTE: Complex and tart-sweet with lots of flower and spice, plus a hint of green pepper.

TEXTURE: Fine-grained and juicy, with a firmness that suggests a good baking apple (it is).

SPENCER

CATEGORY: Tender-sweet.

BEST USE: Spencer is pleasantly sweet, but lacks the spicy flavors of its McIntosh parent, so I use this as a fresh eating apple rather than a cooker.

ORIGIN: This McIntosh–Golden Delicious cross was developed in 1926 at the British Columbia Experimental Station in Summerland and released commercially in 1959.

AVAILABILITY: Look for it at farm stands and farmers' markets on the West Coast. I have also found it at a few orchards in New England and Virginia and at the Union Square Greenmarket in Manhattan.

SEASON: Harvest generally happens between late September and mid-October. The Spencer is considered a good keeper, so you'll likely see it sold through the holidays.

APPEARANCE: In size and shape, Spencer resembles its Golden Delicious parent, being medium-large and generally conical. The skin can be pale green to yellowish with orange-red streaks or a full red blush, depending on how much sun it receives.

TASTE: Exactly like you'd expect a Mac–Golden Delicious cross to taste: sweet, not terribly complex, but mildly spicy and vinous.

TEXTURE: The flesh tends to be on the softer side, though it has some nice crispness when fresh.

SPIGOLD

CATEGORY: Firm-sweet.

BEST USE: This complex, sweet-tart apple is most commonly eaten fresh, but it bakes and cooks well. I like to use it in the Spiced Apple-Cranberry Compote on page 236 because the apple's herbal/floral notes play well off the vanilla and cinnamon in the recipe.

ORIGIN: Another graduate of the Agricultural Experiment Station in Geneva, New York, class of 1962. As its name indicates, it's a cross between Northern Spy and Golden Delicious.

AVAILABILITY: The Spigold needs good sun, but can be grown in both warmer and cooler climates, so look for it at your local farmers' market or pick-your-own orchard.

SEASON: Late September to mid-October. With proper storage, it can keep into early winter.

APPEARANCE: Large, golden, round-to-oblate fruit with a deep red blush and some russeting.

TASTE: Interesting herbal and floral flavors and aromas remind me of orange blossom water, but the sweetness is backed up by the acidity from its Spy parentage.

TEXTURE: The Spigold should be fine-grained and firm, but quick to dissolve in the mouth.

STAYMAN WINESAP
(also known as "Stayman")

CATEGORY: Firm-tart.

BEST USE: A popular fruit for cider, the Stayman is also a very good baker.

ORIGIN: This chance seedling from a Winesap tree was raised in the mid-1800s by Dr. J. Stayman of Leavenworth, Kansas. It was introduced commercially in 1895 and soon became a favorite dessert apple.

AVAILABILITY: Prefers a milder climate and is very popular in Virginia and other apple-growing states in the middle latitudes, as well as in Australia, Italy, and France. Look for it at farmers' markets, pick-your-own orchards, and farmstands.

SEASON: Late September through October. Stores through the winter.

APPEARANCE: Medium to large in size and round, with a green-gold base that is generously overlaid with deep red blushing and stripes and dotted with pale lenticels (essentially "pores" on the apple's skin, which appear as little spots).

TASTE: Very tart, with an almost winelike flavor typical of the Winesap and some spice notes at the finish.

TEXTURE: Very firm, even a bit heavy, and crisp.

SUNCRISP

CATEGORY: Firm-tart.

BEST USE: Most Suncrisps are simply eaten fresh, but the flesh does keep its shape in cooking.

ORIGIN: Developed by Dr. Fred Hough at the Rutgers University Horticultural Research Farm, the Suncrisp is a cultivar of Golden Delicious mixed with Cortland and Cox's Orange Pippin and was introduced commercially in 1994.

AVAILABILITY: Particularly popular in Midwestern and Mid-Atlantic states, though I'm also seeing it in more New England orchards.

SEASON: Ripens in October, but keeps well into January.

APPEARANCE: This apple isn't exactly a beauty, which is probably why it hasn't found the commercial success of, say, the Pink Lady and Jazz. Instead, it's large, conical, and yellow-green, with a dull orange blush on its thin skin.

TASTE: Spicy lemon-lime notes liven up this muncher.

TEXTURE: Fresh fruit is fine-grained, juicy, and crisp.

SWEETANGO

CATEGORY: Firm-sweet.

BEST USE: The SweeTango does hold up well in cooking, but given its incredible crunch and juice, it's best enjoyed fresh. Plus, at about $1 per apple, it makes an expensive dessert.

ORIGIN: Think of this apple as the "It Girl" of the apple world. Developed at the University of Minnesota in the 1990s, it's a cross between Zestar and Honeycrisp, and was bred to meet the demand for crisp, juicy, sweet-tart apples with complex flavor. It first hit store shelves in the fall of 2009.

AVAILABILITY: Now grown in select orchards in Washington, Minnesota, Wisconsin, New York, Quebec, and Nova Scotia, the fruit is gradually being distributed at supermarkets across the country. Like many popular varieties, the SweeTango is grown only on farms licensed by the University of Minnesota, so don't expect to see it at your local farmers' market. You can, however, find a list of growers at sweetango.com.

SEASON: This early season fruit ripens late August through mid-September—unusual for a northern apple.

APPEARANCE: Medium-large to large and conical, with an ample rosy-red blush over a pale yellow background.

TASTE: With concentrated fruit and spice flavors, it's reminiscent of spiced apple cider, and decidedly more complex than the Honeycrisp.

TEXTURE: Crisp and snappy, with an explosive juiciness.

WESTFIELD SEEK-NO-FURTHER

CATEGORY: Tender-tart.

BEST USE: Eat this flavorful apple fresh off the tree or cooked down in applesauce.

ORIGIN: A late eighteenth-century native of Westfield, Massachusetts, a small town along the Connecticut River, it's also known simply as the Seek-No-Further.

AVAILABILITY: This variety once dominated Massachusetts. Today you can find it at some pick-your-own farms on the East Coast, as well as in Michigan and Minnesota.

SEASON: Ripens in September and October; stores through December.

APPEARANCE: No beauty queen, this apple is medium-sized and creamy yellow-green with red striping and some russeting.

TASTE: Tangy and a bit astringent, but very aromatic, with complex flavors of pear, lemon, and vanilla.

TEXTURE: This apple has an unusual creamy mouthfeel, even though it's still crisp and juicy, and a bit coarse in texture.

WINTER BANANA

CATEGORY: Firm-sweet.

BEST USE: While the Winter Banana's flesh is dense and firm and holds up well in baking, the flavor is so subtle that it's best use is really out-of-hand eating. If you use it in baked desserts, combine it with another, more intensely flavored variety, such as Ginger Gold or Grimes Golden.

ORIGIN: Discovered as a chance seedling on the farm of David Flory, Cass County, Indiana, in 1876. It was introduced commercially in 1890.

AVAILABILITY: This variety is popular in warmer climates because it doesn't require an extended period of cold weather in order to produce blooms, but it is grown around the country. Look for it at farmstands and farmers' markets.

SEASON: A late ripening variety, it's ready to be picked around mid- to late October and doesn't keep much beyond December.

APPEARANCE: Very pretty: medium-sized with a roundish conical shape, waxy deep-yellow skin, and a rose-red blush.

TASTE: The name comes from a reported banana-like flavor. I think I've picked it up, but it's hard to deny the power of suggestion. Either way, the sweet-tart balance is refreshing.

TEXTURE: Firm, a bit coarse, and juicy.

ZABERGAU REINETTE

CATEGORY: Firm-sweet.

BEST USE: Its mild flavor can get lost in pies or other baked desserts, but this apple does hold its shape. Most people prefer simply eating it fresh.

ORIGIN: This chance seedling was discovered in Germany's Zaber River region in 1885.

AVAILABILITY: This is another rarity, at least in the United States. I have bought it from Scott Farm in Dummerston, Vermont, and have seen it sold by Vintage Virginia Apples in North Garden, Virginia.

SEASON: Ripens September to October, depending on the latitude where it's grown. It will keep for several months in storage.

APPEARANCE: Some compare this apple to a potato, thanks to its heavily russeted skin and sometimes conical shape.

TASTE: Quite sweet off the tree, it tends to grow sweeter in storage. True to its russeted skin, it has a distinct nutty flavor.

TEXTURE: It feels very solid in the hand. The flesh is fine-grained and firm, and fairly juicy when it's fresh.

HOW TO TELL IF AN APPLE IS FRESH

The best way to know if you're getting a fresh, ripe apple without biting into it is to buy it at a farm stand, orchard, or farmers' market. There, you can ask the grower when the fruit was picked. Short of that, you can buy fruit marked "local" at the supermarket and be reasonably sure that the fruit is fresh.

Looking at an apple, feeling it for firmness, isn't a surefire way to determine if the fruit is ripe and just-picked. Why? For one, color doesn't indicate ripeness in all apple varieties. Also, apple growers and researchers have ways to keep apples firm and crisp for long periods of time, thanks to controlled atmosphere storage, known industry-wide as "CA." This involves keeping apples in a large, refrigerated room in which levels of oxygen, carbon dioxide, and humidity are tightly controlled. In normal conditions, as apples ripen they take in oxygen and release carbon dioxide and in doing so convert their starches to sugar. Limiting the supply of oxygen puts the fruit in a state of suspended animation. Only when it comes out of CA does it "wake up" and finish ripening.

CA has been around since World War II. Many growers and packers have now added a technology called SmartFresh, a synthetic gas (1-methylcyclopropene) that blocks the effects of the fruit's ripening hormone, ethylene. With SmartFresh, apples can stay crisp and tart for months, even a year. Long storage comes at a cost, though. Treatment with 1-MCP tends to block the development of flavor compounds, called esters, that give apples their rich aromas and complex flavors. The fruits recover somewhat when taken out of storage, but they usually lack the vibrancy of fresh-picked.

WHY ARE SOME APPLES SHINY AND OTHERS NOT?

Apples produce a natural wax coating that protects the fruit from drying out and defends it against mold and disease. If you buy your apples at farm stands or farmers' markets, you've probably noticed the wax, which gives the fruit a cloudy appearance.

In contrast, supermarket apples are usually extremely shiny. When apples are processed in commercial packing houses, they're scrubbed to remove dirt and chemical residues. This strips the skin of much of its natural wax. Packers then spray the fruit with protective coatings like carnauba wax or shellac. These coatings are regulated by the FDA and recognized as safe for consumption. But some consumers worry that coatings trap pesticide residue or may contain emulsifying agents such as morpholine. If you have any concerns about waxed fruit, your best bet is to purchase your apples at the source.

DO APPLES EXPRESS *TERROIR*?

To put it simply, yes. The French viticultural term used to describe how a vineyard's location—the soil, the slope of the land, the neighboring plantings—contributes to a wine's flavor can certainly be applied to apples. An apple grown in a very acidic soil will taste different from one grown in basic soil. A steep hillside location might offer the warm days and cold nights in which McIntosh trees thrive, while a lowland meadow location may produce trees with unexceptional fruit.

However, the whole concept of *terroir* is a slippery one. Some use it to refer only to effects of the soil and the landscape. Others include climatic variables such as temperature, sunshine, and rainfall.

So let me offer a broader, more complete statement: Geography most certainly affects flavor. Talk to any Gravenstein grower in Sonoma, California, and he'll explain how the region's loamy soil, seasonal rain, and sun all contribute to his fruit's sweet flavor profile. The northeastern Gravenstein, in contrast, is more tart. The eastern Grav can keep longer in storage, whereas its western siblings, with their more fully converted sugars, must be consumed within a few weeks of harvest. Meanwhile, a Minnesota Honeycrisp grower might adamantly defend her state's acidic soils and cooler temperatures, arguing that they produce brighter, tarter, better structured fruit than the Honeycrisp grown in Washington.

"It's hard to sort out *terroir* from climate, or from what the growing season is like that year," says Ben Watson, the New Hampshire–based author of *Cider, Hard and Sweet*, and a noted apple expert who hosts varietal tastings around the country through Slow Food USA. "I buy apples year after year from not only the same regions but the same orchardists, and I'll still notice differences."

So many things affect the flavor of an apple, from the mineral content of the soil to the amount of rainfall mid-season, to early frosts at harvest time, it's seems a miracle that so much consistently wonderful fruit is available each year. But despite all the variations, at the end of the day a McIntosh is still recognizable as itself, no matter where or how it's grown. "The variety tends to shine through," Watson says.

CHAPTER THREE

COOKING TIPS AND
PANTRY NOTES

Baldwin

First, a pep talk: Excellent, from-scratch, home cooking is really just a matter of understanding a few key principles, learning some techniques, and using good ingredients and the right tools. See? Easy. Restaurant cooking is another matter—there's a reason why people go to culinary school. But we're not talking about high-concept French cuisine here. We're talking about great apple pie.

Let's get you started on the basics. The following pages will tell you everything you need to know in order to cook the recipes in this book—how to keep apples from browning, how to properly mix a cake, and what sort of butter and apple peeler to buy.

Tips and Techniques

HOW TO PEEL AND CORE AN APPLE

Preparing apples for cooking can be quick work if you use this method. In fact, I used to try to peel perfect unbroken spirals until I realized I was wasting time and tiring my hands for a minor thrill. This way is much better.

1. Line your apple corer up so that it's centered around the stem. Push down through the flesh until you come out the other side. Remove and discard the core.
2. Use your peeler to remove the skin around the top of the apple in a circle, leaving the sides intact. Likewise, peel around the bottom.
3. Now use your peeler to remove the skin from the sides in a top-to-bottom motion, turning the fruit as you go.

HOW TO SLICE AN UNCORED APPLE

In many recipes, I ask you to peel, core, and slice apples to an even thickness. This guarantees that everything cooks evenly, and that your pie slices look as good as they taste. But for homier desserts, like the crisps, buckle, pandowdy, and betty, it's fine to simply peel and slice the apple, without taking out the core first. To slice:

1. Set the apple on a cutting board, stem end up.
2. If you're right-handed, start from the right side; if left-handed, start from the left. Cut the apple into ¼-inch-thick slices on that first side, working down from the top (most larger apples allow three slices per side). Turn the apple a quarter-turn and repeat. Repeat through two more turns. The slices won't be the same width, but they will be the same thickness, and that's all that matters.

HOW TO SLICE A CORED APPLE

1. Set the apple on a cutting board, stem end up.
2. Working from the top, cut the apple into quarters lengthwise.
3. Lay the quarters, cut side down, on the board and cut into wedges of even thickness.

HOW TO DICE AN APPLE

It's much easier to dice an apple that hasn't been cored. Follow instructions above for slicing an uncored apple, then:

1. Stack two or three slices of similar width.
2. Cut the slices lengthwise into ¼-inch-wide sticks.
3. Cut sticks crosswise into ¼-inch cubes.

HOW TO KEEP APPLES FROM TURNING BROWN

Most apple cells contain iron-rich chemicals that oxidize (discolor) when exposed to air. Unless you're working with a variety that resists browning when sliced (see page 30), you'll need to soak the slices in lemon water (1 tablespoon lemon juice per 3 cups water) until ready to serve. If your fruit is already a bit brown, soaking it in the same solution will remove some of the discoloration. You can keep the fruit in the liquid for up to four hours.

HOW TO MEASURE INGREDIENTS

The ingredient lists for the recipes in this book are described by volume measurement (teaspoons, tablespoons, cups, milliliters, etc.) and by weight (in ounces and grams). For small measurements in tablespoons and teaspoons, I stick with volumes—who wants to weigh out half a gram of ground cinnamon? But many bakers feel that measuring larger volumes of, say, flour or butter by weight is more accurate.

To measure by weight, you'll need a kitchen scale—I use a digital model, but a good analog one is fine for our purposes. Set the bowl or container in which you'll be weighing the ingredient on the scale and "tare" the scale so it is reset to 0. That way you won't include the weight of the container in the weight of the ingredient. (See the manufacturer's instructions if you need more help with this.) Add the ingredient to the container until you reach the desired amount.

To measure by volume, follow a few rules: Always use liquid measuring cups (the kind made of glass or clear plastic, with a lip and measurements painted on the side) for liquid ingredients and graduated measuring cups (the kind with handles, usually made of plastic or metal) for dry ingredients. To measure flour, sugar, and other powders, use the measuring cup to scoop the material out of the container or bag, then use a knife or other straight utensil to level off the top so it's even with the edge.

HOW TO MAKE PIE CRUST BY HAND

I have experimented with every method under the sun, from making crusts in frozen bowls using frozen butter, to mixing them in a food processor, to cutting in the fat with knives, forks, and pastry cutters. I've made crusts with butter, vegetable shortening, and a combination of both. I've added vinegar and egg to make the dough more pliant. And in the end, I honestly believe the best pie crust is made by hand in a bowl using only flour, salt, chilled butter, and ice water. My hand-mixed crusts turn out nicely flaky with very little fuss, and don't require as much water to bind them. Less water means less opportunity for gluten development, which ensures a more tender product. I also appreciate not having to wash all ten thousand parts of my food processor every time I make a pie.

The technique is simple: Whisk the flour and salt together. Cut the chilled butter into small cubes and sprinkle them over the flour mixture. Alternatively, you can just add a large chunk of butter to the bowl and use a pastry cutter to break it down into small pieces. Use your hands to work the butter into the flour by rubbing your thumbs against your fingertips—just as if you're making the universal sign for "money." Work quickly so the butter doesn't melt—if it's a very warm day, you can chill the flour and the bowl in the freezer for 15 minutes before mixing—and stop when the mixture looks a bit like cornmeal and there are still some pea-sized bits of butter in the mix (I promise that after a few tries, you'll get more confident about knowing when to stop). Add some ice water, stir with a fork, then knead a few times, press the dough into a disk, and chill for at least 30 minutes. That's it—all you need to make a Blue Ribbon pie crust.

HOW TO MAKE PIE CRUST IN A FOOD PROCESSOR

While I prefer to do my crusts by hand, I know there are some cooks who would rather use a food processor, and that's fine. Here's how: Put your dry ingredients in the bowl and pulse until evenly combined. Sprinkle the cold butter cubes over the flour mixture and pulse several times until the mix resembles coarse cornmeal. Transfer the dough to a large bowl and sprinkle with the ice water. Mix with a fork until the dough comes together—if it seems dry, add more water as recommended in the recipe. Gather the dough into a ball and proceed according to the recipe.

HOW TO ROLL OUT PIE CRUST

It's not easy, rolling delicate pastry into a nice even circle while keeping it from sticking to the counter, and *then* transferring the whole business to a pie plate. But it doesn't have to be vexing. The right technique helps.

For free-form rolling, you'll want take a couple of precautions in order to prevent sticking: **Coat the board** with a thin, even sprinkling of flour; **rotate the dough** a quarter turn after every couple of swipes with the rolling pin; and **keep the dough pliant but cold** (this also prevents the butter from melting into the dough, which is important because it's those little lumps of butter melting and creating steam in the heat of the oven that makes the pastry flaky).

My favorite overall strategy is to **roll the dough between sheets of parchment or wax paper** or in a **pie crust bag** (available in multiple sizes from kingarthurflour.com), both of which take care of the sticking problem and don't require the use of extra flour (too much flour makes a dry crust). If you're rolling the dough to a specific width, you can mark that width right on the paper or, if using the bag, simply choose the bag that matches your desired width and roll the dough to the edges. Both methods simplify the dreaded transfer—just pick up the package, peel off the bottom sheet (or unzip the bag), and set the dough in the pan, then peel off the top.

One last tip: To ensure evenness and improve your chances of ending up with a nice circle, always roll out from the center.

HOW TO MIX A CAKE

You'll notice that most of the cake recipes in this book begin by asking you to beat the butter and sugar together for several minutes—up to 10, in some cases. Don't skimp—keep going until the mixture is pale, very fluffy, and mousselike. There's a good reason: For a cake to have some nice height and good texture, it needs lots of little air bubbles in the batter, which then expand in the heat of the oven. Beating the butter with the sugar incorporates lots of air. I use the whisk attachment on my standing mixer, just to maximize aeration.

HOW TO STORE APPLES

Apples keep best when stored in cold, slightly humid conditions. Your best bet at home is to put the fruit in a paper bag rolled up tight or a plastic bag, loosely tied, with some holes punched in the sides. Stash in a produce drawer. How long they last depends entirely on the variety—some of the best keepers are Granny Smith, Idared, Northern Spy, Rhode Island Greening, and Newtown Pippin—but this technique will hold most apples for at least two weeks.

ON COOKING TIMES

You'll notice that every recipe first lists visual cues ("Cook until golden brown"), then time estimates ("10 to 12 minutes") for assessing when any particular step is complete. Always go by the visual cue! Times can vary, as my stove may be quite different from yours.

Ingredient Notes

APPLES

In the "Apple Notes" section of each recipe, I suggest a couple of apple varieties that would work particularly well. However, some aren't readily available in every market. Always feel free to substitute a more common apple from the same category, as listed on page 30. For example, if the recipe recommends Roxbury Russets and all you have are Granny Smiths, that's just fine. At the same time, please do use this book as an excuse to experiment! Go to your local apple orchard or farmers' market in season. Try new varieties within each category. If you're feeling really adventurous, order more exotic types from the companies on page 282.

APPLE SIZES AND EQUIVALENTS

In general, the recipes in this book ask for a specific number of large or medium or small apples, as well as an approximate weight. Large apples aren't hard to find at supermarkets, given the precision with which most growers sort their fruit. But if you have fruit direct from the orchard or farmers' market, you may have to make adjustments.

On average, a standard American large apple:
- Stands 2¾ to 3¼ inches tall
- Weighs about 8 ounces, or 227 grams
- Yields just under 2 cups sliced or diced fruit

A medium apple:
- Stands about 2½ inches tall
- Weighs about 6 ounces, or 170 grams
- Yields about 1¼ cups sliced or diced fruit

A small apple:
- Stands about 2½ inches tall
- Weighs about 4 ounces, or 113 grams
- Yields about ¾ cup sliced or diced fruit

If a baked apple recipe calls for 6 large fruits, you'll want to use 9 medium fruits or 12 small ones. If the recipe calls for chopped or sliced apples, use the above estimates to determine how many fruits you need.

BUTTER

Many pastry chefs eschew salted butter, arguing that the unsalted variety has purer flavor and higher fat content, which is better for pie crust and pastry. I agree, though I still use salted butter for some cakes, muffins, and other dishes when the fat content isn't as critical. For brands, I recommend Kate's (my favorite, made in Maine), Strauss, Cabot, Vermont Butter & Cheese Creamery, and Plugrá.

BUTTERMILK

I love baking with it, and you'll notice that it shows up in many of the cake and biscuit recipes in this book. To me, buttermilk adds a layer of flavor that I can only describe as the pastry equivalent of *umami*—a rich deliciousness. The acid in the milk also relaxes gluten, making dough more tender. While this may not be a standard ingredient on your refrigerator shelf, it is sold at most every supermarket. Low-fat buttermilk is a better choice for baking than fat free, but if the latter is your only option, you can use them interchangably. And if you don't have any buttermilk at all, you can add a tablespoon of lemon juice or white wine vinegar to a cup of milk, let that sit for 10 minutes, and use it in place of the buttermilk.

FLOUR

All the recipes in this book call for all-purpose flour (I like King Arthur brand).

SALT

I'm a fan of kosher salt. It's easy to sprinkle and seems to have a slightly "cleaner" flavor than iodized (table) salt. For this reason many dishes in the book are made with kosher salt, with the exception of cakes and pastries where sifting is required or where finer-grained table salt simply works better.

If you don't happen to have any kosher salt on hand, you can substitute table salt—just use half the recommended amount.

Tools of the Trade

I'm a sucker for interesting kitchen gadgets, and the only thing that keeps me in check is the finite cabinet space in our kitchen. The recipes in this book don't require much in the way of specialized gear, but a few key tools can make quick work of the requisite peeling, coring, slicing, zesting, rolling, and pureeing.

Note: I recommend my favorite brands here based on my own opinion—I have received nothing in the way of cash or free equipment, not even from the OXO Corporation, whose products I recommend frequently.

APPLE CORER

WHY: Digs out the core in one motion with minimal loss of flesh (the apple's, that is—you'll be unharmed).
BRAND: OXO Good Grips Apple Corer. The large handle is much easier to grip. ($7.95 at cooking.com)

APPLE PEELER

WHY: It's much easier than a paring knife.
BRAND: Some people prefer Y-shaped peelers, but I like OXO's Good Grips swivel peeler. ($7.95 at cooking.com)

APPLE PEELER/CORER

WHY: This old-fashioned tool peels, cores, and slices apples into uniform ¼-inch rings, thus cutting down on prep time.
BRAND: Back to Basics Apple Peeler-Corer. ($28.00 at williams-sonoma.com)

APPLE SLICER

WHY: A great tool for cutting apple wedges into an even thickness for apple pie.
BRAND: Dial-A-Slice Apple Divider lets you cut apples into eight or sixteen slices (½- or ¼-inch widths, respectively), while also removing the core. ($19.95 at williams-sonoma.com)

BISCUIT CUTTER

WHY: Standard sizes ensure consistency, sharp edges make clean cuts. You can use the smallest and largest sizes in your set to make the donuts on page 153.
BRAND: RSVP International's four-piece set. ($8.95 at amazon.com)

FOOD MILL

WHY: Makes quick work of pureeing applesauce and apple butter.

BRAND: Cuisipro's stainless steel food mill is the industry standard for home use. ($89.95 at cutleryandmore.com)

MANDOLINE SLICER

WHY: Allows you to slice fruits and vegetables into perfectly even, paper-thin cuts. Fancier models also allow you to do shoestrings, julienne, and waffle cuts.

BRAND: Cadillac models with all the widgets can go up to $400, but my Kyocera ceramic double-edged mandoline does a great job slicing apples and cucumbers for the pickles on page 270 ($19.95 at cooking.com)

MELON BALLER

WHY: Allows you to scoop out apple cores for baked apples, while still preserving the base of the fruit so the filling stays in.

BRAND: OXO Good Grips Melon Baller. ($8.99 at cooking.com)

MICROPLANE

WHY: You may have heard this a thousand times already, but there's no better way to remove zest from a lemon.

BRAND: Microplane Grater/Zester. (about $12.00 at amazon.com)

CHAPTER FOUR

SOUPS AND STARTERS

Cortland

THE FRUIT OF THE FUTURE:

Inside the Cornell Apple Breeding Program

On this late October day, the air is thick with the sweet scent of apples inside Susan Brown's office at Cornell University's New York State Agricultural Experiment Station (NYSAES) in Geneva, New York. Apples are everywhere: in fruit trays and brown paper bags in one corner of the room, on the artwork and vintage fruit labels tacked to a bulletin board, in the photographs of apple varieties that Brown has introduced in her work as a horticulture professor and apple breeder. And in a pile on the desk in front of me, there are several dozen apples of every size and color: tiny yellow and red crab apples, purple-red apples that resemble plums, giant yellow and orange globes.

As a still life, it's beautiful. As an illustration of apple genetics, it's fascinating. Brown is explaining that many of these fruits were produced from the same two parents, the product of a single controlled cross made many years ago. Brown fertilized one tree entirely with the pollen of another, first removing the male parts—the pollen-producing stalks called stamens—of each flower so that the tree had no chance of pollinating itself. (It's rare for apples to be self-fertilizing, but it does happen in some varieties.) Then she and her team brushed pollen from the chosen "father" onto the female parts (the stigmas) of the mother tree and those pollen grains traveled down to the flower's ovaries where, as the blossoms swelled into fruit, they became seeds. Fifty of those seeds were sprouted and then planted in Brown's research orchards, which cover fifty acres of gently sloping land a few miles west of Seneca Lake. After several years, the seedlings became fruit-bearing trees.

"Many of the apples here are from those fifty seedlings," Brown says. Some resemble the parents clearly, some not at all. "My goal as an apple breeder is for the kids to be better than the parents," Brown says. "Just like you hope that your child gets your eyes but doesn't get the snorty laugh from your husband." So she evaluates the fruits and looks for the ones with the best flavor, size, texture, appearance, storage potential, and disease resistance, among other factors. She does this not just for the fruits of this particular cross, but for all of the 5,000 to 10,000 seedlings that she plants each year. The ones that pass muster are grafted onto dwarf rootstocks and tested in a corner of the orchard reserved for the shining stars. If they continue to do well under these conditions, which resemble those of most modern orchards, they will be released to growers worldwide and marketed as the next new apple. Earlier successes produced by the NYSAES in its nearly 130-year history include Cortland, Empire, Jonagold, Jonamac, and Macoun.

It's hard to imagine that many of the fruits before me are siblings, or even distant cousins. But here they are, evidence of how many different traits are coded in the apple's approximately 56,000 genes (the human genome has somewhere between 20,000 and 25,000 genes), the sequence of which was only recently decoded. "The diversity you see here for color and shape is also there for juiciness, acidity, sugar, the whole nine yards," Brown says. "Most consumers want crisp, juicy, firm apples. So I'm trying to up the components of all those things. For example, if you buy an apple in the store and it's 12 degrees brix [a unit for measuring the sugar concentration in a fruit], you're going to like it more if it's 13 degrees brix. We have some apples here that are twenty degrees brix. But then we have to try to balance that with acid." Brown's team has produced apples that are so crisp and densely packed with juicy cells that biting into them feels almost like popping a water balloon. "You could have that apple in your car for six months and it's not going to get mushy and mealy," she says. Others have been bred to contain as much vitamin C as oranges, or high levels of quercetin, a natural antioxidant that may have a role in protecting brain cells from Alzheimer's disease.

In other words, Brown is trying to improve on what nature would produce on its own. Or, rather, she's speeding up the process, both through classic plant breeding experiments and through genetic engineering, in which individual genes for, say, resistance to fire blight, can be inserted into apples while leaving all the other desirable traits intact. And now that the apple's genetic sequence has been mapped out, scientists can even do traditional breeding more efficiently: By analyzing the genetic makeup of a new hybrid and looking for genes associated with red skin, high sugar content, and juiciness, they can have some sense of what sort of fruit a seedling will produce long before its first harvest.

Brown drives me out to her orchards, and here I can see the apple's vast genetic potential displayed in all its glory: rows and rows of gorgeous fruit in every shade; some trees as tall as giants, others just two feet tall. Some of the fruit hangs from widely sweeping branches, some on boughs as tall and straight as columns. These are the so-called columnar apples, which Brown is breeding for home apple growers who may not have the room to grow regular trees, nor the skills to prune them each winter. In another area, Brown is experimenting with a pear-apple cross that could yield a new hybrid with the best traits of both species.

We make our way down several rows, tasting mealy bland apples and richly flavored sweet-tart ones that could've been contenders, if only they weren't so prone to bitter pit, a calcium deficiency. Eventually these undesirables will be ripped out to make room for more seedlings.

As we inspect each tree, it occurs to me that most of my research up to this point has biased me toward historic heirloom apple varieties with charming names like Black Gilliflower or Keswick Codlin, and against newer, seemingly "scientific" breeds like Gala and Fuji. Somehow, they just don't seem as romantic as the fruit of the nineteenth-century pomological golden age. But Brown's work is proof that apples lose none of their beauty when they're produced with modern technology.

"People talk about heirloom varieties," Brown says, "but a lot of them aren't that good. Maybe they were suited to store well in a cellar, maybe they had attributes to survive in a particular climate or handle rough treatment, but a lot of the apples of that time were merely a source of cider." From Brown's perspective, a classic McIntosh may make a great applesauce, but its tart flavor and soft texture would not pass muster in her test orchard.

Then there's the quest for non-browning flesh. "McDonald's became the biggest purchaser of apples in the country once they introduced those Apple Dippers [little packets of apple slices with caramel sauce] to their menu." Brown says. "They want apples with white flesh, so if we can create some that are naturally non-browning, that's a huge market." Apple breeding is an expensive proposition—consider how much land it requires and how long it takes to get a product to the market—and finding ways to subsidize the research is key. Even once a new variety has been bred and selected, it can take fifteen to twenty years for it to gain commercial acceptance. So plant breeders are finding new ways to promote their fruit. The University of Minnesota is a leader in this area, having used a sophisticated marketing campaign and social networking tools such as Facebook and Twitter to build demand for its Honeycrisp and SweetTango varieties, while also charging steep fees to a select group of farmers for the privilege of growing them.

Back at Brown's office, she shows me what all this innovation is for: five new apples at various stages on their way to release, all better than many of the apples that I buy at my local supermarket. The one nearest to its commercial debut, called NY1 until someone comes up with a snazzier name, is exceptional in its crunch and sweet-tart juice. It's a cross between a Honeycrisp and another NYSAES apple called NY752 and has Honeycrisp's signature texture and floral flavors, but with some key improvements. "Only forty to fifty percent of Honeycrisp fruit can be marketed," Brown notes. "Their stems tend to puncture each other, so some growers clip the stems, which adds to the cost. They're also vulnerable to bitter pit." NY1 doesn't have these problems.

Another apple soon to be released, NY2, is deep red and conic in shape. It's so crunchy that the noise seems to echo when I bite into it, but I'm less enamored of the flavor, which strikes me as vegetal. I'm more intrigued by NY118, which tastes of the spice star anise—a first for me in years of apple tasting.

But it's only when Brown hands me a sample of NY109 that I really fall in love. It's a rounder apple, with colors that run from red-orange to yellow and a little russeting on the skin. The flavors are so complex that it's hard for me even to identify them. I taste nut, spice, honey, lemon, and berry in a flood of tart-sweet juice. I want to go and raid the entire tree. Brown says that the russeting will probably be a problem for many consumers, who see it as a defect. She may look for a way to develop a smoother-skinned version. But as far as I'm concerned, this apple is a little taste of paradise. I ask her how long it will take before I can buy this fruit in the supermarket. "Realistically, years," Brown says. Improving on Mother Nature takes time. And changing consumer preferences takes even longer.

Bacon-Wrapped Dates with Curried Apple Hash

Chef Will Gilson serves these delectable hors d'oeuvres at his Cambridge, Massachusetts, restaurant, Garden at the Cellar. He created them for his fall menu, but found that any attempts to take them off the roster during the warm weather months were met with howls of outrage. And so they remain. The genius lies in combining dates and bacon—one of the best of all food pairings—with a sweet-savory mix of grated apples, onion, and curry.

APPLE NOTES: The hash calls for a very tart green apple, such as Granny Smith, Rhode Island Greening, or Roxbury Russet. (See page 30 for more firm-tart apple varieties.)

NOTES: Applewood-smoked bacon is ideal for this dish, but any thick-cut bacon will work well. Medjool dates are available at most supermarkets and Whole Foods stores.

EQUIPMENT: 12-inch heavy-bottomed skillet or sauté pan; 12 toothpicks; mandoline (optional)

MAKES: *6 servings* • ACTIVE TIME: *35 minutes* • TOTAL TIME: *50 minutes*

FOR THE DATES

12 slices thick-cut bacon (see Notes)

¼ cup (55 g) fresh goat cheese

1 teaspoon finely chopped fresh rosemary

12 Medjool dates, pitted (see Notes)

FOR THE HASH

¼ cup (60 ml) extra-virgin olive oil

½ cup (70 g) finely chopped white onion

4 large firm-tart apples (about 2 pounds total; see Apple Notes) peeled, cored, and cut into matchsticks using a knife or mandoline

1 tablespoon curry powder

2 tablespoons finely chopped fresh chives

½ teaspoon kosher salt

½ teaspoon freshly ground black pepper

1 • Prep the dates: In the skillet, cook the bacon over medium heat until just beginning to brown around the edges but still pink and soft, 6 to 8 minutes. Set aside. In a small bowl, stir together the goat cheese and rosemary.

2 • Preheat the oven to 400°F. Stuff a bit of cheese mixture into each date, then wrap each one with a bacon slice and secure with a toothpick. Set aside.

3 • Make the hash: Heat the oil in a medium skillet over medium heat, then add the onion and cook until translucent, about 5 minutes. Add the apples to the pan and cook until they are limp, about 5 minutes. Add the curry powder, chives, salt, and pepper, then stir and let sit over low heat.

4 • Bake the dates until the bacon is fully cooked, 6 to 8 minutes. Remove the toothpicks. Divide the hash among six plates, then top with dates, two per plate.

Chicken Liver Pâté with Apple

I adapted this recipe from a wonderful chicken liver pâté in the 1965 cookbook *Michael Field's Cooking School*. Field was a gifted food writer and teacher who ran a cooking school in Manhattan in the 1960s, and he had a wonderful way of making French cooking seem completely accessible to home cooks. This dish is a perfect example. His chicken liver pâté is as silky as foie gras and the apples and Calvados (apple brandy) add a heady sweetness. It's also quite easy to make. Serve with toasted French bread, walnuts, and fresh apple slices.

APPLE NOTES: This pâté should be as smooth as possible, so tender-tart apples, which cook down easily (see page 30), are best. McIntosh, Macoun, Jonathan, Empire—any and all would be very good here.

EQUIPMENT: 12- to 14-inch skillet or sauté pan; electric blender; large fine-mesh sieve; 3-cup crock, serving bowl, or terrine

MAKE-AHEAD TIP: The pâté will keep, covered, for several days. You can also freeze it for up to three months; let thaw in the refrigerator.

MAKES: *About 3 cups* • ACTIVE TIME: *45 minutes* •
TOTAL TIME: *45 minutes, plus 3½ to 4½ hours cooling and chilling time*

1 pound (454 g) fresh or thawed frozen chicken livers

16 tablespoons (227 g) unsalted butter, divided, at room temperature

½ cup (70 g) finely chopped onion

2 tablespoons finely chopped shallots

1 small tender-tart apple (about 4 ounces; see Apple Notes), peeled, cored, and roughly chopped

¼ cup (60 ml) Calvados (apple brandy) or applejack

2 to 4 tablespoons heavy cream

1 teaspoon lemon juice

1 teaspoon table salt

¼ teaspoon freshly ground black pepper

LEFT: Chicken Liver Pâté with Apple. Calvados and a sautéed apple impart a hint of sweetness.

1 • Prepare the chicken livers: Rinse them quickly in cold water, then pat dry and cut in half. Set aside. In a skillet over medium heat, melt 3 tablespoons butter. Add onions and shallots and cook, stirring often, until lightly golden, 5 to 7 minutes. Add the apple and cook until tender enough to mash with a spoon, about 5 minutes. Transfer the mixture to a blender.

2 • In the same skillet over medium-high heat, melt 3 tablespoons more butter. Add the chicken livers and cook, stirring gently, until they are browned outside and still pink within (cut several with a sharp knife to check), 3 to 5 minutes. Remove the pan from the heat and add the Calvados or applejack. Return to the heat and let simmer for 1 minute to let the alcohol cook off. Add the mixture to the blender. Add 2 tablespoons of the cream to the blender and blend at high speed until the mixture is very smooth. If it seems too thick, add additional cream, one tablespoon at a time. When the mixture looks like velvet, pour through a sieve set over a bowl, using a spatula to push it through. Let cool completely to room temperature, about 30 minutes. (Don't skip this step; it's important.)

3 • Put the remaining butter in the bowl of a standing mixer (or in a large bowl if using a hand-held mixer) and mix with the paddle attachment until it is very smooth. Add ½ cup of the fully cooled liver mixture and beat until well combined. Repeat with the remaining liver mixture, ½ cup at a time, until it is all incorporated. Add the lemon juice, salt, and pepper and stir to combine. Using a spatula, pack the pâté into a serving dish or terrine, cover tightly with plastic wrap, and refrigerate for 3 to 4 hours until firm. Serve chilled.

Apple, Cheddar, and Caramelized Onion Pastry Puffs

Apples and caramelized onions are an unbeatable combination, especially when paired with Cheddar cheese. Using store-bought puff pastry and cooking the onions ahead of time makes this a very simple appetizer that you can assemble and bake right before your party.

APPLE NOTES: Any firm-tart apples (see page 30) will work well here, but I particularly like the more aromatic varieties, such as Arkansas Black, Esopus Spitzenburg, Newtown Pippin, Northern Spy, Sierra Beauty, or Stayman Winesap.

EQUIPMENT: 12-inch skillet or sauté pan; large rimless baking sheet

MAKES: About *40 puffs* • ACTIVE TIME: *45 minutes* • TOTAL TIME: *1 hour, 10 minutes*

2 tablespoons (28 g) salted butter

2 large yellow onions, sliced crosswise into ⅛-inch-thick rings

1 tablespoon fresh thyme leaves

1 teaspoon kosher salt

6 tablespoons (90 ml) fresh apple cider, divided

1 sheet good-quality store-bought puff pastry, such as Dufour, kept cold

1 medium firm-tart apple (about 6 ounces; see Apple Notes) unpeeled, cored and cut into very thin slices

3 cups (290 g) finely grated sharp Cheddar cheese

1 • In a skillet or sauté pan over medium-low heat, melt the butter, then add the onions, thyme, and salt. Cover and cook, stirring occasionally, until the onions are translucent but do not change color, about 10 minutes. Remove the cover, raise the heat to medium, and pour in 4 tablespoons of the cider, scraping the pan with a wooden spoon to pick up any browned bits. Cook this liquid down until reduced to just a tablespoon or so, about 8 minutes, then add the remaining 2 tablespoons of cider, scraping the bottom once more, and cook until the onions are golden brown, about 10 minutes.

2 • Preheat the oven to 375°F and set the rack in the second-to-lowest position. Put the chilled pastry on the ungreased baking sheet and roll out to a rectangle about 12 by 15 inches. If the pastry becomes soft or sticky during this process, put it in the freezer for 10 minutes to chill. Using a sharp knife or pizza cutter, cut the pastry in crisscrossing diagonal lines to form diamond-shaped pieces, each about 3 inches wide at the widest point. Top the center of each piece with an apple slice (trim to fit), a small pile of onions, and a sprinkling of cheese. Bake until the cheese is melted and the pastry is puffed and golden brown, 30 to 35 minutes. Transfer to a warmed platter and serve immediately.

Apple Chips with Spiced Yogurt Dip

This whimsical play on chips and dip packs all the flavor of apple pie into a light and healthy snack. You can also serve the dip with fresh fruit, such as sliced apples, blackberries, strawberries, peaches, or bananas.

MAKES: *2 cups* • ACTIVE TIME: *5 minutes* • TOTAL TIME: *5 minutes*

2 cups (480 ml) lowfat (2%) plain Greek yogurt

3 to 4 tablespoons honey

1 tablespoon plus 1 teaspoon fresh lemon juice

¾ teaspoon vanilla extract

1 teaspoon ground cinnamon

¼ teaspoon ground ginger

Two large bags crisp apple chips, such as Bare Fruit brand (see page 283)

In a medium bowl, combine the yogurt, 3 tablespoons of the honey, the lemon juice, vanilla, cinnamon, and ginger. Stir together and taste; add more honey if you prefer. Transfer to a bowl and serve on a platter with apple chips.

Sweet Potato, Apple, and Ginger Soup

I love making pureed vegetable soups, because you can produce something quite rich and cozy with very little added fat. This one is a superlative warmer, with great body, a bit of sweetness, and a warm hit of ginger.

APPLE NOTES: Here's a rare case (at least in this book) where you could use pretty much any apple variety and have this soup come out beautifully. However, a sweeter apple is ideal, so consult the lists of firm-sweet and tender-sweet apples on page 30.

NOTE: You can adjust the amount of ginger to your taste, depending on whether or not you like a lot of spice. I generally use a 1½-inch-long piece that's a bit wider than my thumb, and the result is identifiably gingery, though not overwhelmingly so.

EQUIPMENT: 4- to 5-quart Dutch oven or other heavy-bottomed pot; large rimmed baking sheet; immersion blender or regular blender

MAKES: *6 cups* • ACTIVE TIME: *30 minutes* • TOTAL TIME: *1 hour, 10 minutes*

1 pound sweet potatoes (455 g, about 2), peeled and cut into ¾-inch cubes

½ pound (227 g) baby-cut carrots

1 large apple (about 8 ounces; see Apple Notes), unpeeled, cored and cut into 1-inch chunks

5 tablespoons (75 ml) olive oil, divided

1½ teaspoons kosher salt, divided, plus more to taste

½ teaspoon freshly ground black pepper, divided

1 medium yellow onion, diced

1- to 2-inch-long piece ginger, peeled and cut into medium chunks (see Note)

3 garlic cloves, coarsely chopped

1 bay leaf

4 cups (945 ml) reduced-sodium chicken or vegetable broth

½ cup (120 ml) fresh apple cider

1 • Preheat the oven to 400°F. In a medium bowl, toss the potato, carrots, and apple with 3 tablespoons of the olive oil, 1 teaspoon of the kosher salt, and ¼ teaspoon of the pepper. Arrange on a foil-lined sheet pan (shiny side up) and roast until tender, about 30 minutes. Set aside.

2 • Meanwhile, add the remaining 2 tablespoons oil to the pot and set over medium-high heat. Add the onion, ginger, garlic, bay leaf, and remaining ½ teaspoon salt and ¼ teaspoon pepper and cook until the onions just begin to turn golden, 8 to 10 minutes. Add the roasted vegetables, broth, and cider, stir, and bring to a simmer. Reduce heat to low, cover, and simmer for 30 minutes.

3 • Remove the bay leaf from the pot and use an immersion blender or regular blender to puree the soup until smooth. If using a regular blender, process the soup in three batches to avoid splattering hot liquid. Return the pureed soup to the pot, taste for seasoning, and serve.

Chestnut Soup with
Spiced Apple-Cranberry Compote

If you've tried a few recipes from this book already, you may have noticed I'm fond of dishes that have sweet and savory elements. This is a terrific example. The soup is nutty and creamy, and the compote adds crunch and sweet contrast. Using pre-roasted, vacuum-packed chestnuts makes it all incredibly easy. And if you don't want to prepare the compote to go with it, the variation below, topped with crumbled bacon, is an easy and delicious alternative.

APPLE NOTES: See page 30 for a list of firm-tart apples. I particularly like green-skinned varieties, such as Granny Smith or Rhode Island Greening here.

NOTE: Vacuum-packed roasted chestnuts are available at gourmet and Whole Foods stores, and at many grocery stores during the holiday season.

EQUIPMENT: 4- to 5-quart Dutch oven or other heavy-bottomed pot; large rimmed baking sheet; immersion blender or regular blender

MAKES: *6 servings* • ACTIVE TIME: *30 minutes* • TOTAL TIME: *50 minutes*

2 tablespoons (28 g) salted butter

1 tablespoon olive oil

1 large red onion, coarsely chopped

1 celery stalk, coarsely chopped

2 medium carrots, peeled and coarsely chopped

1 large firm-tart apple, (About 8 ounces; see Apple Notes), peeled, cored, and coarsely chopped

2 bay leaves

1 teaspoon kosher salt

4 cups (945 ml) low-sodium chicken or vegetable broth

22-ounce jar (624 g) vacuum-packed roasted chestnuts (see Note)

¼ cup (60 ml) heavy cream

Spiced Apple-Cranberry Compote (page 236)

1 • In a pot, melt the butter with the olive oil over medium heat. Add the onion, celery, and carrots, and cook, stirring often, until the onions are golden brown, 12 to 15 minutes. Add the apple, bay leaves, and salt, and cook for 3 minutes, then add the broth, scraping the bottom of the pot with a wooden spoon to pick up browned bits. Add the chestnuts and cook until very tender, about 15 minutes.

$2 \cdot$ Remove the bay leaves, then puree the soup using an immersion blender or process in batches in a regular blender (do not fill more than halfway, to avoid the risk of splattering). Return the pureed soup to the pot. Stir in the cream and taste for salt; add more of either, if desired. Serve warm with a generous dollop of Apple Compote in the center.

Variation • Chestnut Soup with Bacon: In a Dutch oven or other large, heavy-bottomed pot, cook 4 slices bacon over medium heat until very crispy. Set aside the bacon and drain off all but 3 tablespoons bacon drippings, then add 1 tablespoon olive oil and proceed with step 1 as in original recipe. Serve with crumbled bacon instead of compote.

CHAPTER FIVE

VEGETABLE ENTREES, SIDES, AND SALADS

Zabergau Reinette

A Visit to Red Apple Farm
in Phillipston, Massachusetts

Red Apple Farm looks like a New England apple orchard out of central casting: country road lined with maples and stone walls? Check. Rows of apple trees? Check. White farmhouse? Check. Red farmstand stocked with dumplings, apples, and jams? Check. Hay rides and a pumpkin patch? You got it.

But here's something that you probably didn't expect to see, over by the picnic pavilion near the front gate: a craggy old tree, sagging in parts and worse for the wear, but festooned with tiny red fruits on this bough, and yellow ones up above, and big pink globes underneath, and . . . wait, are those McIntosh above that?

Why, yes. And those are crab apples, and that's a Winter Banana, and these are just a few of the 108 varieties growing on this single tree, which, back in 1970 when it was first planted, was just a plain Cortland.

Welcome to the magic of grafting. This tree, which serves no practical purpose other than attracting tourists, is a testament to *Malus domestica*'s hospitality, allowing any number of cuttings to travel from one tree to another and set up house.

I've talked about why grafting is necessary—apples don't reproduce true to seed. But it's also interesting to learn about how it's done. Al Rose, Red Apple Farm's affable proprietor—the fourth generation of his family to farm apples here—took me through the steps.

(I should note that his technique is a popular type of grafting called dormant wood grafting, which is done only during the cold weather months. There is another type, called live wood grafting or budding, which can be performed during the growing season. But because the former type is the most common, I focus on that here.)

You start with two trees. One, the breed of choice, is chosen for the quality of its fruit. The other, called the rootstock, is chosen for being well adapted to its surroundings. Perhaps it's able to resist a common disease in the area, or can tolerate hot or cold temperatures, or has strong roots that can reach a distant water table. In any case, the rootstock is the solid, reliable foundation from which the fruit variety can spring forth.

In the winter, when the trees lie dormant, or, as Al puts it, "when the juices aren't flowing," you cut branches from your favorite fruit trees, and these become the scions. They must be small and young, from last year's growth, and they must go into a cold, dark, moist spot to remain dormant until grafting time.

In order for this type of graft to take, you want the scion and the host tree to essentially wake up from their long winter nap together. So deciding when to perform the graft come spring is a bit of an art. "There are specific windows when the sap starts flowing," Al says. "Around here, its in late March. That's your critical time when the graft is more likely to take. Even if you do it right, you're still not going to get a one hundred percent success rate."

But you cross your fingers and make a cut in the rootstock and a matching cut in the scion, exposing the live inner wood (the cambium) of each to the other and fitting them together like puzzle pieces. "You can do a wedge cut, you can do a z-cut," Al says. "It's very artistic. Everyone has their own preferred way."

Then you seal the graft, using wax or tape, or watertight compounds, and wait, first for several weeks to see if the scion lives, and then for a year or two to learn how it bears fruit. "If all goes well," Al says, "what's growing above the graft joint will be an exact replica of the parent tree, an ongoing continuation of the original." But there are no guarantees. Sometimes the scions are injured by the cold, sometimes the graft dries out or succumbs to disease. Sometimes the cambium tissues fail to line up exactly. As with everything related to apple growing, grafting requires patience. But if you do it right, you get perfect fruit, reproduced ad infinitum. And if you're feeling particularly adventurous, you get a Technicolor tree surrounded by dazzled school kids pointing to their favorite fruit *right up there* . . . no, *there* . . . oh, wait! Up there . . .

Endive Salad with Apples, Walnuts, and Gorgonzola

Apple, walnuts, and Gorgonzola are such a tried-and-true combination: the fragrant cheese is like a little flavor bridge between the fruit and the toasty nuts. Add walnut oil and cider vinegar to the mix, and you have some lovely harmony.

APPLE NOTES: The Cheat Sheet on page 30 lists apple varieties that resist browning and are thus excellent for salads. Some examples: Cortland, Ginger Gold, Spigold, and Fuji.

NOTES: You can find walnut oil in most gourmet, natural, and Whole Foods stores. If necessary, you can substitute any variety of olive oil. Gorgonzola dolce is a popular Italian blue cheese made with cow's milk and aged for just three months. This brief maturation gives it a lighter flavor than most blues—*dolce* means "sweet"—and a softer, creamier texture.

EQUIPMENT: 8- to 12-inch heavy-bottomed skillet

MAKES: *4 servings* • ACTIVE TIME: *25 minutes* • TOTAL TIME: *25 minutes*

FOR THE VINAIGRETTE

- 3 tablespoons cider vinegar
- 1 tablespoon honey
- ½ teaspoon kosher salt
- ¼ teaspoon freshly ground black pepper
- 2 medium shallots, minced
- ½ cup (120 ml) walnut oil (see Notes) or olive oil

FOR THE SALAD

- ¾ cup (65 g) walnut halves, chopped
- 5 Belgian endive, ends trimmed and leaves pulled off and roughly chopped
- 1 large salad-friendly apple (about 8 ounces, see Apple Notes), unpeeled, cored and cut into ⅛-inch-thick wedges
- 2 ounces (57 g) Gorgonzola dolce (see Notes), broken into small pieces

1 • Make the vinaigrette: In a small bowl, whisk together the vinegar, honey, salt, and pepper until the salt dissolves. Add the shallots and let sit for 10 minutes (this is a good time to toast your walnuts; see below). Drizzle in the walnut oil in a thin stream, whisking as you go. Set aside.

2 • Toast the walnuts in a skillet over medium-low heat, stirring occasionally, until brown and fragrant, about 10 minutes. Set out four chilled salad plates and arrange one-fourth of the endive on each. Top with apple slices, bits of Gorgonzola, and walnuts. Serve immediately with the vinaigrette on the side.

Autumn "Coleslaw" with Dates, Apples, and Pecans

This is the perfect fall potluck dish: simple, healthy, ample, and unexpected. The trick is to slice the cabbage very thinly so that the dressing can soften it a bit. You want the cabbage to be silky, in contrast to the crisp apples and crunchy nuts.

APPLE NOTES: The Cheat Sheet on page 30 lists apple varieties that resist browning and are thus excellent for salads. Some examples: Cortland, Ginger Gold, Spigold, and Fuji.

NOTE: To get the best results, use a mandoline. It produces paper-thin ribbons of cabbage—the ideal texture.

EQUIPMENT: 8- to 12-inch heavy-bottomed skillet; mandoline (optional)

MAKES: *6 to 8 servings* • ACTIVE TIME: *40 minutes* • TOTAL TIME: *40 minutes*

FOR THE SALAD

¾ cup (80 g) pecan halves, chopped

1 small head (1.5 pounds or 680 g) red cabbage, cored, with first 2 layers of outer leaves removed

2 large salad-friendly apples (about 1 pound total; see Apple Notes), unpeeled, cored and cut into matchsticks

¾ cup (90 g) chopped pitted dates

⅓ cup (11 g) chopped fresh cilantro

1 large shallot, thinly sliced crosswise

FOR THE DRESSING

¼ cup (45 ml) almond oil or olive oil

¼ cup (45 ml) lemon juice

2 tablespoons honey

½ teaspoon kosher salt

½ teaspoon freshly ground black pepper

1 • In a skillet over medium-low heat, toast the pecans, stirring often, until browned and fragrant, about 10 minutes. Set aside.

2 • Quarter the cabbage lengthwise, then lay each section on its side and slice with a mandoline, or use a knife to slice down as thinly as possible, as if you're shaving the cabbage. As you get to the outer edge of the quarter, feel free to stop. It gets too difficult to thinly cut at that point. You should have 8 cups cabbage. Toss the cabbage with the apples, dates, cilantro, and shallot.

3 • In a small bowl, whisk together the oil, lemon juice, honey, salt, and pepper. Pour over the salad and toss. Sprinkle with toasted pecans.

Apple, Pistachio, Persimmon, and Pomegranate Salad

Apple, Pistachio, Persimmon, and Pomegranate Salad

This salad is inspired by my years in San Francisco, where apples, persimmons, and pomegranates were in season each fall. To a native New Englander, it was incredible that a person could have a pomegranate tree in her backyard, let alone persimmons, which are are so bright and pretty hanging from the branches—like little pumpkins. In this salad, the light honey-lemon dressing complements the brightness of the fruit.

APPLE NOTES: Your best bet for this sweeter salad is to choose a sweeter variety that doesn't brown when sliced. Gala and Fuji are good options, but consult page 30 for a complete list.

EQUIPMENT: 8- to 10-inch heavy-bottomed skillet

MAKES: *6 servings* • ACTIVE TIME: *30 minutes* • TOTAL TIME: *30 minutes*

FOR THE DRESSING

¼ cup (60 ml) freshly squeezed lemon juice

1 tablespoon honey

½ teaspoon kosher salt

½ teaspoon freshly ground black pepper

2 tablespoons olive or grapeseed oil

FOR THE SALAD

½ cup (56 g) shelled unsalted pistachios

8 ounces (225 g) baby arugula

2 medium salad-friendly tender-sweet apples (about 12 ounces total; see Apple Notes), unpeeled, cored, and cut into ¼-inch-thick slices

2 ripe Fuyu persimmons, cut into ¼-inch-thick slices

Seeds from 1 pomegranate (about 1 cup or 155 g)

1 • For the dressing: In a small bowl, whisk together the lemon juice, honey, salt, and pepper until the salt dissolves. Slowly drizzle in the oil, whisking as you go, until the mixture is emulsified. Set aside.

2 • In a skillet over medium-low heat, toast the pistachios, stirring often, until browned and fragrant, about 10 minutes. Set aside.

3 • Set out six serving plates, preferably chilled. Divide the arugula among the plates, then top each plate with equal portions of apples and persimmons. Sprinkle each plate with pistachios and pomegranate seeds. Just before serving, drizzle with dressing.

Chicken Waldorf Salad

The original Waldorf Salad was the creation of Oscar Tschirky, the first maître d'hôtel of the Waldorf Astoria in New York. In his 1896 book, *The Cook Book by 'Oscar of the Waldorf,'* he gives the following instructions: "Peel two raw apples and cut them into small pieces, say about half an inch square, also cut some celery the same way, and mix it with the apple. Be very careful not to let any seeds of the apples be mixed with it. The salad must be dressed with a good mayonnaise." Over the years, walnuts were added, then raisins, and the Waldorf became an American classic. An apple cookbook isn't complete without one, but I've never been a fan of fruit in mayonnaise, or raisins in salads. So I replaced the raisins with red grapes and tossed them with apples and lettuce in a simple lemon vinaigrette. Then I mixed chicken, celery, and lots of toasted walnuts in a creamy dressing of Greek yogurt with mayo, lemon juice, tarragon, and onion. It's like a chicken salad mixed in with a green salad combined with a fruit salad. And all those parts come together in a fresher, more flavorful whole.

APPLE NOTES: Page 30 notes apple varieties that resist browning and are thus good for salads. Some examples: Cortland, Ginger Gold, Spigold, Piñata, and Fuji. Any would go very well here.

NOTES: If you don't like tarragon, you can substitute parsley, chervil, or chives. A 1½ pound rotisserie chicken will give you enough meat for this salad. Of course, you can poach your own chicken breasts, but the pre-cooked chicken is easy and affordable.

EQUIPMENT: 8- to 12-inch heavy-bottomed skillet

MAKES: *4 servings as a lunch entree, 6 as a side dish* •
ACTIVE TIME: *30 minutes* • TOTAL TIME: *30 minutes*

FOR THE DRESSINGS

¼ cup (60 ml) fresh lemon juice, divided

1 tablespoon olive oil

½ teaspoon kosher salt, divided

⅓ cup (about 3 ounces or 100 g) lowfat (2%) Greek yogurt

2 tablespoons mayonnaise

1 tablespoon minced fresh tarragon (see Notes)

1 teaspoon honey

½ teaspoon freshly grated lemon zest

¼ teaspoon freshly ground black pepper

2 tablespoons (about ½ ounce or 18 g) minced sweet onion, such as Walla Walla or Vidalia

⅔ cup (75 g) walnut pieces

½ pound (226 g) breast and/or thigh meat from a rotisserie chicken (see Notes)

1½ large celery stalks (about 4 ounces or 113 g), sliced crosswise very thinly

6 ounces butter (Boston) lettuce

1 cup (about 6 ounces or 175 g) halved seedless red grapes

1 medium salad-friendly apple (about 6 ounces or 170 g; see Apple Notes) cored and cut into thin wedges

1 • First, make the dressings: In a small bowl, whisk together 1 tablespoon lemon juice with the olive oil and ¼ teaspoon kosher salt. Set aside. In another small bowl, stir together the yogurt, mayonnaise, tarragon, honey, remaining lemon juice, lemon zest, remaining salt, and pepper. Stir in the onion. Set aside while you prepare the salad.

2 • Toast the walnuts in a skillet over medium-low heat, stirring occasionally, until brown and fragrant, about 10 minutes. Pour into a medium bowl and let cool as you prepare the chicken: Remove any skin and tear the chicken into 2- to 3-inch strips. Add to the bowl with the walnuts. Add the celery and the yogurt dressing and stir so that everything is evenly covered.

3 • In a serving bowl, toss the lettuce, grapes, and apple slices with the lemon-oil dressing. Spoon the chicken mixture over all. Use your hands to lightly fluff the leaves and grapes, just to make it look pretty. Serve on chilled salad plates.

Spinach, Apple, Pickled Onion, and Bacon Salad with Cider Vinaigrette

Holding true to the old adage that everything tastes better with bacon on it, we have this simple combination of crisp bacon, apple, and pickled onion. Don't be intimidated by the pickling: a quick (20 minute) soak in vinegar, honey, and salt just takes the peppery edge off the onions, while preserving their essential crunch.

APPLE NOTES: The Cheat Sheet on page 30 lists apple varieties that resist browning and are thus excellent for salads. Some examples: Cortland, Ginger Gold, Spigold, and Fuji.

EQUIPMENT: 8- to 10-inch heavy-bottomed skillet

MAKES: *6 to 8 servings* • ACTIVE TIME: *35 minutes* • TOTAL TIME: *35 minutes*

FOR THE VINAIGRETTE

⅓ cup (80 ml) cider vinegar

1 tablespoon honey

½ teaspoon kosher salt

½ medium red onion, cut crosswise into very thin slices

2 teaspoons Dijon mustard

1 tablespoon olive oil

FOR THE SALAD

6 slices bacon

5 to 6 ounces (142 to 170 g) baby spinach leaves

1 large salad-friendly apple (about 8 ounces; see Apple Notes), unpeeled, cored, and cut into ⅛-inch-thick slices

1 • In a small bowl, whisk together the vinegar, honey, and salt until the salt dissolves. Add the onion slices and let sit while you prepare the rest of the salad, 20 to 30 minutes.

2 • Meanwhile, in a skillet over medium heat, cook the bacon until brown and very crisp, about 10 minutes. Crumble and set aside. Reserve 2 tablespoons of bacon drippings in a small bowl; discard the rest.

3 • Using tongs or a slotted spoon, remove the onion slices from the vinegar mixture and set aside. Then finish the vinaigrette: Add the mustard to the vinegar mixture and whisk to combine. Slowly drizzle in the drippings and olive oil, whisking to emulsify.

4 • In a large salad bowl, toss together the spinach, pickled onions, and apple slices. Just before serving, add the vinaigrette to taste. Toss well. Top with crumbled bacon and serve at room temperature.

Cider-Glazed Root Vegetables

Apple cider has a wonderful ability to cook down to a sweet, tangy, lustrous glaze. This is a terrific side dish for the Cider-Brined Pork Chops on page 142 or the Apple and Chestnut–Stuffed Pork Loin on page 145 or as a vegetarian side dish, served with the protein of your choice. (See pages 144 and 146 for photographs of the finished vegetables.)
EQUIPMENT: Large rimmed baking sheet; 12- to 14-inch skillet

MAKES: *6 servings* • ACTIVE TIME • *45 minutes* • TOTAL TIME: *60 minutes*

1 large (about 3 pounds or 1.4 kg) butternut squash, peeled and seeded

2 large parsnips (about 12 ounces or 340 g total), peeled

2 large carrots (about 8 ounces or 230 g total), peeled

2 tablespoons olive oil

1 teaspoon kosher salt

½ teaspoon freshly ground black pepper

2 tablespoons (28 g) salted butter

1 teaspoon minced ginger

1½ cups (357 ml) fresh apple cider

1½ teaspoons cider vinegar

2 teaspoons fresh thyme leaves

1 • Preheat the oven to 400°F and set a rack in the middle position. Cut all the vegetables into sticks about 2 inches long and ⅓ inch wide. In a large bowl, toss the vegetables with olive oil, salt, and pepper until coated. Spread the vegetables out on a baking sheet and roast until they're just beginning to brown at the edges, about 15 minutes.

2 • Meanwhile, in a large skillet, melt the butter over medium heat. Add the ginger and cook for 1 minute. Add the cider and vinegar and bring to a simmer, then reduce the heat to low and cook until reduced by half, 8 to 10 minutes. Remove from the heat, add the thyme, and stir.

3 • Remove the vegetables from the oven and add to the skillet. Stir to coat with the glaze and return to medium heat. Simmer until the vegetables are tender and glossy, about 10 minutes.

Squash and Apple Gratin

This hearty dish is substantial enough to serve as a vegetarian main course, but also makes a nice accompaniment to roast chicken or turkey. The sliced apples and butternut squash lend sweetness, while a crumbly top of garlicky breadcrumbs gives a savory balance.

APPLE NOTES: Any firm-sweet apple (see page 30) will work well in this gratin, and play off the savory crumb topping.

NOTE: In a pinch, you can substitute 1¼ cups (3 ounces; 81 grams) of panko breadcrumbs for the fresh ones. Toss them with 2 tablespoons melted butter, plus the nutmeg and garlic, then sprinkle over the apples.

EQUIPMENT: 2-quart gratin dish or 8-inch square baking dish; 10- to 12- inch skillet; food processor

MAKES: *6 servings* • ACTIVE TIME: *55 minutes* • TOTAL TIME: *1 hour, 25 minutes*

2 tablespoons heavy cream

3 tablespoons chicken or vegetable broth

1 medium (1½ pounds or 680 g) butternut squash, peeled, seeded, and cut into ¼-inch-wide crescents and half moons

4 ounces (115 g) Gruyère cheese, grated

1¼ teaspoons kosher salt, divided

¾ teaspoon freshly ground black pepper, divided

4 tablespoons (½ stick; 56 g) salted butter, divided

1 medium yellow onion, diced

2 teaspoons minced fresh rosemary

2 medium firm-sweet apples (about 12 ounces total; see Apple Notes) peeled, cored, and cut into ½-inch-thick wedges

1½ ounces (46 g) crusty white bread, such as Pullman style or Italian, torn into small pieces (see Note)

1 garlic clove, minced

½ teaspoon freshly grated nutmeg

1 • Preheat the oven to 350°F and set an oven rack to the middle position. In a small bowl, whisk together the cream and broth. In a large bowl, toss the squash with the cheese, cream mixture, 1 teaspoon of the salt, and ½ teaspoon of the pepper. Pour into a gratin or baking

LEFT: Squash and Apple Gratin

dish, cover with foil, and bake until the squash is tender, 35 to 45 minutes, turning the dish and removing the foil halfway through. Remove from the oven and set aside. Leave the oven on.

2 • Meanwhile, melt 3 tablespoons of the butter in a skillet over medium-high heat, add the onion, and cook until it begins to brown, 8 to 10 minutes, stirring occasionally. Add the rosemary, the remaining ¼ teaspoon salt and ¼ teaspoon pepper and cook until fragrant, about 1 minute. Add the apples, and cook until they are tender and beginning to caramelize, 8 to 10 minutes. Spread evenly over squash. Turn the broiler to high.

3 • In a food processor, pulse the bread with the remaining 1 tablespoon butter, the garlic, and nutmeg to create coarse breadcrumbs. Sprinkle over the squash and apples. Broil, uncovered, until the topping is golden brown, 5 to 7 minutes. Let rest for at least 20 minutes before serving.

Parsnip-Apple Puree

I've always thought of parsnips as one of the underappreciated vegetables. The name brings to mind something bitter and wrinkled. But the parsnip's flavor reminds me of tropical fruit, and it plays so nicely off an apple's sweet-tart notes. Add a little ginger, onion, and browned butter, and you have a Thanksgiving side dish that's both sweet and savory, and smooth as silk.

APPLE NOTES: A velvety texture is your goal here, so best to use a tender-sweet apple (see page 30), which will cook down to sauce while the parsnips simmer.

EQUIPMENT: 3- to 4-quart saucepan

MAKES: *3 cups puree, 6 servings* • ACTIVE TIME: *20 minutes* • TOTAL TIME: *45 minutes*

3 tablespoons (43 g) salted butter

2 pounds (908 g) parsnips, peeled and cut into 1-inch pieces

1 large tender-sweet apple (about 8 ounces; see Apple Notes), peeled, cored, and cut into chunks

½ cup (75 g) diced yellow onion

1½ teaspoons grated fresh ginger

1 cup (240 ml) low-sodium chicken broth

2 tablespoons heavy cream

½ teaspoon kosher salt

¼ teaspoon freshly ground black pepper

1 tablespoon finely chopped parsley, for garnish (optional)

1 • In a saucepan, melt the butter over medium heat. Let sizzle until it begins to turn golden brown, then a deep nut brown, 6 to 8 minutes. Add the parsnips, apples, onion, ginger, and chicken broth, then increase the heat to medium-high and bring the liquid to a boil. Reduce the heat to low, cover the pot, and gently simmer until the parsnips are tender, about 25 minutes.

2 • Use an immersion blender or hand mixer to puree the softened mixture to a smooth, velvety consistency. Stir in the cream, salt, and pepper. Taste and add more salt if desired. Serve warm, with the garnish, if you like.

Apple Risotto (Risotto alle Melle)

The *Silver Spoon Cookbook* is the *Joy of Cooking* for Italians, and, flipping through one day, I was surprised to see a recipe for an apple risotto. The mix of savory (cheese, Worcestershire) and sweet (apple) was intriguing, so I played around with it and came up with this adaptation, which replaces the original Worcestershire with saffron. Serve alone or with apple-flavored pork sausages on the side.

APPLE NOTES: A savory dish like this requires firm-tart apples (see page 30) for the proper balance. Green apples, such as Granny Smith or Rhode Island Greening, are particularly tasty.

EQUIPMENT: 2-quart saucepan; 4- to 5-quart saucepan

MAKES: *4 to 6 servings* • ACTIVE TIME: *45 minutes* • TOTAL TIME: *45 minutes*

About 7 cups (1.6 L) vegetable or chicken broth

2 generous pinches saffron

3 tablespoons (43 g) salted butter

2 medium firm-tart apples (about 12 ounces total, see Apple Notes), peeled, cored, and cut into ¼-inch cubes

1 teaspoon freshly grated lemon zest (loosely packed)

2 teaspoons kosher salt, divided

2½ tablespoons olive oil

1 cup diced onions

2 cups (400 g) short-grain rice such as Arborio or Canaroli

¾ cup (180 ml) light, dry white wine, such as Pinot Grigio

⅓ cup freshly grated Parmesan cheese, plus more as desired

½ teaspoon freshly ground black pepper

1 • In a 2-quart saucepan over medium-high heat, bring the vegetable broth to a simmer. Pour about 3 tablespoons of the broth into a small bowl and stir in the saffron. Set aside. Reduce the heat to low and keep at a gentle simmer while you prepare the rest of the dish. Melt the butter in a larger saucepan over medium heat, add the apples, lemon zest, and 1 teaspoon salt, and cook, stirring often, until the apples are tender, about 5 minutes. Transfer the apple mixture with any melted butter to a bowl and set aside.

2 • Return the large pan to medium heat and add the olive oil, onions, and remaining teaspoon salt. Cook until the onions are translucent, about 5 minutes. Add the rice and cook, stirring constantly, until the grains are coated in oil and a little translucent, about 2 minutes.

Add the wine and cook until the rice absorbs it, about 2 minutes. Add a ladleful of hot broth and cook, stirring often, until it's absorbed, about 4 minutes. Add the saffron and its broth and stir. Add the remaining stock, one ladleful at a time as before, stirring often, until the rice is tender with a very delicate bite in the center, about 20 minutes total. Stir in the apple mixture (with any butter), Parmesan, and pepper. Serve warm with an additional sprinkling of Parmesan, if desired.

Apple and Mustard Grilled Cheese Sandwiches

Pretty much anyone can make an acceptable grilled cheese sandwich. But with this technique, you'll have a perfect crispy-melty sandwich without a panini press (though if you do have one, by all means, use it). A number of different cheeses work equally well here, so feel free to experiment and see which one you like best.

APPLE NOTES: The point of this recipe is to be so easy that you can make it with whatever cheese and fruit you have on hand. However, a firm-tart apple (see page 30) goes best with the mustard and cheese in the sandwich.

NOTE: For best results, slice the apple on a mandoline to make the slices thin enough to soften in the time it takes to grill the sandwich.

EQUIPMENT: 10- to 12-inch, heavy-bottomed skillet; 8- to 10-inch heavy-bottomed skillet, preferably cast iron

MAKES: *2 sandwiches* • ACTIVE TIME: *20 minutes* • TOTAL TIME: *20 minutes*

1½ tablespoons (21 g) salted butter, at room temperature

4 slices sourdough bread

2 teaspoons whole-grain mustard

About ⅓ of a large firm-tart apple (about 3 ounces; see Apple Notes), unpeeled, cored, and sliced very thin (see Note)

4 ounces (about 115 g) sharp Cheddar, aged Gouda, Gruyère, or Havarti cheese, thinly sliced

1 • Set the empty skillets over two stovetop burners, both at medium heat. Let them get hot. If using a panini press, set to 350°F (medium heat).

2 • Meanwhile, butter one side of each bread slice, then lay the slices butter side down on your cutting board. Spread equal portions of mustard on two of the bread slices, then divide up the apple slices into two portions and lay on top of the mustard. Divide up the cheese slices and lay over the apples. Top the sandwiches with the remaining bread slices, buttered-side-up.

LEFT: Apple and Mustard Grilled Cheese Sandwiches with Quick Bread-and-Butter Apple Pickles (page 270)

3 • Lay the sandwiches in the large skillet. Cook until the bottom is browned, 3 to 4 minutes, then flip. Set the preheated medium-size skillet on top of the sandwiches so it functions as a press. If your skillet isn't very heavy, weigh it down with a water-filled kettle, a few large cans of tomatoes, etc. Cook until both sides are evenly browned, about 2 minutes more. If using a panini press, lay the sandwiches in the press and bring down the cover. Cook the sandwiches until crisp and bubbling, 4 to 6 minutes.

Welsh Rarebit with Apples

Welsh rarebit is a very old dish, dating back to eighteenth-century England. It was originally called "Welsh Rabbit," and according to the *Oxford Companion to Food*, the name may have been an insult to the good, cheese-loving people of Wales—"Welsh" meaning "faux" in that context.

In any case, this is essentially a very savory beer-accented cheese sauce that is broiled on slices of toast, and it makes a terrific lunch, late-night snack, or light dinner. Adding apple slices balances out the richness of the cheese, and mustard and Worcestershire give the sauce a bit of tang.

APPLE NOTES: Any tender-tart apple (see page 30) will work well because it'll soften up in the short time under the broiler. I particularly like the way Cortland, McIntosh, and Macoun pair with the Cheddar.

NOTE: For best results, slice the apple on a mandoline to make the slices thin enough to soften in the time it takes to broil the cheese sauce.

EQUIPMENT: 10- to 12-inch skillet; large rimmed sheet pan; mandoline (optional)

MAKES: *About 12 toasts* • ACTIVE TIME: *35 minutes* • TOTAL TIME: *35 minutes*

2 tablespoons (28 g) salted butter

1 tablespoon all-purpose flour

2 teaspoons dry mustard powder, such as Colman's brand

6 ounces (175 ml) dry stout, such as Guinness brand

Pinch of cayenne pepper

1 pound (454 g) aged sharp Cheddar cheese, grated

2 teaspoons Worcestershire sauce

1 loaf crusty sourdough bread, cut into ½-inch-thick slices

1 large tender-tart apple (about 8 ounces; see Apple Notes), unpeeled, cored, and cut into ⅛-inch-thick slices

1 • Preheat the broiler on low and set a rack to the top position. Melt the butter in a skillet over medium heat. Sprinkle with flour and mustard powder and cook, stirring, until the mixture looks glossy, about 3 minutes. Add the stout and gently whisk until the sauce is smooth and begins to thicken, about 4 minutes. Reduce the heat to medium-low. Add the cayenne pepper and stir, then add the cheese, one handful at a time, stirring well after each

addition so that it melts completely. Add the Worcestershire and stir well, then pour the sauce into a shallow bowl and refrigerate for 20 minutes until it thickens and becomes spreadable.

2 • Meanwhile, arrange the bread slices on a baking sheet and set under the broiler until lightly toasted, 4 to 5 minutes. You may need to turn the sheet several times for even cooking. Remove the sheet from the oven, turn the bread slices over, and lightly toast the other side, 3 to 4 minutes.

3 • Increase the broiler to high heat. Take the cooled cheese sauce out of the refrigerator and spread about 2 tablespoons sauce on each bread slice. Divide the apple slices among the toasts and lay on top of the sauce. Top the apples with an additional 1 tablespoon dollop of sauce. Return the sheet to the broiler and cook until the cheese is bubbling and begins to brown, 3 to 5 more minutes. Serve warm.

Pumpkin and Apple Custard

Confession: I've always found Thanksgiving dinner to be a bit of a snooze—and I'm not talking about the customary after-dinner nap. Turkey, mashed potatoes, and gravy aren't high on my list of Foods Worth Craving. But *this* dish, which my grandmother served every year next to the bowl of green beans with mushrooms and the bacon-draped turkey (Tip: lay a few strips over the breast meat and it becomes a self-basting bird)—this was the single best reason to dig into the buffet. That's probably because, with all its sweetness and warm spice, and a texture somewhere between a custard and a soufflé, it's a bit like eating dessert for dinner. If you've ever had savory corn pudding, you'll know what I mean. This dish is relatively low in fat, and a sure crowd-pleaser.

NOTE: You can find apple butter at most natural and Whole Foods stores (I recommend Eden brand, though any will do), or you can very easily make your own (page 275).

EQUIPMENT: 1½-quart soufflé dish; 8-inch square baking pan; standing mixer or hand-held mixer

MAKES: *6 servings* • ACTIVE TIME: *15 minutes* • TOTAL TIME: *1 hour, 10 minutes*

3 large eggs

⅓ cup (70 g) granulated sugar

1 cup (240 ml) canned pumpkin puree

¼ cup (60 ml) apple butter (see Note)

½ cup (120 ml) evaporated milk

1 tablespoon all-purpose flour

1 teaspoon ground cinnamon

1 teaspoon kosher salt

¼ teaspoon ground ginger

¼ teaspoon ground cloves

¼ teaspoon ground allspice

1 • Preheat the oven to 425°F and set a rack to the middle position. Butter the soufflé dish. Fill a kettle with about 4 cups water and bring to a simmer.

2 • Meanwhile, in a large bowl, using a standing or hand-held mixer, beat the eggs and sugar at medium-high speed for 2 minutes, until thick and pale yellow. Gently fold in the remaining ingredients.

3 • Pour the custard into the prepared dish and set in the baking pan. Transfer both to the oven, then fill the baking pan with enough of the simmering water to come halfway up the sides of the soufflé dish. Bake for 10 minutes. Reduce the heat to 350°F and bake until the center of the custard barely jiggles when shaken, 30 to 45 more minutes. Let sit for 10 minutes, then serve warm or at room temperature.

Acorn Squash Stuffed with Kasha and Apple

If you've been agonizing about what to serve your vegetarian cousin at Thanksgiving, here's your answer (just make it with vegetable broth). Kasha, also called buckwheat groats, is categorized a "pseudocereal" in botanical terms—that is, it's not related to wheat—which puts it in the same category as amaranth and quinoa. It has a wonderful aromatic quality, and pairs well with nuts, mushrooms, and fruits, all of which are represented here.

APPLE NOTES: This dish has many flavors all meeting up at once, so don't worry about finding a firm-sweet apple with exactly the right flavor profile. Any firm-sweet fruit (see page 30) will taste great.

MAKE-AHEAD TIP: You can prep the entire dish a day ahead of time, then reheat, covered, in a 325°F oven for 30 minutes before serving.

EQUIPMENT: Large baking sheet; 10- to 12-inch skillet

MAKES: *6 servings* • ACTIVE TIME: *1 hour, 10 minutes* • TOTAL TIME: *1 hour*

3 large (each about 1½ pounds or 680 g) acorn squash

2 tablespoons vegetable oil

1½ teaspoons kosher salt, divided

3 tablespoons (43 g) salted butter

1 medium onion, finely chopped

1 celery stalk, finely chopped

5 ounces (142 g) button mushrooms, stems trimmed, finely chopped

¼ cup (38 g) roughly chopped raw (unroasted, unsalted) cashews

1 teaspoon freshly ground black pepper

1 teaspoon ground nutmeg

1 cup (165 g) uncooked kasha

1 egg, beaten

1 large firm-sweet apple (about 8 ounces; see Apple Notes), peeled, cored, and cut into ¼-inch cubes

½ cup (65 g) chopped sweetened dried cranberries

⅓ cup (45 g) chopped pitted dates

2 cups (474 ml) low-sodium chicken broth or vegetable broth

1½ cups (357 ml) moderately sweet hard cider, such as J.K.'s Scrumpy Hard Cider or Woodchuck Hard Cider

1½ ounces (43 g) Cheddar or Gruyère cheese, grated

1 • Preheat the oven to 375°F and set a rack to the middle position. Line a baking sheet with aluminum foil, shiny side up. Prepare the squash cups: Using a sharp chef's knife, cut the squash in half crosswise. Scoop out the seeds and pulp, then trim the bottom of each cup *just* enough so it sits upright. Do not cut so deeply that you lose the bottom. Brush the cups and rims with half the oil, sprinkle with ½ teaspoon of the salt, and put cut side down on the baking sheet. Bake until tender, 30 to 40 minutes.

2 • Meanwhile, heat the butter and remaining 1 tablespoon oil in a skillet over medium-high heat and add the onion, celery, mushrooms, cashews, the remaining 1 teaspoon salt, pepper, and nutmeg. Cook until the moisture from the mushrooms evaporates, the cashews are toasted, and the onion is lightly golden at the edges, 8 to 10 minutes. Meanwhile, in a medium bowl, stir the kasha with the egg until evenly coated; add to the skillet, reduce the heat to medium, and stir until fragrant, 3 to 5 minutes. Add the apple, cranberries, dates, broth, and cider, bring to a simmer, then reduce the heat to low, cover, and cook until the kasha and dried fruit absorb the liquid, about 10 minutes.

3 • Remove the squash cups from the oven. Turn right side up, then fill with equal portions of kasha mixture, top with equal amounts of cheese, and return to the oven for 10 minutes. Serve warm.

Squash Stuffed with Apples, Pancetta, and Walnuts

In a November 2009 *New York Times* column, Mark Bittman published a compendium of more than one hundred Thanksgiving side dish ideas. One suggestion paired acorn squash with a filling of diced apples and bacon. I liked this idea, and decided to expand on it with the addition of onions, walnuts, Gorgonzola cheese, and a panko breadcrumb topping. I also replaced the bacon with pancetta because I like the latter's milder, less smoky flavor, but feel free to substitute if pancetta is difficult to find.

APPLE NOTES: A mix of firm-sweet and firm-tart apples (see page 30) adds an extra layer of flavor to this dish; any apples in those categories will work well here.

EQUIPMENT: Large rimmed sheet pan; 10- to 12-inch skillet

MAKES: *6 servings* • ACTIVE TIME: *1 hour* • TOTAL TIME: *1 hour*

3 medium (about 1½ lb or 680 g each) acorn squash

1 tablespoon vegetable oil

1½ teaspoons kosher salt, divided

4 ounces pancetta or bacon, chopped into ½-inch pieces

1 medium yellow onion (about 7 ounces or 200 g), diced

1½ large firm-sweet apples (about 12 ounces or 340 g total; see Apple Notes), peeled, cored, and cut into ⅓-inch cubes

1½ large firm-tart apples (about 8 ounces or 340 g total), peeled, cored, and cut into ⅓-inch cubes

¼ teaspoon freshly ground black pepper

½ cup (55 g) chopped walnuts

⅓ cup Gorgonzola cheese

2 tablespoons panko breadcrumbs

1 • Preheat the oven to 375°F and set a rack to the middle position. Line a baking sheet with aluminum foil, shiny side up. Prepare the squash cups: Using a sharp chef's knife, cut each squash in half crosswise. Scoop out the seeds and pulp, then trim the bottom of each cup just enough so it sits upright. Do not cut so deeply that you lose the bottom. Brush the cups and rims with the oil, sprinkle with 1 teaspoon of the salt, and place the squash, cut-side down, on the lined baking sheet. Bake until tender, 30 to 40 minutes.

2 • Meanwhile, in a skillet, cook the pancetta over medium heat until crisp, 3 to 5 minutes. Remove the pancetta to drain on paper towels and pour out all but 2 tablespoons of the rendered fat. Add the diced onion and cook, stirring occasionally, until lightly golden, 5 to 7

minutes. Add the apples, the remaining ½ teaspoon salt, and the pepper, and cook until the apples are tender, 5 to 8 minutes. Stir in the walnuts and the pancetta.

3 · When the squash are done, remove them from the oven and turn them over so they're sitting upright. Turn your broiler to low and set the oven rack to the top position. (If your oven is small, you may need to bring the rack down one level so that the squash won't be too close to the heat.) Fill the squash with equal portions of the apple filling, then top each with an equal portion of Gorgonzola (about one tablespoon) and panko breadcrumbs (about a teaspoon). Broil until tops are golden brown, about 3 minutes. Serve warm.

Sweet Potato–Apple Latkes

Every year, we host a big Hanukkah party for a couple of dozen friends, serving up four or five different kinds of latkes (potato pancakes) at a time. These sweeter latkes, accented with the oniony bite of shallots, are always the first to go. And here's a time-saving bonus: Because sweet potatoes contain less water than regular baking potatoes, you can grate them in the food processor without worrying about their releasing too much liquid.

APPLE NOTES: I like a green, firm-tart apple here (see page 30). Rhode Island Greening and Granny Smith would both make excellent choices.

NOTE: Keep the oil at about 370°F while frying to prevent latkes from turning greasy. Check the heat with a candy thermometer (most quick-read thermometers don't go high enough) and adjust accordingly.

MAKE-AHEAD TIP: If making ahead, cool the latkes to room temperature, then freeze in zip-top bags. Re-crisp in a 325°F oven for 15 to 20 minutes before serving.

EQUIPMENT: Food processor or box grater; 10- to 12-inch heavy-bottomed skillet; 3 large baking sheets

MAKES: *25 to 30 latkes* • ACTIVE TIME: *1 hour, 10 minutes* • TOTAL TIME: *1 hour, 10 minutes*

2 pounds (900 g) Garnet or Jewel sweet potatoes

3 large firm-tart apples (about 1½ pounds total; see Apple Notes), unpeeled, cored, and quartered lengthwise

8 medium shallots (7 ounces or 200 g)

6 large eggs, beaten

1 cup (130 g) matzo meal

1 tablespoon coarse kosher salt

1 teaspoon freshly ground black pepper

Vegetable oil for frying (see Note)

Sour cream and Classic Applesauce (page 268), for garnish

1 • Using the coarse side of a box grater or a food processor fitted with a medium grating disk, grate the potatoes, apples and shallots. Toss together in a large bowl. Add the eggs, matzo meal, salt, and pepper and toss to mix well.

LEFT: Sweet Potato–Apple Latkes served with Classic Applesauce (page 268) and sour cream

2 • Preheat the oven to 200°F. Pour ¾ inch of oil into a skillet over medium-high heat. When the temperature reaches 370°F, scoop ¼ cup potato mixture from the bowl, then gently drop that mixture out onto a wide spatula (the point here is to keep your hands as clean as possible). Press into a patty about ⅓ inch thick with your hand, then gently slide the pancake into hot oil. Cook three or four pancakes at a time (do not crowd the pan) until the edges are crispy and well browned and the undersides are golden brown, 4 to 5 minutes. Gently turn and cook until the other sides are golden brown, 2 to 3 minutes longer.

3 • Transfer the pancakes to paper towels to drain briefly, then arrange in a single layer on baking sheets and keep warm in the oven while you cook the remaining pancakes. Serve hot, with sour cream and applesauce.

CHAPTER SIX

POULTRY, MEAT, AND FISH ENTREES

Hidden Rose

FRUIT FROM THE DESERT:

New Mexico's Hidden Apple Country

Nothing about the drive to Dixon's Apple Farm would ever tell you that you're in apple country. The road to the farm heads west from the interstate, passing the man-made expanse of Cochiti Lake and the low-slung buildings of the nearby pueblo. The high desert landscape halfway between Albuquerque and Santa Fe is mostly a flat expanse of ochre-colored earth dotted with sagebrush and piñon trees, framed by the Jemez Mountains in the distance.

That starkness makes the entrance to the farm seem all the more Edenic. Round a corner and head down a little hill past a sign that reads "Apple eaters have the right of way," and you're suddenly overwhelmed by *green*. Neat rows of apple trees—fifty acres' worth—run the length of a wide canyon floor edged by sandstone cliffs, the grass beneath the trees blazing up from the moist, volcanic soil. The heavy fruit on the branches is a testament to the power of ample desert sunshine and a regular supply of water from the narrow Rio Chiquito.

Nearly all year long, this is a quiet place. The farm is surrounded by the vast expanse of Bandelier National Monument, a protected wilderness best known for its collection of twelfth-century Pueblo cliff dwellings. Tourists travel from around the world to visit the park and scramble up ladders to the caves, but few know of this little bit of apple paradise just a few miles away.

But the locals know. Every September, they come in droves to buy the Dixon's apples, snaking down those last few miles of Highway 22 in a long line. The apples sell out within weeks; weekends are a madhouse. The farm grows Red Delicious and Rome apples, but what really attracts the crowds are their signature varieties, which the farm's founder, Fred Dixon, named Champagne and Sparkling Burgundy, after he discovered the two chance seedlings in the late 1940s.

"There are cars backed up for four miles," says Becky Mullane, Dixon's granddaughter, who now runs the farm with her husband, Jim (Dixon passed away in 2009). "People waiting at six a.m. to get in the gate. We sell everything. Being just a family farm, it's hard to pass people through quickly. But we don't want it to be a Walmart experience. We want an apple orchard experience."

In a world of big box stores and commodity fruit, Dixon's is a tonic for the soul. It's fully a family farm, with just one full-time employee and some horses. Becky and Jim's three children are being raised and home-schooled on the property. Until his fragile health forced him to leave the farm in 2007, Fred Dixon lived in a small home next to Becky's. Her devotion to her grandfather goes back to 1986, when she left college at eighteen to move to New Mexico and help him keep the farm after her grandmother, Faye, passed away. "As a kid, I dreamed about living here," Becky says. "And I was worried about him. Once I got involved with the work and saw I could do it and saw people at harvest and what it meant to them, it made me want to be here even more." There was one problem, though: Dixon worried about her prospects as a young woman living on a remote farm with her grandfather. "I didn't want her here," he told me several years ago. "I told her, 'I'll keep the farm until you graduate from college.' I figured she was some scatterbrained eighteen-year-old."

But Becky surprised him by staying.

"Grandad said, 'You're never gonna get married,'" says Becky. "Then Jim showed up and he had to eat his words."

Jim took to the farming life and Fred turned the property over to the couple in 1996. In recent years, they've added a herd of cattle, three thousand more Champagne trees, and a micro-irrigation system, which has helped them survive an ongoing drought. "We have tremendous faith," says Becky. "You have to have faith that you'll get through freezing times and hail. In fifteen minutes you can be wiped out. But I'm not afraid of it."

When I visited Fred Dixon in August 2006, he was spending most days in his green easy chair in his small house behind Becky and Jim's renovated log cabin. Becky and the kids wandered in and out. He was still cooking for the family. He watched television. It was a quiet, happy life.

He first came to New Mexico in 1944, driving from Colorado with Faye and their two children in an old Plymouth. He had been trained as an arborist, and "wanted a chance to do something on my own," as he put it. James Webb Young, the legendary advertising executive who founded the Ad Council, had retired to Peña Blanca, New Mexico, and needed someone to manage the fruit trees on his dude ranch. "There were wild apple trees everywhere," Dixon said. And rocks. Thousands of rocks that had to be moved by hand (the stones now form a wall that you pass on the way into the property). He hated the place at first—its disorder, the hailstorms, the Wild West nature of the surrounding community—and almost headed back to Colorado, but Faye persuaded him to stay. "It was a mess. But Mr. Young let me do what I wanted, as long as I made money." One wild tree in particular caught Dixon's attention. The fruit was juicy and sweet, with bright acidity, and it held up well in baking. Plus, it kept for months in the refrigerator. "Faye said, 'I think we could sell this,'" Dixon said. He named it after the finest thing he could think of: Champagne. "I honestly think it's the best apple in the world," he said.

Once word spread, the apples became a New Mexican tradition. "People tell us that this is a ritual for them like going to the Balloon Fiesta or roasting chiles," Becky says. But while Dixon did trademark his Champagne apples (and another promising variety he named "Sparkling Burgundy"), he decided not to sell his scions to other farmers, preferring to keep the apple on the farm, where its scarcity ensures steady demand. It's a significant revenue loss, but the family is determined. "Other growers don't necessarily take care of the apples the way we do," Becky says. "And we're not in it to get rich. We just want to keep it a family business."

It looks like they're pulling it off. It's enough to give the most jaded city slicker hope for the future. As Becky drives me around the property, she points out her sons' horses, the spot where she and Jim got married during apple blossom time. Without actually saying so, she makes it clear that her "sacrifice" at age eighteen was really no sacrifice at all.

"Becky is more than a granddaughter to me," Fred Dixon told me on that August day. "She's a great friend. And sometimes a friend is the best thing you can have."

Apple Cider–Brined Turkey
with Applejack-Sage Gravy

Brining turkey in a mixture of two ciders, salt, brown sugar, ginger, herbs, and spices gives it the most wonderful deep apple flavor and keeps the meat terrifically moist—even the delicate breast meat.

EQUIPMENT: Large (16- to 19-quart) lobster pot *or* 2 large plastic turkey roasting bags (made by Glad or Regency); roasting rack; large roasting pan; meat thermometer; 4-cup liquid measuring cup

MAKES: 8 to 12 servings • ACTIVE TIME: *1 hour, 45 minutes* •
TOTAL TIME: *About 4½ hours, depending on size of bird, plus at least 12 hours brining time*

FOR THE BRINE

3 quarts (2.8 L) fresh apple cider

1 quart (940 ml) sweet hard cider, such as Magners or Woodchuck Amber, available at most liquor stores

1 cup (227 g) kosher salt

½ cup (115 g) firmly packed light brown sugar

8 slices peeled ginger, each about ⅛ inch thick

4 cinnamon sticks

3 bay leaves

1 tablespoon whole allspice

4 sprigs fresh rosemary

4 sprigs fresh thyme

1 gallon (3.8 L) ice water

FOR THE TURKEY

1 whole fresh turkey (not pre-brined), 10 to 15 pounds

1 apple, any kind, unpeeled, cored, and cut into 1-inch chunks

2 celery stalks, roughly chopped

½ large yellow onion, roughly chopped

2 tablespoons salted butter

1½ cups (355 ml) hard cider, such as Magners or Woodchuck Amber

3 or 4 strips thick-cut bacon (preferably applewood smoked)

Applejack-Sage Gravy (recipe follows)

1 • In a lobster pot or your largest stock pot (at least 8 quarts) over medium-high heat, bring fresh cider, hard cider, kosher salt, brown sugar, ginger, cinnamon sticks, bay leaves, and allspice to a boil. Reduce the heat to medium-low and simmer until the salt and sugar are fully dissolved, about 3 minutes. Turn off the heat and stir in the rosemary and thyme; let steep for

5 minutes. Add the ice water, then check the temperature. It should be cool to the touch. If not, let the mixture sit a while longer until it cools. Meanwhile, remove the giblets and neck from the turkey; discard. Rinse the turkey thoroughly, inside and out. No need to pat dry.

2 • If your pot is large enough to hold the turkey (and your refrigerator can accommodate it), put the turkey in the brine and refrigerate for 12 to 24 hours. Otherwise, double-bag two plastic roasting bags and set them, openings up, in your roasting pan. Add the turkey and carefully pour in the brine. Tie the bags securely with tight knots or twist ties and transfer to the refrigerator for 12 to 24 hours, turning the turkey once to make sure all parts are properly brined.

3 • Preheat your oven to 425°F and set a rack in the second-to-bottom position. Pour off the brine and discard, then rinse the turkey with cold water and pat dry with paper towels. Fill the cavity with apple, celery, and onion, then rub the skin all over with the butter and loosely tie the legs together with kitchen twine. Set the turkey, breast side down, in a rack in the roasting pan and pour hard cider around it. Cover the turkey with tented aluminum foil (just pat it down, over the meat—no need to seal) and transfer to the oven. Reduce the heat to 325°F, and roast the turkey for 10 minutes per pound.

4 • Remove the foil tent and turn the turkey over so that it's breast side up. Depending on the size of your bird, drape 3 or 4 bacon slices over the breast so that the meat is nearly covered. Continue roasting at 325°F for an additional 5 to 6 minutes per pound, until the legs feel loose in their sockets and a thermometer inserted straight down *to the bone* through the thickest part of the breast meat registers 160°F. Remove the bacon and discard or save it for yourself (it's delicious). Remove the apple, onion, and celery from the cavity and set aside for making Applejack-Sage Gravy (recipe follows). Pour the pan juices into a liquid measuring cup and let the fat separate from the juices—you'll also use that for the gravy. Set the roasting pan aside with all the browned bits on the bottom. Transfer the turkey to a platter or carving board and let sit tented loosely with foil for 30 to 45 minutes before carving. This allows the juices to redistribute through the meat and gives you time to prepare the gravy.

5 • Carve the turkey and serve with Applejack-Sage Gravy.

Applejack-Sage Gravy

MAKES: *2½ to 3 cups gravy*
EQUIPMENT: 3- to 4-quart saucepan; roasting pan used for turkey

2½ cups (590 ml) low-sodium chicken broth

6 fresh sage leaves

Apples, onions, and celery from roasted bird

3 tablespoons all-purpose flour

½ teaspoon freshly ground black pepper

Pan juices from roasted turkey

2 tablespoons applejack brandy or Calvados

1 tablespoon heavy cream

Salt to taste

1 • In a saucepan, bring the chicken broth, sage leaves, apples, onions, and celery to a boil, then reduce the heat to medium-low and simmer, uncovered, for 20 minutes. When the broth is ready, set your just-used roasting pan over two burners on your stovetop and turn the heat to medium. Strain the broth into the roasting pan and let it simmer, using a wooden spoon to scrape up all the browned bits from the bottom of the pan. Turn off the heat and set aside.

2 • Set your just-used saucepan over medium heat (no need to wash first). Spoon off 3 tablespoons fat from the reserved pan juices and pour into the saucepan. Discard any remaining fat from the pan juices. Add the flour and pepper to the saucepan and whisk together. Cook until the mixture is bubbling and glossy, about 3 minutes. Add the reserved pan juices and whisk together; the mixture will begin to thicken. Add the broth from the roasting pan and simmer, whisking gently, until smooth and thick, about 3 minutes. Whisk in the applejack and cream. Taste for seasoning; add salt, if needed. Strain the gravy into a gravy boat and serve warm with the turkey.

Braised Brisket with Apples and Hard Cider

Before I tried making this recipe, I doubted that apples and beef could ever go together. Pork and sausages, absolutely. Chicken, perhaps. But not beef. I thought that apples would never complement beef's heartier flavor, much in the same way that white wine doesn't tend to pair well with red meat. Luckily, my editor has more imagination. She suggested a brisket cooked in hard cider and I warily gave it a shot. It was fantastic! The cider has just enough intensity to stand up to the beef, and the onions, apples, brown sugar, spice, and chile cook down into a gravy with the tang of, say, barbecue sauce. A little bacon ties it all together. Serve with buttered egg noodles.

APPLE NOTES: Go for the firmest, tartest apple you can find for this dish. In fact, the best apple for this dish may well be the ubiquitous Granny Smith (see page 30 for more firm-tart varieties).

NOTE: You don't absolutely *have* to salt and pepper the brisket at least 4 hours in advance of cooking, but the flavor is so much richer that it really is worth taking that extra step.

EQUIPMENT: 5- to 6-quart heavy-bottomed pot or Dutch oven

MAKES: 6 servings • ACTIVE TIME: *45 minutes* •
TOTAL TIME: *4 hours, plus at least 4 hours to season the meat in advance*

1 tablespoon plus ½ teaspoon kosher salt

1½ teaspoons freshly ground black pepper

1 teaspoon ground cinnamon

3- to 4-pound (1.4 to 1.8 kg) flat cut beef brisket, extra fat removed

4 ounces (116 g) bacon, diced

3 medium yellow onions, sliced into ½-inch-thick rings

2 large firm-tart apples (about 1 pound total), preferably green (see Apple Notes), peeled, cored, and cut into ¼-inch-thick slices

2 tablespoons firmly packed light brown sugar

1 large jalapeño chile, seeded and diced

1 bay leaf

3 cups (710 ml) semi-sweet hard cider, such as Woodchuck Hard Cider or J.K.'s Scrumpy Hard Cider, both available at many large liquor stores

1 • In a small dish, stir together 1 tablespoon kosher salt and all the pepper and cinnamon. Set the brisket in a large baking dish and sprinkle all over with the spice mixture. Cover the dish with plastic wrap and refrigerate for at least 4 hours and up to 24 hours (see Note).

2 • In a pot or Dutch oven over medium heat, cook the bacon until browned and just crisp, 6 to 8 minutes. Remove with a slotted spoon. Increase the heat to medium-high, add the brisket to the pot, and weigh it down with another heavy pot or skillet to maximize browning. Cook until nicely browned on one side, 5 to 7 minutes, then flip the meat, replace the weight, and brown the other side for 5 to 7 minutes. Remove the meat and set aside.

3 • Preheat the oven to 325°F and set a rack to the second-to-bottom position. Drain all but 2 tablespoons fat from the Dutch oven and add the onions, apples, brown sugar, jalapeño, bay leaf, and remaining ½ teaspoon kosher salt. Cook over medium heat, stirring often, until the onions and apples are golden brown and tender, about 10 minutes. Add the cider and use a wooden spoon to scrape up all the browned bits from the bottom of the pot. Return the meat and any juices to the pot, bring the liquid to a simmer, then cover the pot and transfer to the oven.

4 • Gently simmer the brisket until tender when pierced with a fork, about 3 hours, being sure to turn the meat once with a pair of tongs about halfway through. Check periodically to make sure the sauce isn't boiling; if it is, lower the heat to 300°F. Remove the pot from the oven, transfer the brisket to a platter, and strain the sauce through a sieve to remove the cooked-down apples and onions. You can discard the solids or reserve them to spoon over the meat when you serve it with the sauce.

5 • Let the sauce sit in a glass liquid measuring cup for 5 minutes and skim off any excess fat with a spoon, then return the sauce to the pot and simmer over medium-high heat until thickened and glossy, 10 to 15 minutes. Taste the sauce and add salt or pepper if needed.

6 • Carve the meat across the grain into ¼- to ½-inch-thick slices; serve with the reduced sauce and, if desired, the cooked-down apples and onions.

Pork and Apple Pie with Cheddar-Sage Crust.

A savory pork layer is topped with a mix of sweet and tart apples.

Pork and Apple Pie with Cheddar-Sage Crust

My editor, Maria Guarnaschelli, suggested this recipe, based on her memory of a savory pie served at a London pub. One half of the pie was filled with pork and the other with apples. As I later learned, that dish has its roots in an eighteenth-century workingman's lunch called the Bedfordshire Clanger—a hand-held pie filled with meat on one end and jam on the other. It was a compact way to serve lunch and dessert in one package.

In adapting this idea to my own taste, I decided to layer apples on top of a spiced ground pork filling, rather than setting the two ingredients side by side. The flavors are fantastic together, and this dish has been the hit of many parties. It makes an especially good buffet option, as it can be served warm or at room temperature.

APPLE NOTES: As with all pie recipes, you want firm fruit here (see page 30). Some good examples: Granny Smith, Arkansas Black, and Northern Spy for tart apples; and Golden Delicious, Jazz, or Pink Lady for sweet ones.

EQUIPMENT: 10- to 12-inch skillet; food processor; 9-inch deep-dish pie plate, preferably glass; parchment paper or wax paper

MAKES: *8 to 10 servings* • ACTIVE TIME: *1 hour* • TOTAL TIME: *2 hours*

FOR THE CRUST

2½ cups (350 g) all-purpose flour

2 teaspoons dried sage, finely crumbled

½ teaspoon table salt

16 tablespoons (2 sticks; 255 g) chilled unsalted butter, cut into small cubes

3 ounces (85 g) sharp Cheddar cheese, finely grated

6 to 8 tablespoons (90 to 120 ml) ice water

1 egg blended with 1 tablespoon water

Fresh sage leaves for garnish (optional)

FOR THE FILLING

1½ pounds (about 3 large) firm-sweet apples (see Apple Notes), unpeeled, cored, and cut into ¼-inch-thick wedges

1½ pounds (about 3 large) firm-tart apples, unpeeled, cored, and cut into ¼-inch-thick wedges

2 tablespoons vegetable oil

1 small onion, very finely chopped

2 pounds (900 g) ground pork (preferably 15 to 17% fat)

1 tablespoon firmly packed light brown sugar

1 teaspoon kosher salt

½ teaspoon ground cinnamon

½ teaspoon ground ginger

¼ teaspoon ground cloves

¼ teaspoon ground allspice

3½ tablespoons plain breadcrumbs

Pork and Apple Pie with Cheddar-Sage Crust (page 129), in process

1 • First make the crust: In a medium bowl, whisk together the flour, sage, and salt until well combined. Sprinkle the butter cubes over the flour mixture and use your fingers to work them in (you want to rub your thumb against your fingertips, smearing the butter as you do so). Do this until the mixture looks like cornmeal with some pea-sized bits of butter remaining. Stir in the cheese with a fork until evenly distributed. Sprinkle 6 tablespoons ice water over the mixture and stir with a fork until the dough begins to come together. If needed, add an additional tablespoon or two of ice water (you shouldn't need much more). Turn the dough out onto a lightly floured surface and knead three times. Gather the dough into a ball, then divide into two portions, making one slightly bigger than the other. Press each portion down into a disk and wrap in plastic wrap. Refrigerate for at least 30 minutes.

2 • Make the filling: In a skillet over medium-low heat, cook the apples without any oil, stirring gently, until they just begin to soften, 5 to 7 minutes. Transfer to a dish and set aside. Add oil to the pan and increase the heat to medium-high. Add the onion, pork, brown sugar, salt, and spices. Cook, using a wooden spoon to break up the meat, until it is lightly browned, about 10 minutes. Let the meat mixture cool for 10 minutes, then transfer to a food processor. Add the breadcrumbs and pulse five times until the mixture has the texture of coarse sand. Set aside.

3 • Prepare the crust: Unwrap the larger disk of dough and put it in the center of a large sheet of parchment paper or wax paper. Cover the dough with a second piece of parchment. Roll out, working from the center, to a 13-inch circle. Peel off the top piece of parchment and transfer the dough to a pie plate, peeled side down. Peel off the remaining parchment and press the crust into the sides of the pie plate, draping any excess over the edge. Unwrap the smaller disk of dough and put it in the center of a large sheet of parchment paper. Cover the dough with a second piece of parchment. Roll out, working from the center, to an 11-inch circle. Set aside.

4 • Preheat the oven to 425°F and set a rack to the second-to-bottom position. Fill the pie: Pour the meat mixture into the bottom crust and gently smooth the top with a spatula. Arrange the cooked apple slices over the meat, pressing down to make the whole construction as smooth and neat as possible. Peel the top sheet of parchment off the top crust. Transfer, peeled side down, to the pie, then peel off the remaining parchment. Using a sharp knife, make two 3-inch slashes in the crust to allow steam to escape. Fold the edges of the bottom crust up over the top crust and crimp the edges to seal. Brush the crust with the egg wash and decorate with sage leaves, if desired. Bake at 425°F for 10 minutes, then reduce the heat to 375°F and bake until the crust is golden brown, 25 to 35 minutes more. Remove from oven and let cool 25 minutes before serving.

Tennessee Cornbread Dressing
with Sausage and Apple

Growing up in New England, I was completely unaware of cornbread dressings until I paid a holiday visit to a then-boyfriend's family near Knoxville. I believe I ate that one dish for breakfast and lunch the next day, too. In the end, the boyfriend proved temporary, but the dressing lives on. In my version, I've enhanced the standard sage-and-sausage blend with tart apple, hard cider, and pecans.

APPLE NOTES: There are so many flavors in this dressing that any firm-tart variety will work (see page 30). The point is to have just enough acidity to cut through the richness.

NOTES: This recipe is calibrated for a savory cornbread, not a sweet one, which is why I strongly recommend making your own. If you can't find Southern-style pork sausage, you can substitute sweet Italian sausage. And if you can't find bulk sausage, simply take fresh link sausage out of the casing.

EQUIPMENT: Large rimmed baking sheet; 9- by 13-inch baking dish; 10- to 12-inch skillet

MAKES: *6 to 8 servings* • ACTIVE TIME: *40 minutes* • TOTAL TIME: *1 hour, 45 minutes*

6 cups (640 g) Southern-Style Cornbread (recipe follows), cut into ½-inch cubes (see Notes)

1 cup (240 ml) reduced-sodium chicken broth, divided

1 cup (240 ml) semi-sweet hard cider, such as Woodchuck Hard Cider, available at most large liquor stores, divided

2 large eggs

1 tablespoon (14 g) salted butter, plus more for buttering pan

1 small yellow onion, diced

1 large celery stalk, diced

5 medium shallots, minced

1 pound (450 g) bulk Southern country sausage (such as Neese's brand or Jimmy Dean), broken into small chunks (see Notes)

1 large firm-tart apple (about 8 ounces; see Apple Notes), unpeeled, cored, and cut into ½-inch cubes

1½ tablespoons finely chopped fresh sage leaves

¾ teaspoon kosher salt

¾ teaspoon freshly ground black pepper

1 cup (100 g) chopped pecans or walnuts

1 • Preheat the oven to 350°F and set a rack to the middle position. Arrange the cornbread cubes on a baking sheet and bake until golden brown and crispy, about 30 minutes. Remove from the oven and cool for 15 minutes. Transfer the cubes to a large bowl.

2 • Butter a baking dish and set aside. In a small bowl, whisk together ⅔ cup of the broth, ⅔ cup of the hard cider, and the eggs. Pour over the cornbread cubes and toss very well to combine (don't worry if some cubes crumble; the dressing will have better texture). Set aside.

3 • Melt the butter in a skillet over medium-high heat. Add the onion, celery, and shallots. Cook just until the onions are translucent, 3 to 5 minutes. Add the sausage and cook, breaking up with a wooden spoon, until it begins to brown, about 10 minutes. Add the apple, sage, salt, and pepper and cook, stirring, until the apples are softened and the sausage is browned, 5 to 7 minutes more. Pour the mixture, fat and all, over the cornbread cubes and toss well.

4 • Increase the oven heat to 400°F. Return the skillet to the stovetop over medium-high heat and add the remaining ⅓ cup broth and ⅓ cup cider. Simmer, using a wooden spoon to scrape browned bits from the bottom, until the liquid is reduced by half, about 5 minutes. Pour the liquid over the dressing and toss well.

5 • Pour the dressing into the prepared baking dish and spread evenly. Scatter pecans over the top and bake until the top is golden brown, about 35 minutes.

Southern-Style Cornbread

In this case, "Southern-style" means savory. It's a point of pride for many Southern cooks to eschew the sweet breads favored by us Northerners—breads that one friend of mine calls, with no apparent affection, "dessert." I can assure any Southern readers that the 2 teaspoons of sugar in this recipe merely enhance the corn flavor, and are barely detectible.

NOTE: If you're using this bread for dressing, make it up to two days ahead (wrap tightly in plastic wrap and store at room temperature). For straight eating, consume within a day or so. You can also freeze the bread, wrapped tightly in plastic and foil, for up to one month.

EQUIPMENT: 10-inch cast iron skillet, or other oven-safe frying pan of same size

MAKES: *1 loaf; 6 cups cubed bread for dressing* • ACTIVE TIME: *15 minutes* • TOTAL TIME: *40 minutes*

2 tablespoons (7 g) salted butter

1 cup (170 g) medium grind cornmeal, such as Bob's Red Mill (bobsredmill. com) or Anson Mills (ansonmills.com) brands

½ cup (73 g) all-purpose flour

2 teaspoons granulated sugar

1¼ teaspoons baking powder

½ teaspoon baking soda

1 teaspoon kosher salt

1¼ (295 ml) cups buttermilk

1 large egg

2 teaspoons vegetable oil

1 • Preheat the oven to 400°F and set a rack to the bottom position. Put the skillet in the oven.

2 • In a microwave oven, melt the butter. Let it cool while you prep the batter. In a medium bowl, whisk together the cornmeal, flour, sugar, baking powder, baking soda, and salt. In a small bowl, whisk together the buttermilk and egg, then add to the dry ingredients. Stir in the melted butter. Fold everything together very gently and briefly with a spatula; stop as soon as the mixture is combined. Some lumps are fine.

3 • Retrieve the pan from the oven and add the oil; swirl to coat the pan (I use a silicone pastry brush around the sides). Pour in the batter (it may sizzle) and bake until the bread is golden brown on top and has pulled away from the sides, 15 to 20 minutes. Cool in the pan on a rack for 10 minutes before removing.

Sausage and Red Onion Sandwich

My friend Adeena Sussman created this sandwich, and I hate to go more than a few months without making it. It requires a few steps, but it actually goes very quickly and the sandwich tastes best when each component is made separately.

APPLE NOTES: The Cheat Sheet on page 30 lists firm-sweet apple varieties. Some good examples: Golden Delicious, Ginger Gold, Pink Lady, Jazz, and Piñata.

EQUIPMENT: 10- to 12-inch skillet

MAKES: 4 servings • ACTIVE TIME: *45 minutes* • TOTAL TIME: *45 minutes*

1 medium red onion, sliced into ¼-inch-thick rings

7 tablespoons (104 ml) olive oil, divided

1½ teaspoons kosher salt, divided

1½ teaspoons freshly ground black pepper, divided

4 uncooked sweet Italian sausages (about 1 pound or 450 g total)

4 garlic cloves, very thinly sliced

1 (10-ounce or 285 g) package baby spinach

4½ tablespoons (67 ml) cider vinegar, divided

2 tablespoons Dijon mustard, divided

2 medium firm-sweet apples (about 12 ounces total; see Apple Notes), cored and cut into ¼-inch-thick wedges

4 large, crusty French or ciabatta rolls

1 • Preheat a skillet over medium heat. In a bowl, toss the onion rings with 1 tablespoon of the olive oil, 1 teaspoon of the salt, and 1 teaspoon of the pepper. Cook the onions in the pan, turning once, until lightly browned, about 10 minutes total; remove and set aside. Put the sausages in the pan and cook until cooked through and browned all over, about 15 minutes. Set aside, drain on paper towels, and keep warm in the oven. Wipe the skillet with paper towels to remove the grease.

2 • Preheat the oven to 200°F and set a rack in the middle position. Heat 3 tablespoons of the olive oil in the skillet over medium heat. Add the garlic and brown for 30 seconds. Add the spinach and stir with a wooden spoon until wilted, 2 to 3 minutes. Remove from the heat and use a wooden spoon to press excess liquid from the spinach; discard the liquid, but retain the garlic. Remove the spinach and garlic to a bowl and toss with the remaining ½ teaspoon of the salt and ½ teaspoon of the pepper; keep warm in the oven.

3 • In same skillet, heat the remaining 3 tablespoons olive oil over medium-low heat. Add 2½ tablespoons of the cider vinegar and 1 tablespoon of the mustard. Add the apples and cook, stirring often, until they soften slightly, 5 to 6 minutes. With a slotted spoon, remove the apples to a plate and keep warm. Add the remaining vinegar and mustard to the pan and whisk until slightly emulsified, adding a little more salt and pepper to taste, if desired.

4 • To assemble the sandwiches, split the rolls in half. Drizzle some warm dressing from the skillet on both sides of each roll. Divide the spinach-garlic mixture among the rolls. Place the sausage on the spinach, layer with apples, and top with onion. Serve immediately.

Sausage with Braised Cabbage and Apples

My mother makes a similar dish every fall, only with sauerkraut instead of fresh cabbage. By cooking cabbage in cider vinegar and apple cider rather than starting with sauerkraut, you get a more delicate sweet flavor. Adding sausages gives everything a hint of smoke. Served with some crusty bread, it's a complete meal unto itself.

APPLE NOTES: The goal here is twofold: You want a tender-sweet apple to cook down and form a sauce (see page 30 for list of varieties), and then a firm-sweet fruit to keep its shape and not melt into the cabbage. As long as you manage to do that, you really don't need to worry about specific varieties; all will do well here.

EQUIPMENT: 4- to 5-quart Dutch oven

MAKES: *6 servings* • ACTIVE TIME: *40 minutes* • TOTAL TIME: *1 hour, 35 minutes*

1 small head (1½ pounds; 680 g) red cabbage, cored, with first 2 layers of outer leaves removed

1 tablespoon olive oil

6 uncooked pork sausages such as bratwurst or sweet Italian (about 1 pound; 454 g)

1 medium red onion, sliced thin

1½ teaspoons kosher salt

1 teaspoon caraway seeds

6 tablespoons (90 ml) cider vinegar

¾ cup (180 ml) fresh apple cider

1 large tender-sweet apple (about 8 ounces; see Apple Notes), peeled, cored, and cut into ½-inch cubes

1 large firm-sweet apple (about 8 ounces), peeled, cored, and cut into ¼-inch cubes

2 tablespoons (28 g) salted butter

1 • Quarter the cabbage lengthwise, then lay each section on its side and slice down lengthwise as thinly as possible, as if you're shaving the cabbage with your knife. As you get to the outer edge of the quarter, feel free to stop if it gets too difficult to thinly cut.

2 • Heat the olive oil in a Dutch oven over medium-high heat. Add the sausages and cook until lightly browned all over but not cooked through, about 5 minutes. Transfer to a plate.

3 • Add the onion and salt to the pot and cook until it begins to brown, about 8 minutes. Add the caraway, cider vinegar, and apple cider and bring to a simmer, scraping up any brown bits. Add the cabbage and apples and cook 10 minutes. Return the sausages to the pot, cover, and continue to simmer until the cabbage is tender, about 20 minutes. Add the butter and stir until melted. Serve immediately.

Duck Panzanella with Apples and Thyme

Traditional Italian panzanella is a summer dish made from leftover bread mixed with tomatoes, red onion, cucumber, basil, olive oil, and vinegar. This variation takes it into the fall by using duck, apples, and thyme. Serve it for lunch or as a light supper.

APPLE NOTES: Any firm-sweet apple will do well here. For a complete list, see page 30.

NOTE: Since most bread loaves weigh 1 pound, you need about ¼ loaf.

EQUIPMENT: Large rimmed baking sheet; 10- to 12-inch skillet

MAKES: *4 servings* • ACTIVE TIME: *45 minutes* • TOTAL TIME: *45 minutes*

¼ pound (113 g) day-old sourdough or olive bread, crusts on, cut into 1-inch cubes (see Note)

1 large duck breast (about 1 pound or 454 g, thawed if frozen)

1 teaspoon kosher salt, divided

½ teaspoon freshly ground black pepper, divided

2 teaspoons canola oil or other vegetable oil

½ teaspoon freshly ground black pepper

1 large sweet onion, such as Vidalia or Walla Walla, sliced

2 large, firm-sweet apples (about 1 pound; see Apple Notes), peeled, cored, and cut unto 1-inch cubes

1 tablespoon fresh thyme leaves, plus more for garnish

3 cups (about 12 ounces or 340 g) baby arugula leaves

FOR THE DRESSING

½ cup (120 ml) olive oil

⅓ cup (80 ml) cider vinegar

1 teaspoon Dijon mustard

1 shallot, minced

½ teaspoon kosher salt

¼ teaspoon freshly ground black pepper

1 • Preheat the oven to 300°F and set a rack to the middle position. Arrange the bread on a baking sheet and bake until lightly toasted, 4 to 5 minutes. Remove from the oven and let cool. Pat the duck breast dry with paper towels and use a sharp knife to score the skin in a crisscross pattern. Season all over with ½ teaspoon of the salt and ¼ teaspoon of the pepper.

$2 \cdot$ Add the oil to a skillet and heat over medium-high heat until it's thin and glossy. Place the duck breast skin side down in the skillet and cook, without moving it, until the skin is crisp and has rendered some of its fat, 6 to 7 minutes. Turn the duck over and cook for an additional 2 minutes until bright pink in the center, but not rare (cut to check). Remove and let rest on a cutting board. Discard all but 2 tablespoons of rendered duck fat from the skillet.

$3 \cdot$ Add the onion to the skillet and cook, stirring, until it's soft but not browned, about 5 minutes. Add the apples, 2 tablespoons water, thyme, and an additional ½ teaspoon salt and ¼ teaspoon pepper and cook until the apples have just begun to soften, about 6 minutes. Transfer the mixture to a large bowl, toss with the arugula, and set aside (the arugula will start to wilt).

$4 \cdot$ Make the dressing: In a bowl, whisk together the olive oil, vinegar, mustard, shallot, salt, and pepper until emulsified. Add the bread cubes to the apple-onion-arugula mixture, then add the vinaigrette and toss to coat. Divide the salad among four plates (or arrange on a platter). Slice the duck against the grain into ¼-inch-thick slices, divide into four portions, and arrange on top of the salad. Serve warm, sprinkled with fresh thyme leaves.

Cider-Braised Pork with Calvados and Prunes

Pork and apples are a classic pairing—the trick is to get the right mix of sweet and savory flavors. A braising liquid of hard cider and Calvados (apple brandy) perfumes the meat; prunes add sweetness and turn silky during cooking.

MAKE-AHEAD TIP: Like most braises, this dish is even better when made a day ahead. Prepare the recipe through step four, then cool and refrigerate overnight. An hour before serving, skim fat from the surface, then bring the sauce to a simmer on the stovetop, reduce the heat to low, add the marjoram, and proceed according to instructions.

EQUIPMENT: 5- to 6-quart Dutch oven; 6-cup liquid measuring cup

MAKES: *6 servings* • ACTIVE TIME: *45 minutes* • TOTAL TIME: *4 hours*

¼ cup (36 g) all-purpose flour

2 tablespoons kosher salt, plus more to taste

2 teaspoons freshly ground black pepper

4- to 5-pound (1.8 to 2.3 kg) boneless pork shoulder (Boston butt)

3 tablespoons olive oil

15 medium shallots

Cinnamon stick

1¾ cups (415 ml) semi-sweet hard cider, such as Woodchuck Hard Cider, available at most large liquor stores

1¾ cups (415 ml) low-sodium chicken broth

½ cup (120 ml) Calvados (apple brandy) or applejack

35 pitted prunes (not in syrup)

3 fresh marjoram sprigs

1 • In a large baking dish, stir together the flour, salt, and pepper. Roll the pork shoulder in the flour mixture to coat, then shake off any excess.

2 • In a Dutch oven, warm the oil over medium-high heat. Ad the pork to the pot and brown all over, 3 to 4 minutes per side, adjusting the heat as needed to keep the flour from burning. Remove the pork and drain all but 2 tablespoons fat from the pot. Set aside.

3 • Preheat the oven to 325°F and set a rack to the middle position. Return the Dutch oven to the heat on the stovetop and add the shallots; cook, stirring, until lightly browned, about 5 minutes. Add the cinnamon stick, then pour in the cider, broth, and Calvados, scraping the bottom of the pot with a wooden spoon to remove the brown bits. Return the meat to the pot.

Bring to a simmer, then add the prunes, cover the pot, and put in the oven. Cook the pork for 2½ hours, then remove from the oven.

4 • Add the marjoram sprigs to the pot, stir, and put the pot on stovetop over medium-low heat with the lid ajar. Maintain a gentle simmer for an additional 30 minutes, or until the pork is tender when pierced with a fork and the sauce has thickened a bit. Remove the pork from pot and let it rest on a carving board for 10 minutes.

5 • Pour the sauce, along with the shallots and prunes, into a liquid measuring cup. Let sit for 10 minutes, then skim off any fat that rises to the surface. Taste the sauce and add more salt as needed. Slice the pork into ¼-inch-thick slices and serve immediately with buttered noodles, polenta, or spaetzle.

Cider-Brined Pork Chops
with Mustard Pan Sauce

The only time-consuming part of this recipe is brining the pork, which you will do a few hours ahead of time. The simple sauce is easy to prepare, incredibly flavorful, and a beautiful caramel color. Apples flavor the dish throughout, from the brine to the sauce.

MAKE-AHEAD TIP: Place the chops in the brine in the morning and you can have dinner on the table in 40 minutes.

EQUIPMENT: 10- to 12-inch heavy-bottomed skillet; 9- by 13-inch baking dish

MAKES: *6 servings* • ACTIVE TIME: *35 minutes* •
TOTAL TIME: *35 minutes, plus at least 3 hours brining time*

FOR THE BRINE

3½ cups (830 ml) fresh apple cider

¼ cup (70 g) kosher salt

2 teaspoons whole black peppercorns, divided

2 bay leaves, divided

4 crushed garlic cloves, divided

6 bone-in pork rib chops (each about 1 inch thick)

FOR THE SAUCE

2 tablespoons (28 g) salted butter

¾ cup (180 ml) fresh apple cider

1 cup (240 ml) chicken broth

⅓ cup (80 ml) heavy cream

1 tablespoon whole-grain mustard

¼ teaspoon kosher salt

1 • First make the brine: In a large bowl, whisk together the cider and salt until the salt dissolves. Divide the brine between two zip-top freezer bags, then add 1 teaspoon peppercorns, 1 bay leaf, and 2 garlic cloves to each. Put 3 chops in each bag, seal, and chill for at least 3 hours and up to 1 day.

2 • Preheat the oven to 325°F and set a rack to the middle position. Drain the chops and blot dry. In a large skillet over medium-high heat, melt the butter and add 3 pork chops. Cook (no need to stir or turn) until browned on one side, 3 to 5 minutes. Turn the chops and cook until browned on the other side, 3 to 4 minutes more. Repeat with the second batch. Set the skillet aside.

3 • Layer the chops in a 9- by 13-inch baking dish and bake until very pale pink in the center (cut to check), 15 to 20 minutes. Remove the dish from the oven and transfer the chops to a serving platter.

4 • Make the sauce: Return the skillet to medium-high heat and add the cider. As it bubbles, use a wooden spoon to scrape up brown bits on the bottom. Add the broth, turn the heat to high, and boil until the liquid is reduced to about ½ cup, 8 to 10 minutes. Remove from the heat and stir in the cream and mustard. Season with salt. Pour the sauce over the chops and serve with mashed or steamed potatoes and a green salad.

Apple and Chestnut–Stuffed Pork Loin with Cider Sauce and Cider-Glazed Root Vegetables (page 99)

Apple and Chestnut–Stuffed Pork Loin with Cider Sauce

A simple stuffing, sweetened with apples and chestnuts and lightly accented with cinnamon and sage, is rolled up inside a butterflied pork loin in this centerpiece dish. When you slice the loin, you see the swirl of stuffing. Served with a very simple cider pan sauce, it's impressive enough for company, but quite easy to do.

APPLE NOTES: A certain amount of acidity is needed here to stand up to the stuffing, but any firm-tart variety will work well (see page 30).

MAKE-AHEAD TIP: You can prep the loin through step 3 up to a day in advance. Cover with plastic wrap and refrigerate.

NOTES: You can butterfly your own pork loin if you like, but if you're not confident of your meat-cutting skills, my advice is to ask your butcher to butterfly it to a ¾-inch thickness. Vacuum-packed roasted chestnuts are available at gourmet and Whole Foods stores.

EQUIPMENT: 12- to 14-inch skillet; small (approximately 12- by 14-inch) roasting pan; six 18-inch lengths of butcher's twine; 1-quart saucepan

MAKES: *8 servings* • ACTIVE TIME: *45 minutes* • TOTAL TIME: *2 hours*

FOR THE PORK

3-pound boneless pork loin roast, butterflied (see Notes)

2 teaspoons kosher salt

½ teaspoon freshly ground black pepper

FOR THE STUFFING

2 tablespoons olive oil

1 tablespoon (14 g) salted butter

1 small white onion, finely chopped

1 celery stalk, ends trimmed, cut into ¼-inch cubes

1 large firm-tart apple (about 8 ounces; see Apple Notes), unpeeled, cored, and cut into ½-inch cubes

7 fresh sage leaves, finely chopped

½ teaspoon kosher salt

½ teaspoon freshly ground black pepper

¼ teaspoon ground cinnamon

5 ounces (142 g) white or whole-wheat bread, crusts removed, torn into 1-inch pieces

5 ounces (142 g) vacuum-packed roasted chestnuts (see Notes)

1 egg, lightly beaten

½ cup (120 ml) low-sodium chicken broth

FOR THE SAUCE

1½ cups (240 ml) fresh apple cider, divided

2 teaspoons cornstarch

Sliced Apple and Chestnut–Stuffed Pork Loin with Cider Sauce (page 145) and Cider-Glazed Root Vegetables (page 99)

1 • The night before you roast the pork, season all over with salt and pepper. Using a meat pounder or a rolling pin, pound the meat out to an even ½-inch thickness. Cover with plastic wrap and refrigerate (you can skip this step and season the meat right before cooking, but the results of pre-salting are incredibly good).

2 • Combine the olive oil and butter in a skillet over medium heat. Add the onion and celery and cook, stirring occasionally, until the onion is translucent, about 5 minutes. Add the apple, sage, salt, pepper, and cinnamon. Stir and cook for 5 more minutes, until the apples are tender. Pour the mixture into a large bowl. In a food processor, pulse the bread until it forms fluffy breadcrumbs. Add the chestnuts and pulse until they're roughly chopped. Add the breadcrumbs and chestnuts to the onion-apple mixture. Add the egg and chicken broth and stir to mix evenly. Let cool to room temperature. Meanwhile, preheat the oven to 375°F and set a rack to the middle position.

3 • Unfold the pork loin and lay horizontally on the counter. Spoon the stuffing over the meat, spreading it evenly with a spatula and leaving a 2-inch border along the top edge. Roll the meat up over the stuffing, jelly-roll style, from the bottom to the top. Turn seam side down. Using a sharp knife, lightly score any extra fat on the surface of the loin in a diamond pattern. Tie the loin up at regular intervals with pieces of twine and transfer it to the roasting pan.

4 • Pour ½ cup of the cider in the bottom of the pan and put the pan in the oven. Roast the loin for 30 minutes. Baste the meat with the pan juices, then add another ½ cup of cider. Return to the oven and roast, basting regularly, until a quick-read thermometer inserted into the middle of the loin reads 150°F, 50 to 60 more minutes.

5 • Transfer the meat to a cutting board and cover loosely with aluminum foil. Scrape the pan bottom with a wooden spoon to dislodge any browned bits, then pour the pan juices into a large glass measuring cup and add the remaining cider. You should have about 1½ cups liquid. Pour ¼ cup of the cider mixture into a small saucepan over medium-high heat. Add the cornstarch and whisk until it's dissolved. Add the remaining cider mixture and bring to a simmer. Reduce the heat to medium and cook, gently stirring with the whisk, until the sauce is slightly thickened, about 5 minutes. Taste and add salt and pepper as needed. Pour the sauce into a warmed bowl.

6 • Cut the loin into ¾-inch-thick slices and arrange on a warmed platter. Serve the hot cider sauce on the side.

Pan-Seared Salmon with Cider-Glazed Onions

It's the Holy Grail of dinner party recipes: something fancy enough for company, but with just a handful of ingredients and two steps, easy enough to have on the table in just 45 minutes. You'll be amazed at how nicely apple cider complements the caramelized onions. You can also serve the glazed onions with grilled steak, chicken, or pork.

MAKE-AHEAD TIP: Prepare the onions up to one day ahead, then gently warm before serving.

EQUIPMENT: 12- to 14-inch skillet; 10- to 12-inch ovenproof skillet, preferably nonstick

MAKES: 4 servings • ACTIVE TIME: *35 minutes* • TOTAL TIME: *45 minutes*

2 tablespoons olive oil, divided

1 red onion, cut into very thin rings

1 teaspoon kosher salt, divided

1 teaspoon granulated sugar

2 cups (480 ml) fresh apple cider

½ teaspoon freshly ground black pepper

4 (5-ounce or 140 g) center-cut pieces salmon fillet (1 to 1½ inches thick)

1 tablespoon minced chives (optional)

1 • Heat 1 tablespoon of the olive oil in a large skillet over medium heat. Add the onion, ½ teaspoon of the salt, and the sugar. Cook, stirring often, until the onions are lightly golden, 8 to 10 minutes. Add the cider and bring to a boil, scraping the bottom of the pan with a wooden spoon to lift any brown bits. Cook, stirring occasionally, until the sauce is reduced to a glaze and the onions are very soft, 8 to 10 minutes more. Cover the pan and keep it warm over low heat while you prepare the fish.

2 • Preheat the oven to 400°F and set a rack to the middle position. In a small bowl, stir the pepper and remaining ½ teaspoon salt together, then sprinkle the mixture over the salmon flesh (not skin). In the smaller skillet over medium-high heat, warm the remaining tablespoon of oil until shimmering. Put the salmon skin side up in the pan and cook, without moving or poking, until it has a nice sear, 3 to 5 minutes. With tongs, gently flip the salmon over and transfer the skillet to the oven. Roast until cooked through (cut in middle to check), 5 to 10 minutes more. Serve in the pan or on a warmed platter, topped with the glazed onions and, if you'd like, a sprinkling of chives.

CHAPTER SEVEN

PANCAKES, DONUTS, BISCUITS, AND BREADS

Melrose

A Visit to Poverty Lane Orchards in Lebanon, New Hampshire

"You gotta see this one. This is one wild apple."

Stephen Wood bounds over to a large tree hanging heavy with pale green, russeted fruit. He pulls an apple off a branch, and hands it to me. It's crisp, a bit rough-textured, and sweet, but also astringent, like tea from leaves left too long in the cup. This is a Medaille d'Or, one of dozens of traditional French, British, and American apples that Wood grows at his Poverty Lane Orchards in the rolling hills of Lebanon, New Hampshire.

The apple in my hand is one of many varieties that Wood blends into his acclaimed Farnum Hill ciders, which rank among the best ciders in the country. And though it's not a fruit I'd gladly eat out of hand, the bitterness I taste is all for a good cause, deriving from the same tannins (or, in science-speak, plant polyphenols) that give red wine structure and nuance. Much like a winemaker, Wood oversees a process in which his apples are pressed to extract the juice, which is then fermented, blended, bottled, and aged.

In making his ciders, Wood says his goal is not just to preserve his childhood home, and his family's orchards and way of life, but to educate consumers about fine ciders and, ultimately, to reestablish Americans' affection for cider. And it's easy to cheer his efforts. Not just because the ciders are so delicious, but also because, if you believe in eating locally and supporting local farmers and don't live in California, it makes so much more sense to drink more local cider and less shipped-from-afar wine.

But back to the apples! With names like Chisel Jersey, Ashton Bitter, Somerset Redstreak, Foxwhelp, and Kingston Black, most of Wood's apples are heirlooms. But what does "heirloom" mean, exactly?

Put simply, heirloom apples are antiques—traditional varieties reproduced for some number of decades or centuries via grafting to perpetuate winning characteristics. In common parlance, heirlooms are defined by what they are *not*: that is, newly bred, mass-produced commodity fruit. That's not a terribly scientific definition, but it functions well. The Granny

Smith you buy at Safeway? Not an heirloom. The Seek-No-Further you picked up at the local farmers' market? An heirloom.

With other plants, such as berries and tomatoes, heirlooms are defined more rigorously, describing varieties grown from seed and pollinated by natural means, such as insects or wind (this is in contrast with hybrid plants, in which one plant is deliberately hand-pollinated with the pollen from another plant).

Apples don't reproduce true from seed, so the rigorous definition can't apply. Throughout history, the whole business of perpetuating one apple variety or another has been covered with human fingerprints. And yet, the "heirloom" or "antique" label is more than just a charming bit of marketing language. It hints at the historic diversity of this ancient fruit—and reminds us how much of that has been lost.

Which is just one reason why Wood's efforts are so important. Most of the British and French varieties that he is growing date back much further than their American counterparts—hundreds if not thousands of years.

He's quick to point out that Farnum Hill isn't simply an apple museum, and he doesn't only grow heirlooms. "We grow things that grow well here in our glacial till and that aren't grown commonly. Most of them are old varieties but some are from as recently as the 1920s."

A noble effort, and a practical one. Wood has been growing these odd apples for nearly thirty years, since realizing in the early 1980s that the commodities market for his standard issue McIntosh and Golden Delicious fruits was evaporating. Why this was happening is complicated, but one clear reason is the public's taste for larger, more uniform, waxed apples from the warmer, sunnier West Coast (and, in the spring, from Southern Hemisphere locales like New Zealand and Australia). "I ripped out acres and acres of Macs and Cortlands and replanted them with the weird varieties that are now our mainstay," he says. Wood argues that what some of his apples lack in lush good looks, they make up for in flavor. "The cold nights here in New Hampshire, the moderate frosts that threaten but don't destroy apples lead to a rush of photosynthates [specifically, sugars] in the apples," Wood says. "The conditions that make our apples grow to stunning standards also threaten our crop."

He started making ciders in 1992 as an attempt to market a more profitable product while remaining what he most wanted to be, an apple man. "If we were going to do this with any satisfaction, we had to make something with high inherent value," he says. "We came this close to expanding our retail, but the thought of coming home smelling of potpourri and candles to say we were 'making a living off the land' didn't do it."

He began experimenting with antique European cider varieties like the tiny red Wickson and the Ashton Bitter, and traveled to England to study cider-making. "I spent a lot of time sniffing through stuff." By 2001, he had become a skilled enough cidermaker that Farnum Hill earned raves in publications like the *New York Times*, *Saveur*, and *Martha Stewart Living*.

It's tempting to end this story by simply saying that Stephen Wood saved his farm through cider. But, of course, it's never that simple. Cider remains a niche product, and as well as Farnum Hill has done, it remains a struggle to get the product into restaurants and stores around the country. Still, Wood has reason to be optimistic, given the growing interest in artisanal products. He's also encouraged by the growing cider market that has given rise to regional groups like the Northwest Cider Society, the Michigan Hard Cider Club, and fan websites like oldtimecider.com. Wood knows that if he can get enough people to try his ciders or his fresh apples, they pretty much speak for themselves.

Case in point: At the end of our visit, Wood says he wants to show me his all-time favorite cooking apple (his overall favorite is Spitzenburg). What an offer! We walk down a long row of heirloom trees, kicking through the long grass, until we reach a craggy specimen with pale green, knobby fruit with the faintest blush of pink. This, he says, is the Calville Blanc d'Hiver, the most prized heirloom of France, and the traditional apple used in the famous French tarte tatin. The apple feels dense and heavy in my hand—a sure sign of a good baker that won't dissolve in the oven. I take a bite, eyes widening at the amazing flood of tart, honeyed juice. I taste lemons and spice and raspberries. It's startlingly good, and I immediately lament the fact that I can't simply walk down to my local market to buy more. Wood wraps up several apples in tissue (they bruise easily) and sends me on my way. That night I make the tarte tatin of my dreams. For the recipe, see page 203.

Vermont Apple Cider Donuts

It's a cider-maker's tradition to use some of the freshly pressed juice to make lightly tangy, apple-scented donuts like these. The cider adds more than flavor, though; its acidity makes donuts more tender.

I have two favorite spots for buying these treats: Atkins Farm in Amherst, Massachusetts, and Cold Hollow Cider Mill in Waterbury, Vermont. And when I can't be there, I make my own.

NOTES: Boiled apple cider gives these donuts a very rich, slightly tangy flavor. You can buy boiled cider in some gourmet and Whole Foods stores; from Wood's Cider Mill in Springfield, Vermont (woodscidermill.com); or from the King Arthur Flour catalog. Alternatively, you can boil your own cider by simmering 1½ cups of fresh apple cider down to ⅓ cup in about 25 minutes—it just won't be as concentrated as the commercial product.

Frying foods at the proper temperature guarantees crisp and light results. Use an instant-read thermometer to monitor the temperature during frying, and adjust the heat as needed.

EQUIPMENT: Hand-held or standing mixer; 2 large baking sheets; parchment paper or wax paper; 3-inch donut cutter or 2 biscuit cutters (one 3 inches and one 1 inch); 4- to 5-quart Dutch oven or other heavy-bottomed pot; instant-read thermometer (see Notes)

MAKES: About eighteen 3-inch donuts • ACTIVE TIME: *1½ hours* •
TOTAL TIME: *1 hour, 45 minutes*

1 cup (210 g) granulated sugar

5 tablespoons (70 g) unsalted butter, at room temperature

2 large eggs, at room temperature

3½ cups (505 g) all-purpose flour, plus additional for work surface

1¼ teaspoons table salt

2 teaspoons baking powder

1 teaspoon baking soda

1½ teaspoons ground cinnamon

½ teaspoon freshly grated nutmeg

½ cup (120 ml) lowfat buttermilk

⅓ cup (80 ml) boiled apple cider (see Notes)

1 tablespoon vanilla extract

Canola or safflower oil for frying

Cinnamon-sugar (1½ cups sugar mixed with 3 tablespoons ground cinnamon) or confectioners' sugar for sprinkling

1 • In a large bowl using a hand-held or standing mixer fitted with the whisk attachment, beat together the sugar and butter until the mixture is pale and fluffy, 4 to 6 minutes. Add the eggs, one at a time, beating for a minute after each. In a medium bowl, whisk together flour, salt, baking powder, baking soda, cinnamon, and nutmeg; set aside.

2 • Pour the buttermilk, boiled cider, and vanilla into the sugar-butter-egg mixture. Mix well, and don't worry if the mixture looks a bit curdled; it'll smooth itself out. Add the flour mixture and gently mix just until fully moistened. The mixture may appear a bit lumpy, but the most important thing is not to overmix.

3 • Line the baking sheets with wax paper or parchment paper and dust generously with flour. Turn the dough out onto one baking sheet and gently pat into a ¾-inch-thickness. Sprinkle dough with additional flour, cover with plastic wrap and put in the freezer for 10 minutes to firm up. Remove the dough from the freezer and use a lightly floured 3-inch donut cutter (or two concentric biscuit cutters) to cut out about 18 donuts with holes. You can gather the scraps and re-roll as needed, but you may need to chill the dough more to firm it up. Put the cut donuts on the other baking sheet as you go, then transfer to the freezer for 5 minutes to firm up again.

4 • Preheat the oven to 200°F and set a rack in the middle position. Set a plate lined with a few layers of paper towels nearby. In a Dutch oven or large pot, heat 3 inches of oil to 370°F (test with a thermometer). Drop 3 or 4 donuts into the oil, being careful not to crowd the pan. Cook until browned on one side, about 1 minute, then flip over and cook until browned on that side, about one minute more. Transfer the donuts to the paper-towel-lined plate and keep warm in the oven as you cook the rest. Repeat with the remaining dough (if you find it getting too soft as you work your way through the batches, pop it in the freezer again for 10 minutes). When the donuts are cool enough to handle, but still warm, sprinkle all over with the cinnamon-sugar or confectioners' sugar. Serve immediately.

LEFT: Vermont Apple Cider Donuts (page 153) with Mulled Apple Cider (page 276)

Baked Apple French Toast with Hazelnut Crumb Topping

Here's my go-to brunch dish for company. It's like light bread pudding with apples, and the hazelnut crumb topping gives it a nutty flavor kick and welcome crunch. While it looks impressive, it's so easy to put together that I've prepped it half-asleep after waking at midnight with the realization that guests were due the next morning.

APPLE NOTES: The crumb topping provides plenty of crunch in this dish, so I prefer a tender-sweet apple (see page 30), which will cook up soft and silky and melt nicely into the bread and custard. Any variety in the category will work well, but if you're lucky enough to get your hands on the Cox's Orange Pippin, this dish is a great way to enjoy its rich flavor.

NOTE: Don't worry about removing the hazelnuts' papery skin. The topping is so finely chopped in the food processor that the skins won't be detectable.

EQUIPMENT: 9- by 13-inch baking dish

MAKES: *6 to 8 servings* • ACTIVE TIME: *30 minutes* •
TOTAL TIME: *1 hour, 30 minutes, plus at least 2 hours chilling time.*

FOR THE FRENCH TOAST

Butter for greasing pan

6 large eggs

3 cups (710 ml) whole or 2% milk

¼ cup (60 g) packed light brown sugar

2 teaspoons vanilla extract

1 teaspoon kosher salt

1 teaspoon ground cinnamon

½ teaspoon freshly grated nutmeg

1 pound (450 g) loaf challah or brioche, cut in half lengthwise, then cut crosswise into ¾-inch-thick slices

2 large tender-sweet apples (about 1 pound total: see Apple Notes), peeled, cored, and sliced ¼-inch thick

FOR THE TOPPING

¾ cup (100 g) whole hazelnuts (see Note)

⅓ cup (75 g) firmly packed light brown sugar

¼ cup (36 g) all-purpose flour

4 tablespoons (½ stick; 57 g) salted butter, cut into small cubes

1 • The night before (or at least 2 hours ahead), generously grease the baking dish with butter. Whisk together the eggs, milk, brown sugar, vanilla, salt, cinnamon, and nutmeg. Arrange the bread slices in the prepared dish so that they overlap. Stick apple slices in between the bread slices, then pour the egg mixture over all. Cover with plastic wrap and chill for at least 2 hours and up to overnight.

2 • Preheat the oven to 350°F. In a food processor, pulse the hazelnuts, brown sugar, flour, and butter to form a crumbly mixture. Sprinkle the topping over the bread.

3 • Bake until the custard is set and the topping is golden brown, about 1 hour. Let cool on a rack for 15 minutes, then serve from the dish with maple syrup.

Dutch Baby

Dutch Baby

Also called a German pancake, this egg-leavened breakfast dish is like a sweeter version of Yorkshire pudding and a close cousin of the popover. I love it because it solves my eternal breakfast dilemma, providing the sweetness of pancakes, without the sleepiness that follows an all-carb feast. It also takes very little time to make, but looks so impressive, all golden and puffed up, when you bring it to the table.

APPLE NOTES: A sweeter apple pleases my morning taste buds better than an acidic one. Favorite firm-sweet varieties include Baldwin, Ginger Gold, Gravenstein, Honeycrisp, Jazz, and Piñata.

EQUIPMENT: 12-inch cast iron or other heavy-bottomed skillet

MAKES: 4 servings • ACTIVE TIME: *20 minutes* • TOTAL TIME: *35 minutes*

¾ cup (110 g) all-purpose flour

1 tablespoon granulated sugar

½ teaspoon ground cinnamon

1 teaspoon kosher salt

3 tablespoons (43 g) unsalted butter

1½ large firm-sweet apples (about 12 ounces total; see Apple Notes) peeled, cored, and cut into ⅛-inch-thick rings

5 large eggs

1 cup (240 ml) whole or 2% milk

Confectioners' sugar for sprinkling

Lemon wedges

1 • Sift the flour into a medium bowl, then stir in the sugar, cinnamon, and salt. In a separate bowl, whisk together the eggs and milk for about 1 minute; the mixture should be frothy and drizzle from the whisk in a thin stream. Set aside.

2 • Preheat the oven to 425°F and set a rack in the middle position. Melt the butter in a skillet over medium heat. Lay the apple slices in the butter and cook, without stirring, for 2 minutes. Gently flip the slices and cook until tender, about 2 more minutes.

3 • Working quickly, add the flour mixture to the egg mixture and whisk just to combine. Pour the batter into the hot skillet with the apples, then transfer the skillet to the oven. Bake until the pancake is puffed and golden, 10 to 14 minutes. Sprinkle with confectioners' sugar and serve immediately from the skillet, with lemon wedges to squirt over the top.

Dutch Baby pancakes (page 159) puff up in the oven but quickly lose their height.

Oatmeal-Apple Pancakes

The first really great pancakes I ever made came from a recipe in the 1970s classic *The Vegetarian Epicure* by Anna Thomas. They were made with cottage cheese, eggs, and a little flour, and required you to separate the egg yolks from the egg whites and beat the yolks with the cheese while whipping the whites into a foam. It seemed like a lot of work, but the results were so fantastically light and fluffy that I was sold.

That same technique guides this recipe, which folds hearty oats and diced apples into a standard buttermilk pancake batter, but, thanks to those whipped whites, still cooks up to an airy lightness that will forever change how you think about pancakes. Serve with maple syrup.

APPLE NOTES: Tender-sweet varieties, such as Fameuse, Cox's Orange Pippin, Fuji, and Gala will soften quickly, just in the time it takes to cook the pancake. For a complete list, see page 30.

NOTE: Quick-cooking oats are not the same thing as instant oats. If you're having difficulty identifying them, look for the type that cook in 3 to 5 minutes.

EQUIPMENT: Food processor; 12- to 14-inch skillet

MAKES: *20 pancakes* • ACTIVE TIME: *45 minutes* • TOTAL TIME: *45 minutes*

1½ cups (215 g) all-purpose flour

½ cup (45 g) quick-cooking oats, also called quick oats (see Note)

¾ teaspoon table salt

½ teaspoon baking soda

½ teaspoon ground cinnamon

¼ teaspoon freshly grated nutmeg

2 cups (475 ml) buttermilk

4 tablespoons (½ stick; 57 g) salted butter, melted and cooled

2 eggs, yolks and whites separated

½ cup (75 g) diced tender-sweet apple (see Apple Notes)

Vegetable oil or butter for frying

1 • Preheat the oven to 200°F. In a food processor, combine the flour, oats, salt, baking soda, cinnamon, and nutmeg. Whirl for 10 seconds to break the oats into small flakes. Set aside.

2 • In a medium bowl, whisk together the buttermilk, melted butter, and egg yolks. Set aside. In another bowl using a whisk, a hand-held mixer, or a standing mixer, whip the whites to soft peaks—that is, until they are firm and glossy but not stiff.

3 • Pour the flour mixture into the buttermilk mixture and whisk until just combined but still fairly lumpy. Using a spatula, gently fold about a third of the whipped egg whites into the batter. Add the remaining egg whites and gently fold again. Gently fold in the apples.

4 • Set a skillet over medium heat and add a tablespoon of vegetable oil or butter. Swirl to coat the pan. When the fat is sizzling, drop the batter in ¼-cup portions and cook until the pancakes are browned on the bottom and the edges begin to look dry, about 5 minutes. Turn the cakes with a spatula and brown on the other side, 1 to 2 minutes more. Add more oil or butter as necessary to keep the pancakes from sticking. Serve pancakes as you cook them (my preference) or keep them warm in a single layer on a baking sheet in the oven.

Baked Apple Oatmeal Pudding

This is like a bread pudding made with oatmeal. It's just as delicious when made ahead and reheated, so it's great to serve for overnight guests. Or bake a batch on Sunday for cozy and nutritious breakfasts through the week. Serve with plain yogurt or a dollop of crème fraîche.

APPLE NOTES: Firm-sweet apples (see page 30) provide just the right texture for this dish, and their milder acidity adds a nice contrast to the dried fruit. I like aromatic varieties like Jonagold, Ginger Gold, Piñata, Jazz, and SweeTango.

MAKE-AHEAD TIP: Bake the pudding up to three days ahead, then cover with foil and reheat at 250°F until warmed through, about 25 minutes.

NOTE: Rolled oats are thicker than instant or quick-cooking oats and take longer to cook, but they have a nice chewiness that works very well in this dish.

EQUIPMENT: 2½-quart soufflé dish or an 8- by 8-inch baking pan

MAKES: *6 servings* • ACTIVE TIME: *20 minutes* • TOTAL TIME: *1 hour, 15 minutes*

Butter for greasing pan

2 cups (180 g) rolled oats, also called old-fashioned oats (see Note)

1½ teaspoons baking powder

¾ teaspoon kosher salt

⅓ cup (40 g) chopped pecans

⅓ cup (about 55 g) roughly chopped dried fruit, such as cranberries, apricots, and raisins

1¾ cups (175 g) diced firm-sweet apple (about 1½ large; see Apple Notes)

2 cups (474 ml) 2% milk or 1% milk

3 large eggs

⅓ cup (75 g) firmly packed light brown sugar

½ teaspoon ground cinnamon

1 • Preheat the oven to 325°F and set a rack to the middle position. Grease the soufflé dish or baking pan. In a large bowl, stir together the oats, baking powder, and salt. Add the pecans, dried fruit, and apple.

2 • In another bowl, whisk together the milk, eggs, brown sugar, and cinnamon. Pour this mixture over the oat mixture and stir to combine.

3 • Pour the pudding into the prepared dish. Bake until the top is golden brown and the center is no longer liquid, 55 to 65 minutes. Spoon into bowls and serve warm.

Apple-Stuffed Biscuit Buns

I love a good cinnamon bun—even more with some diced apples wrapped up in the swirls—but I'm rarely organized enough to prep a yeast dough hours in advance of baking. These buns, inspired by the ones I once tasted at the River Run Café in Plainfield, Vermont, are made with a quick biscuit dough. Problem solved!

APPLE NOTES: This is, indeed, a rich dish. And normally, I like a more acidic apple when cooking with a fair amount of butter. However, these buns just needed something sweet, but still firm. Some favorites for this dish include Jazz, Pink Lady, and Piñata, for their bright, vibrant flavors. See page 30 for a complete list of firm-sweet apples.

EQUIPMENT: 8- by 8-inch baking pan; parchment paper

MAKES: *9 servings* • ACTIVE TIME: *40 minutes* • TOTAL TIME: *1 hour, 15 minutes*

FOR THE FILLING

1¼ cups (290 g) firmly packed light brown sugar

5 tablespoons (70 g) salted butter, cut into chunks, plus more for greasing pan

1½ teaspoons ground cinnamon

1 large firm-sweet apple (about 8 ounces; see Apple Notes), peeled, cored, and cut into ¼-inch cubes

FOR THE BUNS

½ cup (120 ml) buttermilk

1 large egg

3 cups (435 g) all-purpose flour

1 tablespoon granulated sugar

2½ teaspoons baking powder

1½ teaspoons kosher salt

½ teaspoon baking soda

12 tablespoons (1½ sticks, 170 g) cold salted butter, cut into small cubes

1 • Grease the baking pan with a little bit of butter; set aside. Make the filling: In a medium bowl, combine the brown sugar, the 5 tablespoons butter, and the cinnamon. Using a pastry cutter (or fork), cut the butter into the sugar, working it in until the mixture looks like wet sand. Put in the refrigerator to chill while you prepare the dough.

RIGHT: Apple-Stuffed Biscuit Bun

2 • In a small bowl, whisk together the buttermilk and egg; set aside. In a medium bowl, whisk together the flour, sugar, baking powder, salt, and baking soda. Sprinkle the butter over the flour mixture and use your fingers to work it in (rub your thumb against your fingertips, smearing the butter as you do). Stop when mixture looks like sand studded with little chunks. Add the egg mixture and stir with a fork just until the dough begins to hold together. It will look quite ragged and not fully blended, but stop there. You want to prevent the butter from melting into the dough—those little chunks will create a flakier texture once baked.

3 • Preheat the oven to 350°F and set a rack to the middle position. Dump the dough out onto a piece of parchment paper and knead *just* enough to bring it all together into a ball. Using a rolling pin and bench scraper (or spatula), roll the dough (still on parchment) into a 9- by 15-inch rectangle with straight sides.

4 • Sprinkle the dough all over with the brown sugar mixture, leaving a 1-inch border across one of the longer edges. Top with the apples and gently press down. Working from the long edge *opposite* the border, roll the dough up tightly, jelly-roll-style, using the parchment as an aid. When you reach the border, give the roll a squeeze and turn seam side down.

5 • Cut the roll crosswise into 9 equal buns and arrange in the prepared pan. Bake until golden brown and bubbling, 30 to 35 minutes. Serve warm, right from the pan.

Apple Cranberry Scones

Scones and biscuits can be intimidating for first-timers, with all the dire warnings about working fast and not over-kneading. Here's the simple trick: Err on the side of a shaggier, rougher dough, rather than a perfectly smooth one. As long as it holds together, it's fine. Another trick: Use dried fruit, which keeps the dough lighter by not adding a lot of extra moisture. Serve with the jam of your choice, extra butter, or clotted cream.

EQUIPMENT: Large unrimmed baking sheet; parchment paper

MAKES: *12 servings* • ACTIVE TIME: *25 minutes* • TOTAL TIME: *55 minutes*

⅓ cup (80 ml) buttermilk

1 large egg

3 cups (435 g) all-purpose flour

⅓ cup (70 g) granulated sugar

2½ teaspoons baking powder

¾ teaspoon table salt

½ teaspoon baking soda

12 tablespoons (1½ sticks; 170 g) cold unsalted butter, cut into small cubes

½ cup (40 g) chopped dried apples

¼ cup (33 g) chopped dried sweetened cranberries

1 tablespoon freshly grated orange zest (optional)

1 • Preheat the oven to 350°F and set a rack to the middle position. In a small bowl, whisk together the buttermilk and egg. Set aside.

2 • In a medium bowl, whisk together the flour, sugar, baking powder, salt, and baking soda. Sprinkle the butter over the mixture and use your fingers to work it in, rubbing your thumb against your fingertips, smearing the butter as you do. Stop when the mixture looks like cornmeal studded with pea-sized bits of butter (work quickly so the butter doesn't melt).

3 • Add the egg mixture to the flour mixture, together with the apples, cranberries, and orange zest (if using) and use a fork to combine. The mixture will still look ragged; don't overmix. Dump the dough out onto a lightly floured work surface and knead *just* enough to bring it all together into a ball. Divide in half and press each half into a 6- to 7-inch disk.

4 • Transfer the disks to a parchment-lined baking sheet. Use a knife or bench scraper to cut the disks into six wedges each (do not separate the pieces). Bake until golden brown and puffed—turning the baking sheet halfway through—25 to 30 minutes. Transfer to a serving plate and serve warm.

Apple-Studded Brown Butter Streusel Coffee Cake

Apple-Studded Brown Butter Streusel Coffee Cake

Cooking butter until it turns a rich brown color adds a nutty flavor to this addictive coffee cake. In fact, I don't think it's possible to pack in more appealing elements here: buttermilk batter, warm spices, streusel topping, the browned butter, and lots of apples.

APPLE NOTES: The texture of this cake should be extremely tender, which is why a tender-sweet apple is important. The apples shouldn't add crunch in the cake as much as little pockets of flavor. The popular supermarket varieties, Fuji and Gala, are a great choice here. For a complete list, go to page 30.

EQUIPMENT: 9-inch cake pan with removable sides

MAKES: *8 to 10 servings* • ACTIVE TIME: *30 minutes* • TOTAL TIME: *1 hour, 15 minutes*

FOR THE TOPPING

½ cup (115 g) firmly packed light brown sugar

½ cup (72 g) all-purpose flour

½ teaspoon ground cinnamon

3 tablespoons (57 g) butter, cut into ½-inch cubes, plus more for greasing pan

8 firm-sweet apple slices (see Apple Notes), unpeeled, for garnish

FOR THE CAKE

10⅔ tablespoons (⅔ cup; 151 g) salted butter

2 cups (290 g) all-purpose flour

½ cup (115 g) firmly packed light brown sugar

½ cup (105 g) granulated sugar

2 teaspoons baking powder

½ teaspoon baking soda

½ teaspoon table salt

1 teaspoon ground cinnamon

¼ teaspoon freshly grated nutmeg

1 large egg, plus 1 egg yolk

1 cup (240 ml) buttermilk

2 medium tender-sweet apples (about 12 ounces total; see Apple Notes), peeled, cored, and cut into ½-inch cubes

1 • Butter the cake pan. Set aside.

2 • Make the topping: In a small bowl, stir together the brown sugar, flour, and cinnamon. Sprinkle the 3 tablespoons of butter cubes over the mixture and use your fingertips to work it in to form a crumbly topping. Chill in the refrigerator while you prepare the cake.

3 • Preheat the oven to 350°F. Make the cake: In a small pan, melt the butter over medium heat until it begins to turn a medium nut brown, 6 to 8 minutes. Remove from the heat and set aside to cool slightly. In a large bowl, whisk together the flour, sugars, baking powder, baking soda, salt, and spices. In a medium bowl, beat the egg and egg yolk to blend. Whisk in the butter and buttermilk, then pour the liquid mixture into the flour mixture and stir just to combine. Fold in the apple cubes and pour the batter into the prepared pan. Sprinkle the topping over the cake and arrange the apple slices around the top, lightly pressing them into the topping. Bake until the top is golden brown and a cake tester inserted into the center comes out clean, 45 to 55 minutes. Set on a cooling rack for 20 minutes, then check to see if the sides of the cake are sticking to the pan in any spots. If so, use a thin knife to loosen them. Carefully remove the sides of pan, transfer to a platter, and serve warm or at room temperature.

Apple-Apricot Kuchen

A kuchen is traditionally a rich German yeast-raised cake filled with fruit or cheese and dotted around the top with jam or fresh fruit. It's like a cross between a coffee cake and a tart. My friend Adeena Sussman, a food writer, came up with the time-saving idea of using baking powder as the rising agent. It worked beautifully, and I'm for anything that can get fresh pastry on the table sooner. As with traditional kuchen, this dish can be served for breakfast or as a dessert. Serve from the pan as is, or with a dollop of whipped cream and a sprinkle of cinnamon sugar.

APPLE NOTES: I particularly like Piñata and Jazz varieties in this recipe because both have tropical flavors that complement the apricot jam. However, you really can't go wrong with any firm-sweet variety (see page 30 for a list), so feel free to mix it up.

MAKE-AHEAD TIP: You can prep the dough through step 1 a day ahead of baking; just wrap and refrigerate.

EQUIPMENT: 10-inch deep-dish pie plate

MAKES: *8 servings* • ACTIVE TIME: *40 minutes* • TOTAL TIME: *1 hour, 45 minutes*

FOR THE DOUGH

2⅓ cups (338 g) all-purpose flour

1 cup (210 g) granulated sugar

4 teaspoons baking powder

½ teaspoon table salt

2 large eggs, at room temperature

16 tablespoons (2 sticks; 227 g) salted butter, at room temperature

FOR THE FILLING

4 large firm-sweet apples (about 2 pounds total; see Apple Notes)

¼ cup (51 g) plus 1 teaspoon granulated sugar

1 tablespoon freshly squeezed lemon juice

2 tablespoons apricot jam

2 teaspoons ground cinnamon

1 • To make the dough, put the flour, sugar, baking powder and salt in a standing mixer (or in a large bowl if using a hand-held mixer). With the whisk attachment, stir the mixture on low speed for 10 seconds to combine, then add the butter and eggs and mix at medium-high speed until the ingredients form a ball, about 1 minute. Divide the dough into two equal pieces, wrap each in plastic wrap, and chill for 30 minutes.

2 • Meanwhile, make the filling: Peel, core, and slice the apples into ¼-inch-thick slices. Sprinkle ¼ cup sugar and the lemon juice over the apples and stir. Set aside.

3 • Preheat the oven to 350°F, and set a rack to the middle position. Press one ball of dough into the pie plate so that it covers the bottom. Cover with the sliced apples. Top all over with small dabs of jam. Divide the remaining ball of dough into 10 equal-sized balls and distribute evenly on top of the apples. They will spread out as they cook. Sprinkle with the remaining 1 teaspoon sugar and the cinnamon. Bake for 40 minutes, or until the dough is golden brown. Remove to a rack and let cool for 20 minutes.

Apple Pumpkin Walnut Muffins

Here's a great way to start off a fall morning: flavors of pumpkin, spice, apples, and walnuts will warm you up, and the simple method makes these muffins easy to prepare on short notice.

APPLE NOTES: I like firm-sweet apples (see page 30) in these muffins for their more delicate flavor, but firm-tart apples will also work well.

MAKE-AHEAD TIP: You can prep this recipe through step 1 the night before, then finish it in the morning. You can also freeze the finished muffins in a zip-top bag for up to two months.

NOTE: I love the subtle nutty flavor that walnut oil brings to the mix, but vegetable oil (such as canola or corn oil) is fine too.

EQUIPMENT: One 15-cup muffin tin or two 12-cup tins of ⅓-cup capacity.

MAKES: *15 muffins* • ACTIVE TIME: *20 minutes* • TOTAL TIME: *45 minutes*

1⅔ (242 g) cups all-purpose flour

½ cup (105 g) granulated sugar

½ cup (115 g) firmly packed light brown sugar

1 teaspoon ground cinnamon

1 teaspoon kosher salt

½ teaspoon baking powder

½ teaspoon baking soda

½ teaspoon ground ginger

¼ teaspoon ground cloves

1 cup (240 ml) canned pumpkin puree (not pumpkin pie filling)

2 large eggs

½ cup (120 ml) walnut oil or vegetable oil (see Note)

1 large firm-sweet apple (about 8 ounces; see Apple Notes), peeled, cored, and cut into ¼-inch cubes

¾ cup (65 g) walnuts, chopped

1 teaspoon vanilla extract

15 walnut halves for garnish (optional)

1 • Preheat the oven to 375°F. Line the muffin cups with paper liners or grease with butter. In a large bowl, whisk together the flour, sugar, cinnamon, salt, baking powder, baking soda, ginger, and cloves. In a medium bowl, whisk together the pumpkin puree, eggs, oil, apple, chopped walnuts, and vanilla.

2 • Add the wet ingredients to the dry and stir to combine (do not overmix). Divide the batter among the 15 muffin cups, filling each about three-quarters full, and top each with a walnut half if desired. Bake until the muffins are puffed and golden and a cake tester comes out clean, 20 to 25 minutes. Let the muffins cool on a rack for 15 minutes, then serve warm.

Morning Glory Muffins

The Morning Glory Café was a famous Nantucket Island gathering spot in the 1970s and 1980s; it was there that chef/owner Pam McKinstry introduced the muffins that would immortalize her restaurant. *Gourmet* magazine printed the recipe in 1981, and they began appearing at bakeries and cafés around the country. Packed as they are with apples, walnuts, coconut, pineapple, and carrots, they're like a healthy wake-up call for your taste buds.

APPLE NOTES: There are so many other flavors in this muffin, truly any firm-sweet apple (see page 30) will work well.

MAKE-AHEAD TIP: You can prep this recipe through step 1 the night before, then finish it in the morning. You can also freeze the finished muffins in a zip-top bag for up to two months.

EQUIPMENT: One 15-cup muffin tin or two 12-cup tins of ⅓-cup capacity

MAKES: *15 muffins* • ACTIVE TIME: *25 minutes* • TOTAL TIME: *50 minutes*

2¼ cups (325 g) all-purpose flour

1¼ cups (255 g) granulated sugar

1 tablespoon ground cinnamon

1 teaspoon baking powder

1 teaspoon baking soda

¾ teaspoon table salt

2 cups (180 g) grated carrots

⅔ cup (125 g) canned crushed pineapple, drained

½ cup (45 g) shredded sweetened coconut

1 large firm-sweet apple (about 8 ounces; see Apple Notes), unpeeled, cored, and grated

½ cup (65 g) roughly chopped walnuts

3 large eggs

¾ cup (177 ml) vegetable oil, such as canola or corn

1 teaspoon vanilla extract

1 • Preheat the oven to 350°F and set a rack to the middle position. Line the muffin cups with paper liners or grease with butter. In a large bowl, whisk together the flour, sugar, cinnamon, baking powder, baking soda, and salt. Add the carrots, pineapple, coconut, apple, and walnuts, and stir to combine. Add the eggs, oil, and vanilla and stir to combine.

2 • Divide the batter among the 15 muffin cups, filling each ⅔ of the way to the top. Bake until the muffins are puffed and golden and a cake tester comes out clean, about 25 minutes. Let the muffins cool in the pan on a rack for 10 minutes, then turn them out to cool for another 10 minutes; serve warm.

Sausage, Apple, and Cheddar Strata

Savory bread puddings, or stratas, are another great brunch option.
They're endlessly versatile, allowing for a whole range of flavor combinations, and can be prepared the night before you serve them. This strata combines some of my favorite breakfast flavors: sausage, eggs, maple syrup, and fried apples. Tossed with bread cubes and Cheddar and soaked in custard, the ingredients all come together in sweet and savory harmony.

APPLE NOTES: Firm-tart apples (see page 30) are the best choice for this dish because they have the acidity to stand up to the rich sausage and Cheddar. I particularly like the Northern Spy, because it tends to be just a bit sweeter, and that makes it a nice match for the maple flavors. Other good choices: Esopus Spitzenburg, Sierra Beauty, and Arkansas Black.

EQUIPMENT: 9- by 13-inch baking pan; 10- to 12-inch skillet

MAKES: *8 servings* • ACTIVE TIME: *45 minutes* •
TOTAL TIME: *1 hour, 45 minutes, plus at least 2 hours chilling time*

Butter for greasing pan

6 large eggs

3½ cups (830 ml) whole or 2% milk

1 tablespoon Dijon mustard

1 teaspoon kosher salt, divided

6 ounces (170 g) grated Cheddar cheese

2 scallions, ends trimmed, cut into ½-inch lengths

12 ounces (340 g) fresh pork breakfast sausage, such as Jimmy Dean brand, in bulk or in links

1½ cups (210 g) chopped yellow onion

2 large firm-tart apples (about 1 pound total; see Apple Notes), peeled, cored, and cut into ½-inch-thick wedges

1 tablespoon maple syrup mixed with 1 tablespoon water

14 ounces (450 g; about ¾ of a standard loaf) crusty white bread, such as Italian or Pullman style, cut into 1-inch cubes

1 • The night before serving (or at least 2 hours ahead), whisk together the eggs, milk, mustard, and ½ teaspoon of the kosher salt. Set aside. Toss the Cheddar with the scallions and set aside. Generously grease a baking pan with butter. Set aside.

2 • In a skillet over medium-high heat, cook the sausage, stirring occasionally, until fully cooked through and browned, 7 to 10 minutes. If using link sausages, turn to brown all over. If using bulk sausage, break up the pieces with a wooden spoon as they cook. Remove the sausage, drain on paper towels, and set aside. If using links, cut into half-inch pieces.

3 • Drain all but 2 tablespoons sausage drippings from the pan, then add the onion and remaining ½ teaspoon salt. Cook over medium-high heat, stirring frequently, until the onions are translucent, about 5 minutes. Reduce the heat to medium and add the apples and maple syrup mixture. Cook, stirring often, until the apples are tender and the maple syrup has reduced to a glaze, 4 to 6 minutes more.

4 • Arrange half the bread cubes in the bottom of the prepared dish and top with a third of the grated Cheddar-scallion mixture, half the onion-apple mixture, and half the sausage. Repeat with the remaining bread, a third of the cheese-scallion mixture, and the remaining onion-apple mixture and sausage. Top with the remaining cheese-scallion mixture. Pour the egg mixture over all, making sure that all the bread is coated. Cover with foil or plastic wrap and chill for at least 2 hours and up to overnight.

5 • Preheat the oven to 350°F. Bake, uncovered, until the custard is set and the top is golden brown, about 1 hour. Let cool on a rack for 20 minutes, then serve warm from the pan.

Irish Soda Bread with Apples and Currants

Boston is a great place to live around Saint Patrick's day because even the Italian bakeries turn out respectable rounds of soda bread. And why not? Made without yeast, this bread requires no rising time—instant gratification! Typically, these loaves are studded with raisins, but I like a combination of apples and currants, along with the traditional caraway seeds.

APPLE NOTES: Firm-tart apples (see page 30), such as Granny Smith and Rhode Island Greening, are best.

EQUIPMENT: 8 or 9-inch round cake pan

MAKES: *1 loaf* • ACTIVE TIME: *25 minutes* • TOTAL TIME: *65 minutes*

2¼ cups (325 g) all-purpose flour

¼ cup (51 g) plus 2 teaspoons granulated sugar, divided

1½ teaspoons baking powder

1 teaspoon table salt

¾ teaspoon baking soda

4 tablespoons (58 g) melted unsalted butter, plus more for greasing pan

1 cup (240 ml) buttermilk

1 large firm-tart apple (about 8 ounces; see Apple Notes), peeled, cored, and cut into small cubes

½ cup (65 g) currants

1 teaspoon caraway seeds

1 • Preheat the oven to 375°F and set a rack to the middle position. Generously grease a cake pan with butter. In a large bowl, whisk together the flour, ¼ cup sugar, the baking powder, salt, and baking soda. Add the butter and stir until the flour is mostly coated. Make a well in the center and add the buttermilk. Gently stir just until moistened. The dough should look very shaggy. Add the apples, currants, and caraway seeds and stir just to combine.

2 • Using floured hands, shape the dough into a ball. Transfer to the prepared pan and flatten slightly (the dough will not reach the edges). Sprinkle with the remaining 2 teaspoons sugar.

3 • Bake until the top of the loaf is golden brown and a tester inserted into the center comes out clean, 45 to 50 minutes. Transfer to a rack and cool for 15 minutes. Gently turn the bread out of the pan and cool on the rack for an additional 15 minutes. Serve warm or at room temperature.

Holiday Apple-Raisin Challah

The trick to making great challah is to add just enough eggs and oil to the dough so that it tastes rich and moist without becoming heavy and sticky. My friend Kathy Cohen gets it exactly right—her bread, stuffed with apples, raisins, and cinnamon, is the highlight of her annual Jewish New Year feast. For years, I'd count the days between slices, until I finally decided to ask for the recipe.

APPLE NOTES: There aren't a lot of apples in this bread, so you want a variety that really stands out. Therefore, green firm-tart apples (see page 30), such as Granny Smith and Rhode Island Greening, are the perfect choice here.

EQUIPMENT: 2 large baking sheets, rimmed or unrimmed

MAKES: *2 loaves* • ACTIVE TIME: *45 minutes* • TOTAL TIME: *4 hours*

FOR THE BREAD

2 tablespoons dry yeast

1 tablespoon plus ¾ cup (155 g) granulated sugar

5 large eggs

¾ cup (180 ml) vegetable oil, such as canola or safflower

¾ teaspoon kosher salt

6 cups (870 g) all-purpose flour

FOR THE FILLING

1 large firm-tart apple (about 8 ounces; see Apple Notes), peeled, cored, and cut into small cubes

½ cup (65 g) raisins

3 tablespoons lemon juice

2 tablespoons honey

½ teaspoon ground cinnamon

1 egg yolk

1 • Combine ½ cup warm water, the yeast, and 1 tablespoon of the sugar in a small bowl. Stir until the yeast dissolves. Let it activate for 10 minutes—the mixture should look foamy.

2 • In the large bowl of a standing mixer with the paddle attachment or with a hand-held mixer, beat the eggs at medium speed until blended. Add the oil, salt, and remaining ¾ cup sugar. Beat until pale in color, about 4 minutes. Beat in ⅔ cup water, then add the yeast mixture. Beat in the flour 1 cup at a time.

LEFT: Holiday Apple-Raisin Challah

3 • Turn the dough onto a floured surface and knead for 2 minutes (or use the dough hook on your mixer for 1 minute at low speed). Put the dough in a lightly oiled bowl and turn to coat. Cover with plastic wrap and a kitchen towel and put in a warm corner of your kitchen to rise. I like to use my (unheated) oven with the lightbulb on. You want the dough to double in size, which takes just about an hour.

4 • Punch down the dough, rewrap with plastic wrap and a kitchen towel, and let the dough rise for 30 minutes. It won't quite double in this time, but it will puff up.

5 • Meanwhile, make the filling: In a small bowl, toss the apples with the raisins, lemon juice, honey, and cinnamon. Let sit for 20 minutes, then drain any liquid.

6 • Turn the dough out onto a lightly floured surface and divide in half. Divide each half into three equal parts, for a total of six pieces. Roll out each piece to form a 12-inch strand, then pat each strand down into a flat rectangle shape. Spoon a bit of apple mixture down the center of each rectangle, then fold dough over the filling, roll into a 15-inch rope, and pinch the ends tight.

7 • Form the loaves: Put three of the apple-filled "ropes" on each baking sheet. Braid the ropes together (fold right rope over center, then fold left rope over center, repeat). Pinch at bottom. Repeat with the other loaf. Cover the loaves with kitchen towels, and let rise for 45 minutes.

8 • Preheat the oven to 400°F and set a rack to the middle position. Whisk the egg yolk with 1 tablespoon water and brush over the tops of the loaves. Bake for 10 minutes, then reduce the heat to 350°F and bake until the crusts are browned and the bread is puffed and light, 30 minutes more. Transfer the loaves to a rack and let cool for 30 minutes before serving.

CHAPTER EIGHT

PIES, CRISPS, COBBLERS, BUCKLES, AND BETTIES

Spencer

A Tour of Washington's Wenatchee Valley, "Apple Capital of the World"

Wenatchee, Washington doesn't look like Eden, though the local Visitor's Bureau would have you believe so. Promotional photos depict a landscape of lush, green, orchard-lined hills rolling down from the Cascade Mountains to the confluence of the Wenatchee and Columbia rivers, the trees heavy with ripe apples, cherries, peaches, and pears. So it's startling to enter this valley in late summer, just before the start of apple season, and find a dry, high desert landscape.

In fact, the region only greens up during the spring, after the rains, and the orchards are kept alive solely through ample irrigation from the rivers. The sun shines three hundred days out of the year in Wenatchee, and without human intervention, the land would revert to a brown, rocky landscape dotted with sage and bitterbrush.

Yet central Washington is America's most prolific apple-growing region. More than half the apples grown in the United States come from this state—a volume more than four times than that of number two finisher New York—and nearly 38 million boxes of apples were shipped from Wenatchee alone in 2008. Nearby Yakima produces even more apples—about 50 percent more in any given year. But Wenatchee still claims to be "The Apple Capital of the World," a slogan trumpeted on a large, apple-shaped neon sign at the edge of town.

How such abundance came from the desert seems a puzzle at first. But the answer can be found not far from that sign, in a low-slung brown building on Euclid Avenue, where the Washington Apple Commission hosts a modest visitors center. The exhibits there tell a story of how, in the early 1800s, the first pioneers discovered that the region's clear Cascade mountain water and bright sunshine, hot days and crisp autumn nights, and rich volcanic soil replenished by Mount St. Helens' periodic blasts made this prime apple country. Yes, scarce rainfall necessitates irrigation, and the hot summer temperatures aren't good for many breeds of apples, but the dry climate also keeps insect populations in check. In fact, Washington is the country's leading producer of organic apples, and even non-organic farms require fewer pesticide applications per season than farms in other regions. The sunshine helps the fruit grow big and ripe—premium-grade apples weigh about half a pound each—while the controlled water supply can concentrate the flavor of the fruit. Suddenly, a desert Eden makes sense. And here, apples are a very big, very modern business.

If this paradise could be said to have an operations center, it can be found in the sprawling warehouses of Stemilt Growers, one of the largest growing, packing, and shipping operations in the state. Here, popular supermarket varieties such as Braeburn, Gala, and Fuji—some grown on Stemilt-owned land, others on smaller family farms—are graded, sorted, stored, and packed for transport on an automated assembly line that's decidedly more high-tech than home spun. Along the line, apples are systematically photographed, weighed, and routed by computer; sent down long water-filled flumes; and gently slapped with the tiny PLU stickers that are the bane of home cooks worldwide. Some below-grade apples are siphoned off for the juice factory while premium fruits are sent straight to market, and still others are housed in giant controlled atmosphere storage rooms where the fruit is held in suspended animation for months at a time.

It's an operation of mind-boggling complexity, so different from the simple family-run orchards selling paper sacks of apples at the farmers' market. Though the business has been owned and run by members of the Mathison family since 1893—they first arrived as homesteaders, and began raising fruit soon after—it has evolved into an international corporation with annual revenues exceeding $100 million. On this stage, innovation is essential.

"We continue to find better ways grow, better ways to pick and transfer fruit," says Roger Pepperl, the company's marketing manager, whose office in the company's sleek corporate headquarters is just up the hill, but a world away from the warehouses. "We're continually upgrading machines on the sorting line. We have the capability to sample the fruit's sugars and test pressure levels, to determine crunch." He shakes his head. "There always seems to be something new, and the standards continue to rise."

Today's standards call for sweet, juicy, and very crunchy apples, so most of the growers in the Wenatchee Valley favor just a handful of varieties, including Golden Delicious, Granny Smith, Honeycrisp, Cameo, Jonagold, and Pink Lady. Not a bad mix, but hardly the diversity once cultivated on American farms. The market demands large, uniform, storable, transportable fruit, and many heirloom breeds can't compete.

And so, rather than relying on a roll of the genetic dice, as the first American apple farmers did, today's large-scale growers turn to market research, focus groups, and controlled breeding methods to find the next winning variety. Red Delicious, long lamented as a mealy, flavorless fruit, is, thankfully, in the sunset of its career, while Pink Lady, Gala, Fuji, and Jazz apples are leading the charge. Stemilt is even marketing its own proprietary variety, called Piñata (see page 51)—a three-way cross between Golden Delicious, Cox's Orange Pippin, and Duchess of Oldenburg that's prized for exceptional crunch and juiciness. Securing the exclusive rights to trademarked varieties is a tremendous competitive advantage in the current market, and other large growers and cooperatives are scrambling to snap up their own signature varieties (or, in the case of the foreign-bred varieties such as the Jazz, the exclusive American rights). It's hard to imagine a more contrary approach to Johnny Appleseed's seed-scattering free-for-all.

But just as in the nineteenth century, a modern home-run apple breed can mean big money, and since U.S. apple consumption has generally been flat over the past decade, thanks in part to competition from an increasingly diverse fruit market (have you noticed those winter grapes and raspberries from Chile?) and junk food, growers are hungry for new ways to grab market share.

"The fruit business is definitely becoming more vertically integrated, and there's been a ton of consolidation," says Pepperl. "Fifteen years ago, there were maybe fifty to sixty shippers in the state of Washington, all shipping around the country. Since then, we've consolidated to maybe fifteen players."

International markets hold promise, and the Washington Apple Commission has pushed hard to make inroads in Mexico, India, and Asia. But on the international market, China is casting a very long shadow. According to the United States Department of Agriculture, China produced nearly 30 million metric tons of apples in 2008—some of which reached the American market in the form of inexpensive apple juice. Meanwhile, in that same year, the United States harvested just over 4.4 million metric tons.

"China is interesting," says Pepperl. "They produce eight, nine times what we produce, but that doesn't take into account quality. A lot of their stuff is produced and sold within China, but they still imported 1 or 2 million pounds of our apples last year. Why? Because we grow fantastic apples."

In a global market, Wenatchee is counting on that combination of high desert sunshine and high-tech savvy to keep its "Apple Capital" sign shining—if not in terms of quantity, then certainly in quality.

"At the end of the day, certain areas are going to grow better fruit," Pepperl says. "Washington State is the premiere area for growing apples. One of the best in world."

Grandma's Apple Crisp

My grandmother, Mary Quagliaroli, made this buttery, cinnamon-scented crisp every fall, and to me, it's the flavor of home. This is her adaptation of a recipe from the November 1945 issue of *Country Gentleman* magazine; I still have the original, now tissue-thin and torn at the creases, which she passed along to me in a little plastic bag filled with some of her favorite recipes. Now I make it in summer or fall, filling it with whatever's fresh: apples, blueberries, peaches, nectarines, raspberries, or pears.

Not your usual oat-and-brown-sugar blend, it has a simple, sweet biscuit topping made with flour, baking powder, salt, sugar, and eggs. That's it. Just drizzle with the butter and sprinkle with cinnamon. Serve with a scoop of ice cream, a drizzle of heavy cream, or no topping at all.

APPLE NOTES: For the perfect texture, I like to mix tender-tart apples (see page 30), such as McIntosh or Jonathan, with firm-sweet ones, such as Jazz or Ginger Gold. The tender apples cook down and create a sort of thick sauce, in which the firmer slices are suspended—a mixture of smoothness and texture.

NOTE: You can cut your prep time in half by using an old-fashioned apple corer/peeler, which makes short work of cutting the apples into perfect, even slices.

EQUIPMENT: 9- by 13-inch baking dish

MAKES: *8 servings* • ACTIVE TIME: *30 minutes* • TOTAL TIME: *1 hour, 15 minutes*

FOR THE FILLING

5 large tender-tart apples (about 2½ pounds total; see Apple Notes), peeled, cored, and cut into ¼-inch-thick rings or slices

5 large firm-sweet apples, (about 2½ pounds total), peeled, cored, and cut into ¼-inch-thick rings or slices

FOR THE TOPPING

2 cups (290 g) all-purpose flour

2 teaspoons baking powder

1½ teaspoons kosher salt

1 cup (210 g) granulated sugar

2 large eggs, lightly beaten

8 tablespoons (1 stick; 120 g) salted butter, melted and cooled

2 teaspoons ground cinnamon

1 • Preheat the oven to 350°F, and set a rack to the middle position. Arrange the sliced apples in an even layer in a baking dish (no need to grease it); set aside.

2 • In a large bowl, whisk together the flour, baking powder, salt, and sugar. Add the eggs and, using a fork or a pastry cutter, work in until crumbly. The mixture will look like streusel, with a mix of wet and dry bits. Have no fear; the eggs provide enough liquid.

3 • Spread the topping evenly over the apples, then drizzle all over with the melted butter. Sprinkle with cinnamon and bake until the topping is golden brown and apple juices are bubbling, 45 to 55 minutes. Let cool 20 minutes, then serve warm from the pan.

Oatmeal-Topped Apple Crisp

Apple crisp is, hands-down, my favorite dessert, which is why there are two versions in this book: my grandmother's cake-topped recipe (page 185), and this more traditional variation, in which the apples are blanketed in a thick layer of oats, pecans, and spices. Both are so delicious that if I were to stage a head-to-head apple crisp bake-off, I'd have to declare a tie, but only after repeated samplings for, ahem, research purposes. Serve with a scoop of ice cream, a drizzle of heavy cream, or no topping at all. Like Grandma's Apple Crisp, this is also delicious when made with blueberries, mixed berries, sliced peaches, or nectarines.

APPLE NOTES: As with Grandma's Apple Crisp, I think any combination of tender-tart apples (see page 30) and firm-sweet ones is ideal here, both from a taste and texture perspective. However, because this crisp has pecans and a bit more spice, you'd do especially well with apples with spicy notes, such as Baldwin, Braeburn, Ginger Gold, Jonathan, and McIntosh.

NOTE: Rolled oats are thicker than instant or quick-cooking oats and take a bit longer to cook, but they have a nice chewiness that works very well in this dish.

EQUIPMENT: 9- by 13-inch baking dish; food processor

MAKES: *8 servings* • ACTIVE TIME: *30 minutes* • TOTAL TIME: *1 hour, 25 minutes*

FOR THE FILLING

5 large tender-tart apples (about 2½ pounds total; see Apple Notes), peeled, cored, and cut into ½-inch chunks

5 large firm-sweet apples (about 2½ pounds total), peeled, cored, and cut into 1-inch chunks

FOR THE TOPPING

1 cup (145 g) all-purpose flour

½ cup (45 g) rolled oats, also called old-fashioned oats (see Note)

½ cup (115 g) firmly packed light brown sugar

½ cup (105 g) granulated sugar

1 teaspoon ground cinnamon

scant ½ teaspoon freshly grated ground nutmeg

½ teaspoon kosher salt

10 tablespoons (1¼ sticks; 142 g) chilled salted butter, cut into small pieces

¾ cup (80 g) pecan halves

1 • Preheat the oven to 375°F, and set a rack to the middle position. Arrange the apples in a baking dish (no need to grease it).

2 • In a food processor, pulse the flour, oats, sugars, cinnamon, nutmeg and salt to blend. Sprinkle the butter on top and pulse four times (1 second each)—the mixture will look like rough sand. Add the pecans and pulse until they are the size of peas—about three pulses.

3 • Spread the mixture over the apples and bake until the topping is golden brown and apple juices are bubbling, 50 to 60 minutes. Let cool 20 minutes, then serve warm from the pan.

Swedish Apple Pie

My friend Aaron Cohen, a food writer, shared this crustless apple pie recipe, and I was so impressed with its ease of preparation and fantastic flavor that I had to include it here. It's even easier to make than my grandmother's apple crisp on page 185, and that's saying something. In this case, all you do is peel and slice five apples and then top them with a quick batter of flour, sugar, butter, and an egg. That's it. Spread that over the apples and pop in the oven. The batter settles down around the fruit as it cooks, so you end up with slices of fruit suspended in a cakelike filling.

APPLE NOTES: Any firm-tart apple (see page 30) will do very well here. All that matters is that the fruit has enough acidity to stand up to the rich batter.

EQUIPMENT: 9- or 10-inch deep-dish pie plate

MAKES: *8 servings* • ACTIVE TIME: *20 minutes* • TOTAL TIME: *60 minutes*

4 large firm-tart apples (about 2 pounds total; see Apple Notes), peeled, cored, and cut into ¼-inch-thick slices

1 teaspoon ground cinnamon

1 tablespoon plus 1 cup (145 g) all-purpose flour

2 tablespoons plus 1 cup (210 g) granulated sugar

10 tablespoons (1¼ sticks; 142 g) salted butter, at room temperature, plus more for greasing pan

1 large egg

1 • Preheat the oven to 375°F. Grease a pie plate and set aside.

2 • In a medium bowl, toss the apple slices with the cinnamon, 1 tablespoon of the flour, and 2 tablespoons of the sugar. Arrange the slices flat and in an even layer in the pie plate (if using a 9-inch pie plate, it will look quite full; don't worry, there will still be room for the topping).

3 • In a standing mixer or with a hand-held mixer, combine the remaining flour and sugar with the butter and egg. Mix until combined. Use a spatula to spread the batter over the apples. Bake until the top is golden brown and crusty, 40 to 45 minutes. Let cool on a rack for 30 minutes, then serve warm from the pan.

Double-Crust Apple Pie

Here's the classic American apple pie, the result of many rounds of baking. I found my ideal in a blend of sweet and tart apples piled between fantastically flaky and buttery crusts. The filling has a hint of warm spice, with a just a little lemon to brighten the flavors. Meanwhile, cornstarch keeps the juices thicker, so your slices look beautiful.

APPLE NOTES: Pies require firm apples, I think. A mix of sweet and tart fruit is best to give the pie the richest flavor. Some of my favorite pie apples include Northern Spy, Sierra Beauty, and Esopus Spitzenburg in the tart family, and Ginger Gold, Golden Delicious, Jazz, and Jonagold from the sweet.

MAKE-AHEAD TIP: You can prepare the crust through step 1 and refrigerate for up to five days. You can also freeze the dough for up to three months. Defrost overnight in the refrigerator before using.

EQUIPMENT: Parchment paper; 9-inch pie plate (not deep-dish; preferably glass); baking sheet (any size)

MAKES: *8 servings* • ACTIVE TIME: *50 minutes* • TOTAL TIME: *2 hours*

FOR THE CRUST

2½ cups (360 g) all-purpose flour

2 tablespoons granulated sugar

1 teaspoon kosher salt

18 tablespoons (2¼ sticks; 255 g) chilled unsalted butter, cut into small cubes

6 to 8 tablespoons (90 to 120 ml) ice water

Milk for brushing over crust

FOR THE FILLING

1½ pounds (680 g, or about 3 large) firm-tart apples (see Apple Notes), peeled, cored, and cut into ½-inch-thick wedges

1½ pounds (680 g, or about 3 large) firm-sweet apples, peeled, cored, and cut into ½-inch-thick wedges

¼ cup (51 g) granulated sugar

2 tablespoons firmly packed light brown sugar

1 tablespoon lemon juice

1½ tablespoons cornstarch

¼ teaspoon ground cinnamon

¼ teaspoon freshly ground nutmeg

¼ teaspoon kosher salt

$1 \cdot$ First, make the crust: In a medium bowl, whisk together the flour, sugar, and salt until well combined (for instructions on using a food processor, see page 67). Sprinkle the butter over the flour mixture and use your fingers to work it in (rub your thumb against your fingertips, smearing the butter as you do). Stop when the mixture looks like cornmeal with some pea-sized bits of butter remaining. Sprinkle 6 tablespoons ice water on top and stir with a fork until the dough begins to come together. If needed, add more ice water, a tablespoon at a time. Turn out onto a lightly floured surface and knead three times, or just enough to make a cohesive dough—do not overmix! Gather into a ball, then divide into two pieces, one slightly larger than the other. Press each piece into a disk and wrap in plastic wrap. Refrigerate for 30 minutes.

$2 \cdot$ Meanwhile, prepare the filling: In a large bowl, toss the apples with the sugar, brown sugar, lemon juice, cornstarch, cinnamon, nutmeg and salt. Set aside.

$3 \cdot$ Preheat the oven to 425°F and set a rack to the lowest position. Unwrap the larger disk of dough and put it in the center of a large sheet of parchment paper. Cover with a second piece of parchment and roll out, working from the center, to a 13-inch circle about ⅛ inch thick. Peel off the top piece of parchment and transfer the dough to a pie plate, peeled side down. Peel off the remaining parchment and press the crust into the sides of the plate draping any excess over the edge. Fill the crust with the apple mixture, making the pile a bit higher in the center. Set aside (if it's a warm day, transfer to refrigerator to chill while you roll out the top crust).

$4 \cdot$ Unwrap the smaller disk of dough and put it in the center of a large sheet of parchment paper. Cover with a second piece of parchment and roll out, working from the center, to a 10-inch circle about ⅛ inch thick. Peel off the top piece of parchment and transfer the dough to the pie, peeled side down. Peel off the remaining parchment and, using a sharp knife, make two 3-inch slashes in the top crust to allow steam to escape. Fold the bottom crust up over the top crust and crimp to seal. If you don't have a favorite crimping technique, you can always simply pinch the crust between your thumb and forefinger at regular intervals around the crust, but I like to make a scalloped edge by holding my right thumb and forefinger in a "U" shape, then poking the crust between them using my left forefinger. Brush the crust all over with milk.

$5 \cdot$ Put the pie on a baking sheet and bake on the lowest rack for 10 minutes. Reduce the heat to 350°F and bake until juices are bubbling and the crust is golden brown, another 40 to 50 minutes. Let cool on a rack for at least 45 minutes before serving.

Blue Ribbon Deep-Dish Apple Pie

Blue Ribbon Deep-Dish Apple Pie

When it comes to apple pie, the more fruit the merrier. Except the more apples you pile into the dish, the more likely you are to end up with a big gap between the crust, which sets early in the baking, and the filling, which softens and shrinks by the time the pie is done. The answer, in a technique I adapted from *Cook's Illustrated* magazine, is to pre-cook the apples just a bit to "set" their shape. The result is a pie that's good enough for a bake-off: tall, beautifully domed, and filled to the very top with juicy apples.

APPLE NOTES: Again, any combination of firm-tart and firm-sweet apples is fine (see page 30). But, as with the classic Double-Crust Apple Pie on page 190, I particularly like Northern Spy, Sierra Beauty, and Esopus Spitzenburg for tartness, and Ginger Gold, Golden Delicious, Jazz, and Jonagold for sweetness.

MAKE-AHEAD TIP: You can prepare the crust through step 1 and refrigerate for up to five days. You can also freeze the dough for up to three months. Defrost overnight in the refrigerator before using.

EQUIPMENT: 5- to 6-quart Dutch Oven or other large, heavy-bottomed pot; parchment paper; 9-inch deep-dish pie plate (preferably glass); baking sheet (any size)

MAKES: *8 servings* • ACTIVE TIME: *1 hour, 15 minutes* • TOTAL TIME: *2 hours, 45 minutes*

FOR THE CRUST

2½ cups (360 g) all-purpose flour

3 tablespoons granulated sugar, divided

1 teaspoon kosher salt

18 tablespoons (2¼ sticks; 255 g) chilled unsalted butter, cut into ¼-inch cubes

6 to 8 tablespoons (90 to 120 ml) ice water

Milk for brushing over crust

FOR THE FILLING

2½ pounds (1.13 kg, or about 5 large) firm-tart apples (see Apple Notes), peeled, cored, and cut into ½-inch-thick wedges

2½ pounds (1.13 kg, or about 5 large) firm-sweet apples, peeled, cored, and cut into ½-inch-thick wedges

⅓ cup (70 g) granulated sugar

2 tablespoons firmly packed light brown sugar

1½ tablespoons (22 ml) freshly squeezed lemon juice

½ teaspoon ground cinnamon

½ teaspoon kosher salt

1½ tablespoons cornstarch

1 • First, make the crust: In a medium bowl, whisk together the flour, 2 tablespoons of the sugar, and salt until well combined (for instructions on making crust in a food processor, see page 67). Sprinkle the butter cubes over the flour mixture and use your fingers to work them in (you want to rub your thumb against your fingertips, smearing the butter as you do). Stop when the mixture looks like cornmeal with some pea-sized bits of butter remaining. Sprinkle 6 tablespoons ice water on top and stir with a fork until the dough begins to come together. If needed, add 1 or 2 tablespoons more of ice water. Turn the dough out onto a lightly floured surface and knead three times, or just enough to make a cohesive dough—do not overmix! Gather the dough into a ball, then divide into two pieces, one slightly larger than the other. Press each piece into a disk and wrap in plastic wrap. Refrigerate for 30 minutes.

2 • Preheat the oven to 425°F and set a rack to the lowest position. Meanwhile, prepare the filling: In a Dutch oven over medium heat, stir the apples with the sugar, brown sugar, lemon juice, cinnamon, and salt. Cook, stirring gently, until the apples just begin to turn tender, about 10 minutes. Reduce the heat if apples begin to sizzle vigorously.

3 • Remove the apples from the heat, stir in the cornstarch, and spread the apples out on a large baking sheet. Put in the freezer to cool to room temperature, 12 to 15 minutes.

4 • Meanwhile, unwrap the larger disk of dough and put it in the center of a large sheet of parchment paper. Cover with a second piece of parchment. Roll out, working from the center, to a 13-inch circle. Peel off the top piece of parchment and transfer the dough to a pie plate, peeled side down. Peel off the remaining parchment and press the crust into the plate, draping any excess over the sides. Unwrap the smaller disk of dough and put it in the center of a large sheet of parchment paper. Cover with a second piece of parchment. Roll out, working from the center, to an 11-inch circle. Set aside.

5 • Remove the apples from the freezer, and use a spatula to transfer them, with any juices, into the pie plate. Peel the parchment off the top crust. Transfer, peeled side down, to the pie, then peel off the remaining parchment and, using a sharp knife, make three slashes in the crust to allow steam to escape. Fold the bottom crust up over the top crust and crimp to seal. If you don't have a favorite decorative crimping technique, you can always simply pinch the crust between your thumb and forefinger at regular intervals around the crust, but I like to make a scalloped edge by holding my right thumb and forefinger in a "U" shape, then poking the crust between them using my left forefinger. (For the photo of this dish on page 192, food stylist

Blue Ribbon Deep-Dish Apple Pie (page 193) à la mode and Apfel Eis apple ice wine

Michael Pederson used the handle of his offset spatula to make diagonal indentations around the edge.) Brush the crust all over with milk and sprinkle with the remaining sugar.

6 • Put the pie on a baking sheet and bake on the lowest rack for 10 minutes. Reduce the heat to 350°F and bake until the pie is golden brown, another 40 to 50 minutes. Let cool on a rack for at least 45 minutes before serving.

THE BEST APPLES FOR PIE

I always recommend using a mix of firm-sweet and firm-tart apple varieties (see page 30) in your pies. That way, you get a broader spectrum of apple flavors. However, if you're eager to try a single variety pie, here's a list of my favorites:

FIRM-TART	FIRM-SWEET
Arkansas Black	Gravenstein
Calville Blanc d'Hiver	Jonagold
Newtown Pippin	
Northern Spy	
Rhode Island Greening	
Roxbury Russet	
Sierra Beauty	
Stayman Winesap	

Apple Pie with Crumb Topping

If it's at all possible to improve on a great apple pie, this is the way: Pile on a thick layer of nutty, crumbly topping made with pecans, brown sugar, flour, and butter. If I had to pick favorites among all the pies in this book, this would be it. It's like the best of apple crisp and apple pie all in one delicious package.

APPLE NOTES: In any pie recipe, I'll always recommend firm apples, preferably a mix of tarter and sweeter varieties (see page 30). As with the Oatmeal-Topped Apple Crisp on page 187, you'll do especially well with apples that have a spicier profile, such as Baldwin, Goldrush, Ginger Gold, and Suncrisp.

MAKE-AHEAD TIP: You can prepare the crust through step 1 and refrigerate for up to five days. You can also freeze the dough for up to three months. Defrost overnight in the refrigerator before using.

EQUIPMENT: Parchment paper; 9-inch deep-dish pie plate (preferably glass); baking sheet (any size)

MAKES: *8 servings* • ACTIVE TIME: *60 minutes* • TOTAL TIME: *2 hours*

FOR THE CRUST

1¼ cups (180 g) all-purpose flour

1 tablespoon granulated sugar

½ teaspoon kosher salt

9 tablespoons (128 g) chilled unsalted butter, cut into small cubes

3 to 4 tablespoons (45 to 60 ml) ice water

FOR THE FILLING

1½ pounds (680 g, or about 3 large) firm-tart apples (see Apple Notes) peeled, cored, and cut into ¼-inch-thick wedges or slices

1½ pounds (680 g; or about 3 large) firm-sweet apples, peeled, cored, and cut into ¼-inch-thick wedges or slices

¼ cup (55 g) granulated sugar

2 tablespoons firmly packed light brown sugar

2 tablespoons cornstarch

1 tablespoon lemon juice

¼ teaspoon kosher salt

FOR THE STREUSEL TOPPING

½ cup (55 g) pecan halves, chopped fine

1 cup (145 g) all-purpose flour

½ cup (115 g) packed light brown sugar

¼ teaspoon kosher salt

7 tablespoons (100 g) salted butter, melted

1 • First, make the crust: In a medium bowl, whisk together the flour, sugar, and salt until well combined (for instructions on making crust in a food processor, see page 67). Sprinkle the butter cubes on top and use your fingers to work them in (you want to rub your thumb against your fingertips, smearing the butter as you do). Stop when the mixture looks like cornmeal with some pea-sized bits of butter remaining. Sprinkle 3 tablespoons ice water on top and stir with a fork until the dough begins to come together. If needed, add a tablespoon more of ice water. Turn the dough out onto a lightly floured surface and knead three times. Gather into a ball, then press into a disk and wrap in plastic wrap. Refrigerate for at least 30 minutes.

2 • Meanwhile, prepare the filling: In a large bowl, toss the apples with the sugar, brown sugar, cornstarch, lemon juice, and salt. Set aside.

3 • Preheat the oven to 400°F and set a rack to the lowest position. Make the streusel topping: Stir together the pecans, flour, brown sugar, and salt in a small bowl. Add the butter and stir with a fork until small clumps form. Set aside.

4 • Unwrap the dough and put it in the center of a large sheet of parchment paper. Cover with a second piece of parchment. Roll out, working from the center, to a 13-inch circle. Peel off the top piece of parchment and transfer the dough to a pie plate, peeled side down. Peel off the remaining parchment and press the crust into the sides of the plate. Trim the crust so it hangs about ½ inch over the edge, then tuck under and crimp. If you don't have a favorite decorative crimping technique, you can always simply pinch the crust between your thumb and forefinger at regular intervals around the crust, but I like to make a scalloped edge by holding my right thumb and forefinger in a "U" shape, then poking the crust between them using my left forefinger. Fill the crust with the apple mixture, then top evenly with the streusel (press down a bit to make the topping as even as possible).

5 • Put the pie on a baking sheet and bake on the bottom rack for 15 minutes. Reduce the heat to 350°F and bake until the topping is golden brown and juices are bubbling, 50 to 60 minutes. Let cool on a rack for at least 45 minutes before serving—the apples stay very hot for quite a while and the pie slices better if you give it a chance to set up. However, if you can't bear to wait, be my guest.

Skillet Apple Pie

If double-crust pies sound like too much effort, opt for this rustic single-crust variation, served in a skillet. The flavors are the same; there's just less crust to roll out and transfer and worry about. You don't even have to crimp any edges—just tuck the dough down around the pre-cooked fruit. Serve with vanilla or maple walnut ice cream.

APPLE NOTES: Use exactly the same apples I recommend for two-crust pies: a mix of firm-sweet and firm-tart fruit (see page 30), only with proportions slightly favoring the sweet. My favorite pie apples include Northern Spy, Sierra Beauty, and Rhode Island Greening in the tart family, and Ginger Gold, Gravenstein, and Jonagold from the sweet.

MAKE-AHEAD TIP: You can prepare the crust through step 1 and refrigerate for up to five days. You can also freeze the dough for up to three months. Defrost overnight in the refrigerator before using.

EQUIPMENT: Heavy-bottomed 10-inch skillet (preferably cast iron) with sides at least 2¼ inches high

MAKES: *8 to 10 servings* • ACTIVE TIME: *45 minutes* • TOTAL TIME: *1 hour, 45 minutes*

FOR THE CRUST

1¼ cups (180 g) all-purpose flour

2 tablespoons granulated sugar, divided

½ teaspoon kosher salt

9 tablespoons (126 g) chilled unsalted butter, cut into small cubes

3 to 4 tablespoons (45 to 60 ml) ice water

Milk for brushing over crust

FOR THE FILLING

¼ cup (60 ml) fresh apple cider

3 tablespoons firmly packed light brown sugar

1 tablespoon cornstarch

¼ teaspoon table salt

¼ teaspoon ground cinnamon

1 teaspoon lemon juice

2 tablespoons (28 g) salted butter

4 large firm-tart apples (about 2 pounds; see Apple Notes), peeled, cored, and cut into ½-inch-thick wedges

5 large firm-sweet apples (about 2½ pounds), peeled, cored, and cut into ½-inch-thick wedges

1 • First, make the crust: In a medium bowl, whisk together the flour, 1 tablespoon of the sugar, and salt until well combined (for instructions on making crust in a food processor, turn to page 67). Sprinkle the butter cubes on top and use your fingers to work them in (you want to rub your thumb against your fingertips, smearing the butter as you do). Stop when the mixture looks like cornmeal with some pea-sized bits of butter remaining. Sprinkle 3 tablespoons ice water on top and stir with a fork until the dough begins to come together. If needed, add 1 more tablespoon of ice water. Turn out onto a lightly floured surface and knead three times. Gather into a ball, then press into a disk and wrap in plastic wrap. Refrigerate for at least 30 minutes.

2 • Meanwhile, prepare the filling: Preheat the oven to 450°F and set a rack to the lowest position. In a small bowl, combine the apple cider, brown sugar, cornstarch, salt, cinnamon, and lemon juice. Set aside.

3 • Set a skillet over medium-high heat. Melt the butter, then add the apples and cook, stirring only occasionally, until they begin to soften and brown a bit, 10 to 12 minutes. Stir in the cider mixture, cook for a minute, remove from the heat, and set aside.

4 • Assemble the pie: Unwrap the dough and put it in the center of a large sheet of parchment paper. Cover with a second piece of parchment paper. Roll out, working from the center, to an 11-inch circle. Peel off the top piece of parchment and transfer the dough to the skillet, peeled side down. Peel off the remaining parchment and tuck the dough down around the fruit. Using a sharp knife, make four 3-inch slashes in the top crust to allow steam to escape. Brush the crust with milk and sprinkle with the remaining sugar.

5 • Bake for 10 minutes. Reduce the heat to 350°F and continue baking until the juices are bubbling and the crust is deep golden brown, about 30 more minutes. Let cool on a rack for at least 20 minutes, then serve from the pan.

Marlborough Pie

I always assumed this dish was a Massachusetts native, associating it with Boston's Marlborough Street, which is very posh and lined with nineteenth-century townhouses. I pictured some proper Bostonian's clever cook inventing an apple custard pie and serving it at a dinner attended by Fannie Farmer, who took it from there (never mind that the godmother of American cooking didn't travel in those circles).

In reality, this custard pie filled with shredded apples and flavored with lemon and sherry goes back much further, first appearing in a 1660 British book, *The Accomplisht Cook*, written by a Paris-trained chef named Robert May. It traveled to the New World with the colonists and became hugely popular in Massachusetts, where it was also called Deerfield Pie.

APPLE NOTES: The most important thing for this pie is that the apples be firm enough not to completely melt away in the cooking. You do want a little bit of texture. If you can get your hands on some Golden Russets, you'll find that their lemony flavor works beautifully here. But really, any firm-tart and firm-sweet apples will do (see page 30). The more varieties, the merrier in this tipsy pie!

MAKE-AHEAD TIP: You can prepare the crust through step 1 and refrigerate for up to five days. You can also freeze the dough for up to three months. Defrost overnight in the refrigerator before using.

EQUIPMENT: 9-inch pie plate, preferably glass; baking sheet (any size)

MAKES: *6 servings* • ACTIVE TIME: *50 minutes* • TOTAL TIME: *2 hours*

FOR THE CRUST

1¼ cups (180 g) all-purpose flour

1 tablespoon granulated sugar

½ teaspoon kosher salt

9 tablespoons (126 g) chilled unsalted butter, cut into small cubes

3 to 4 tablespoons (45 to 60 ml) ice water

FOR THE FILLING

2 large firm-tart apples (about 1 pound total; see Apple Notes), peeled and cored

2 large firm-sweet apples (about 1 pound total), peeled and cored

3 tablespoons lemon juice

3 tablespoons dry sherry

2 tablespoons (28 g) salted butter

⅔ cup (140 g) granulated sugar

3 large eggs

1 cup (240 ml) light cream

¼ teaspoon ground cinnamon

¼ teaspoon freshly grated nutmeg

¼ teaspoon table salt

1 • First, make the crust: In a medium bowl, whisk together the flour, salt, and sugar until well combined (for instructions on making crust in a food processor, turn to page 67). Sprinkle the butter cubes on top and use your fingers to work them in (you want to rub your thumb against your fingertips, smearing the butter as you do). Stop when the mixture looks like cornmeal with some pea-sized bits of butter remaining (try to work quickly so the butter doesn't melt). Sprinkle 3 tablespoons ice water on top and stir with a fork until the dough just begins to come together. If needed, add one more tablespoon ice water. Turn the dough out onto a lightly floured surface and knead just until smooth—three times should do it. Gather into a ball, then press into a disk and wrap in plastic wrap. Refrigerate for 30 minutes.

2 • Preheat the oven to 400°F and set a rack to the middle position. On a floured surface, roll the dough out, working from the center, to a 10-inch circle, about ⅛-inch thick. Carefully transfer the dough to a pie plate and press into the sides. Drape any excess crust over the edge, then fold under and crimp. If you don't have a favorite decorative crimping technique, you can always simply pinch the crust between your thumb and forefinger at regular intervals around the crust, but I like to make a scalloped edge by holding my right thumb and forefinger in a "∪" shape, then poking the crust between them using my left forefinger. Use a fork to prick holes in the bottom of the dough. Line the dough with foil and fill with dried beans or pie weights. Bake for 8 minutes. Carefully remove the weights and foil, then continue baking for another 5 minutes (the crust will still look pale). Remove from the oven and set aside.

3 • Reduce the oven temperature to 350°F. Using a box grater, grate the apples down to the core. Transfer to a medium bowl and stir in the lemon juice and sherry. In a large, heavy-bottomed skillet over medium-high heat, melt the butter, then add the apples (with their liquid) and the sugar and cook, stirring, until the liquid begins to boil. Reduce the heat to a simmer, then continue cooking, stirring occasionally, until the apples are tender and most of the liquid evaporates, about 10 minutes. Remove from the heat and let cool for 10 minutes.

4 • Meanwhile, in a large bowl, whisk together the eggs, cream, cinnamon, nutmeg, and salt. Stir in the apple mixture. Pour the filling into the crust, then bake until the custard is set but not browned, about 35 minutes. Let cool on a rack for 30 minutes, then serve warm or at room temperature.

Tarte Tatin

Tarte tatin is one of France's great contributions to the culinary world, a simple layering of caramelized apples on pastry that is so much more than its parts. Traditionally, it's made with a tart dough similar to that of pie crust, but I prefer it with puff pastry. One French purist friend actually look horrified when I told her this, and if the thought offends you, by all means make your own crust. But puff pastry is both easier (assuming you use the store-bought kind) and, in my opinion, more delicious. Serve with ice cream or whipped cream on the side.

APPLE NOTES: The Calville Blanc d'Hiver is *the* classic tarte tatin apple, perfect in its bright acidity, ability to hold its shape, and slightly dry texture. However, Granny Smith is a good substitute, as are Northern Spy and Rhode Island Greening.

NOTE: Dufour puff pastry is sold at gourmet and Whole Foods stores.

EQUIPMENT: Rimless baking sheet; 12-inch heavy-bottomed skillet, preferably cast iron

MAKES: *8 servings* • ACTIVE TIME: *30 minutes* • TOTAL TIME: *60 minutes*

1 (14 ounce or 400 g) sheet store-bought puff pastry, preferably Dufour brand (see Note)

8 tablespoons (1 stick; 113 g) butter

¾ cup (155 g) granulated sugar

6 large firm-tart apples (about 3 pounds, or 1.36 kg; see Apple Notes), peeled, cored, and quartered lengthwise

1 • Preheat the oven to 425°F and set a rack to the upper-middle position. Dust the baking sheet with flour, then set the pastry on it and dust it with flour. Roll the dough out to a square about 15 inches wide. Using a sharp knife, trim the square to create a 14-inch circle. Transfer the pastry on the baking sheet to the refrigerator while you prepare the apples.

2 • Melt the butter in a skillet over medium-high heat, then add the sugar and cook, stirring often, until the mixture begins to turn golden, about 4 minutes. The sugar won't melt completely into the butter. Instead, the mixture will look rather cloudy. Remove the pan from the heat.

3 • Look at your apple wedges. They'll have two cut edges and a round back side. Starting from the outside and working in, carefully arrange the apples on one of the cut edges (that is, set them on their sides), so that they overlap slightly and lean onto each other. You want to

form concentric circles in the pan (don't touch the hot caramel!). Arrange the inner circle as you did the outer, only a bit more tightly. Return the skillet to the heat and cook the apples on one side for 3 minutes, then flip them so that they're now sitting on the other cut edge, but still overlapping in concentric circles. Cook another 3 to 4 minutes until the caramel is toffee-colored. Remove the pan from the heat and lay the pastry over the apples. Use a spatula to tuck the extra dough down around the apples in the pan. Transfer the pan to the oven and bake until the crust is browned, 20 to 25 minutes.

4 • Remove the pan from the oven and let it sit at room temperature for 20 minutes to allow the caramel to cool and thicken. Run a butter knife around the edge of the crust, then lay a round platter (at least 13 inches wide) over the skillet, serving-side down. Holding the pan tightly against the platter, flip the whole contraption so that the tart drops out of the pan and onto the platter with the pretty side facing up. Don't worry if any apples stick to the pan; just use a spoon to scrape them off and put them back in the tart. Serve warm or at room temperature.

Gravenstein Apple-Raspberry Tart

In his terrific book *Apple Pie Perfect*, Ken Haedrich observes that apples pair best with other fruits that ripen at the same time, such as pears and cranberries. True to form, the Gravenstein, which comes to market as early as July on the West Coast, pairs beautifully with raspberries.

APPLE NOTES: This is one of the few recipes in this book that recommends a specific apple variety. You want the sweet western Gravenstein here. But if you can get your hands on the Pink Pearl or Hidden Rose, they make a delicious and, with their bright fuchsia flesh, seriously pretty alternative.

EQUIPMENT: 9½-inch fluted tart pan with removable rim; parchment paper

MAKES: *8 servings* • ACTIVE TIME: *45 minutes* •
TOTAL TIME: *1 hour, 10 minutes, plus 30 minutes chilling time*

FOR THE CRUST

1¼ cups (180 g) all-purpose flour

1 tablespoon granulated sugar

½ teaspoon kosher salt

9 tablespoons (126 g) chilled unsalted butter, cut into small cubes

3 to 4 tablespoons (45 to 60 ml) ice water

FOR THE FILLING

3 large Gravenstein, Pink Pearl, or Hidden Rose apples (about 1½ pounds total; see Apple Notes), peeled, cored, and cut into ¼-inch-thick wedges

3 tablespoons firmly packed brown sugar

1 tablespoon fresh lemon juice

¾ cup (130 g) fresh raspberries

1 • First, make the crust: In a medium bowl, whisk together the flour, salt, and sugar until well combined (for instructions on making pie crust in a food processor, see page 67). Sprinkle the butter cubes on top and use your fingers to work them in (you want to rub your thumb against your fingertips, smearing the butter as you do). Stop when the mixture looks like cornmeal with some pea-sized bits of butter remaining (try to work quickly so the butter doesn't melt). Sprinkle 3 tablespoons ice water on top and stir with a fork until the dough just begins to come together. If needed, add one more tablespoon ice water. Turn the dough out onto a lightly floured surface and knead just enough to fully combine—three times should do it. Gather into a ball, then press into a disk and wrap in plastic wrap. Refrigerate for at least 30 minutes.

2 • Preheat the oven to 350°F and set a rack to the second-to-bottom position. In a large bowl, gently toss the apple slices with the brown sugar and lemon juice. Set aside. Unwrap the dough and put it in the center of a large piece of parchment paper. Cover with a second piece of parchment paper. Roll out the dough, working from the center, until you have a 10½-inch circle. Peel off the top sheet of parchment and carefully transfer the dough to a tart pan, peeled side down. Peel off the remaining parchment and press the dough into the sides of the pan. Drape any excess over the edge, then run a rolling pin over the edge to trim.

3 • Prick the bottom of the crust all over with a fork. Arrange apple slices over the crust, then dot with raspberries. Pour juices from the bowl over the fruit. Bake until the pastry is golden brown and the apples are soft, 35 to 45 minutes. Let cool on a rack for 30 minutes, then serve warm or at room temperature.

LEFT: Gravenstein Apple-Raspberry Tart (page 205)

Free-Form Apple-Pear-Cranberry Tart

I love the rustic look of this tart filled with sliced apples, pears, and cranberries. Rather than baking it in a pie plate, you simply roll out the crust into a circle, fill it with fruit, and fold the sides up around the filling. It's sweet and tangy, doesn't require any fussiness on your part, and makes an impressive Thanksgiving centerpiece. It's best served with vanilla ice cream.

APPLE NOTES: Consult the Cheat Sheet on page 30 for a list of firm-tart apple varieties. Any will work very well here.

EQUIPMENT: Parchment paper; large rimmed baking sheet

MAKES: *8 medium servings, 6 large servings* • ACTIVE TIME: *45 minutes* •
TOTAL TIME: *1 hour, 20 minutes, plus 30 minutes chilling time*

FOR THE CRUST

1¼ cups (180 g) all-purpose flour

1 tablespoon granulated sugar

½ teaspoon kosher salt

8 tablespoons (1 stick; 113 g) chilled
   unsalted butter, cut into small cubes

1 large egg yolk mixed with 2
   tablespoons ice water

FOR THE FILLING

2 medium (or 1½ large) firm-tart apples
   (about 12 ounces total; see Apple
   Notes)

1 large ripe pear, such as d'Anjou or
   Bartlett

½ cup (103 g) plus 1 teaspoon granulated
   sugar

1 tablespoon cornstarch

1 teaspoon freshly grated orange zest

⅛ teaspoon ground cloves

⅓ cup fresh or thawed frozen
   cranberries

1 large egg, beaten well

1 • First, make the crust: In a medium bowl, whisk together the flour, salt, and sugar until well combined. Sprinkle the butter cubes on top and use your fingers to work them in (you want to rub your thumb against your fingertips, smearing the butter as you do). Stop when the mixture looks like cornmeal with some pea-sized bits of butter remaining (try to work quickly

RIGHT: Free-Form Apple-Pear-Cranberry Tart

so the butter doesn't melt). Sprinkle the egg yolk–water mixture on top and stir with a fork until the dough begins to come together. If needed, add one more tablespoon water. Turn the dough out onto a lightly floured surface and knead three times. Gather into a ball, then press into a disk and wrap in plastic wrap. Refrigerate for at least 30 minutes.

2 • Meanwhile, preheat the oven to 400°F and set a rack to the second-from-the bottom position. Peel, core, and cut the apples into ¼-inch-thick wedges. Peel and cut the pear into ½-inch-thick slices. Gently toss together in a bowl and set aside. In a small bowl, combine ½ cup of the sugar, the cornstarch, orange zest, and cloves; set aside.

3 • On a lightly floured surface, roll the dough into a circle about 16 inches wide and ⅛ inch thick. The circle doesn't have to be perfect—this is a rustic dessert—but try to get it as round as possible, even if that means cutting a little dough off one side to add to the other. Transfer the dough to a baking sheet lined with parchment paper.

4 • Arrange half the apple and pear slices over the dough, leaving a 2½-inch border all around. Sprinkle half the cranberries over the apples. Sprinkle half the sugar-cornstarch mixture over the fruit, then repeat with the fruit and then the sugar mixture. Fold the sides of the dough up and over the edge of the filling, allowing the dough to drape over itself at each fold. Brush the dough with the beaten egg, and sprinkle all with one teaspoon of sugar. Bake for 10 minutes; lower the temperature to 375°F, and bake until golden brown, about 25 minutes more. Let cool on a rack for at least 30 minutes, then transfer to a serving platter and serve warm.

Rustic Apple Brown Betty

This is perhaps the least-known member of the apple crisp/cobbler/ buckle family of recipes. Like the others, it's an American original dating back to the nineteenth century. And like many recipes from that period, it's a testament to economy, turning apples and some stale bread into a sweet, nutty, and cozy fruit dessert that takes very little time to put together. The trick is to make your own crumbs and toast them in the skillet before you assemble the dish. It's the only way to get the proper toasty, buttery flavor and light texture. Serve with vanilla or maple nut ice cream or a drizzle of fresh cream.

APPLE NOTES: Firm-tart apples (see page 30) are ideal here, but I like those on the sweeter end of the tart spectrum for this dessert. Try Arkansas Black, Ashmead's Kernel, Esopus Spitzenburg, Northern Spy, Sierra Beauty, or Stayman Winesap, if you can.

NOTE: Most standard bread loaves weigh about a pound, so use about a third of a loaf here.

EQUIPMENT: 12-inch heavy-bottomed, ovenproof skillet (preferably cast iron)

MAKES: *6 servings* • ACTIVE TIME: *25 minutes* • TOTAL TIME: *45 minutes*

⅓ pound (151 g) crusty white (not sourdough) bread, preferably a bit stale (see Note)

⅓ cup (50 g) chopped walnuts

4 tablespoons (½ stick; 57 g) salted butter

5 large firm-tart apples (about 2½ pounds total; see Apple Notes), peeled and cut into ¼-inch-thick slices

⅓ cup (80 ml) maple syrup

1 • Preheat the oven to 350°F and set a rack to the middle position. Break the bread into large chunks. In a food processor, pulse the bread until it forms fine, fluffy crumbs. Add the walnuts and pulse about four more times, until the nuts are broken into small pieces.

2 • Melt the butter over medium heat in a skillet. Add the bread and nuts. Cook, stirring often, until the bread looks golden brown and toasted, 6 to 8 minutes. Using a slotted spoon, remove the crumb mixture from skillet. Transfer to a bowl, and set aside.

3 • Add the apples, maple syrup, and ¾ cup water to the skillet, increase the heat to medium-high, and cook until some water is evaporated and the apples are just becoming tender, 6 to 8 minutes. Sprinkle the crumb mixture over the apples and bake until the apples are fully cooked and the sauce is bubbling, 15 to 20 minutes. Let cool on a rack for 20 minutes. Serve warm in the skillet.

Apple-Pear Cobbler with
Lemon-Cornmeal Biscuits

You know you have a good dessert when, after spending all day in the kitchen developing it, you still choose to eat another serving instead of a proper dinner. This is a fresh and unexpected take on a New England classic, topped with tender but crunchy cornmeal biscuits, laced with lemon and glazed with cream and sugar. The apples and pears in the filling are fully complementary (remember: fruits that sweeten together can be eaten together!) and really pop with a hit of lemon juice. Serve with vanilla ice cream, a drizzle of fresh cream, or simply by itself.

APPLE NOTES: The lemon flavors in this dessert make it a natural match for the Rhode Island Greening, Pink Pearl, or Roxbury Russet, while pears go very well with Ribston Pippins. However, you can't go wrong with any firm-tart apples (see page 30).

MAKE-AHEAD TIP: You can prepare the fruit through step 1 up to a day ahead of time (you may need to drain the excess juice), but don't make the biscuits until just before baking.

EQUIPMENT: 3- to 4-quart Dutch oven or other deep baking dish with sides at least 3½ inches high

MAKES: *8 servings* • ACTIVE TIME: *45 minutes* • TOTAL TIME: *1 hour, 20 minutes*

FOR THE FILLING

2½ pounds (1.13 kg, or about 5 large) firm-tart apples (see Apple Notes)

1½ pounds (680 g, or about 3 large) ripe pears, such as Bosc or Bartlett

⅓ cup (75 g) granulated sugar

3 tablespoons fresh lemon juice

2 tablespoons all-purpose flour

1½ tablespoons (21 g) chilled salted butter, cut into ½-inch cubes

FOR THE TOPPING

1 cup (145 g) all-purpose flour

1 cup (170 g) cornmeal (white or yellow, not stone-ground)

3 tablespoons plus 2 teaspoons granulated sugar

2½ teaspoons baking powder

1 teaspoon kosher salt

1 teaspoon freshly grated lemon zest

1½ tablespoons (21 g) chilled salted butter, cut into small pieces

1 cup (240 ml) plus 2 tablespoons chilled heavy cream

1 • Preheat the oven to 400°F, and set a rack to the middle position. Peel and core the apples and pears. Cut the apples into ¼-inch-thick slices and the pears into ½-inch-thick slices. Put in a Dutch oven. Add the sugar, lemon juice, flour, and butter, and toss to combine. Bake, uncovered, for 20 minutes.

2 • Meanwhile, prepare the topping: In a medium bowl, whisk together the flour, cornmeal, the 3 tablespoons sugar, the baking powder, salt, and lemon zest. Sprinkle the butter on top and use your fingers to work it in, forming thin flakes. When the dough begins to look like cornmeal, add the 1 cup cream and stir with a fork until the dough just comes together. Gently pat out on a well-floured surface to a ¾-inch thickness. Use a biscuit cutter or juice glass with a 2- to 3-inch diameter to cut out biscuits, scraping and re-rolling the dough as needed. Chill the biscuits in the refrigerator while the fruit finishes the first round of cooking.

3 • Remove the fruit mixture from the oven and give it a quick stir—it should look softer and a little glossy. Arrange the biscuits on top, overlapping slightly in concentric circles, brush with the remaining 2 tablespoons cream, and sprinkle with the remaining 2 teaspoons sugar. Bake, uncovered, until the top is golden brown and sauce is bubbling, about 35 minutes. Cool on a rack for at least 20 minutes, then serve warm.

Buttermilk Apple Buckle

I love the whole class of homey fruit-based desserts like buckles, grunts, slumps, pandowdies, crisps, and cobblers, as much for their irresistibly old-fashioned names as for the eating. By definition, a buckle is a cake studded with fruit and capped with a crumble topping. In this one, the spiced apples settle down into the cake batter during cooking, while most of the pecan crumble mixture stays on top. Buttermilk lends extra tenderness and a delicate tang to the cake.

APPLE NOTES: No need to seek out specific varieties here. Any firm-tart fruit (see page 30) will do a good job of distinguishing itself from the sweet cake.

NOTE: If you don't have buttermilk on hand, you can substitute clabbered milk: Add one tablespoon of lemon juice or white wine vinegar to 1 cup of whole or 2% milk and let stand for 10 minutes before using.

EQUIPMENT: 9- by 13-inch baking pan

MAKES: *10 servings* • ACTIVE TIME: *35 minutes* • TOTAL TIME: *1 hour, 10 minutes*

FOR THE TOPPING

2 large firm-tart apples (about 1 pound total; see Apple Notes), peeled, cored, and cut into ⅛-inch-thick slices

¼ teaspoon plus 1 teaspoon ground cinnamon

1 tablespoon granulated sugar

½ cup (115 g) firmly packed light brown sugar

⅓ cup (48 g) all-purpose flour

¼ teaspoon freshly grated nutmeg

½ cup (50 g) finely chopped pecans

3 tablespoons (46 g) cold salted butter, cut into small cubes, plus more for greasing pan

FOR THE CAKE

7 tablespoons (100 g) salted butter, at room temperature

¾ cup (155 g) granulated sugar

2¼ cups (325 g) all-purpose flour

1½ teaspoons baking powder

½ teaspoon baking soda

1½ teaspoons kosher salt

1 cup (240 ml) buttermilk (see Note)

1 large egg

1 • Preheat the oven to 350°F, and set a rack to the middle position. Grease a baking pan. In a medium bowl, toss the apple slices with the ¼ teaspoon cinnamon and 1 tablespoon sugar. Set aside at room temperature.

2 • Meanwhile, in a small bowl, toss the remaining 1 teaspoon cinnamon with the brown sugar, flour, nutmeg, and pecans. Scatter the cold butter over all and use a pastry cutter or fork to work it in until the mixture looks like wet sand and the largest pieces are pea-sized. Refrigerate until ready to use.

3 • Make the cake: Using a standing or hand-held mixer with a whisk attachment, cream together the butter and sugar in a large bowl until the mixture is fluffy, very pale, and mousselike in texture, 6 to 10 minutes. In a separate bowl, whisk together the flour, baking powder, baking soda, and salt. In a third bowl, whisk together the buttermilk and egg. Add one-third of the flour mixture to the butter mixture. Mix briefly, then add half the buttermilk-egg blend and mix again. Repeat, adding another third of the flour mixture and the remaining buttermilk-egg mixture, then finish with the remaining third of the flour mixture and stir just until combined.

4 • Spread the batter evenly into the baking pan (it will be quite thick). Lay apple slices, overlapping slightly, over the batter in neat rows. Sprinkle the crumble topping over all. Bake until the top is golden and a toothpick inserted into the center comes out clean, 35 to 45 minutes. Let cool on a rack for 30 minutes, then serve warm from the pan.

Williamsburg Wrapples

The Williamsburg General Store in Williamsburg, Massachusetts, where I worked for a summer during college, is a favorite stop on the old two-lane highway from Boston to the Berkshires. Now refashioned for tourists, the store has an ice cream shop, a wall of penny candy, hundreds of kitchen gadgets, and a bakery where customers line up for fresh-baked breads, cakes, and Wrapples, the signature pastry rolls stuffed with apples and cinnamon and glazed with sugar. They're like apple pies, repackaged. The store has its own winning recipe, but I reverse-engineered a close approximation, heavier on the lemon flavor, that earns its own raves.

APPLE NOTES: I recommend using only firm-tart apples (see page 30) in this recipe because with its high crust-to-filling ratio, it needs a little acidity to balance out all that richness. Any firm-tart variety will do nicely.

NOTE: A bench scraper is a useful tool when rolling up these wrapples. It can get under the dough and help lift any spots that are sticking to the counter.

EQUIPMENT: Bench scraper; large rimmed baking sheet

MAKES: *8 servings* • ACTIVE TIME: *60 minutes* • TOTAL TIME: *1 hour, 30 minutes*

FOR THE CRUST

2½ cups (360 g) all-purpose flour

1 teaspoon kosher salt

3 tablespoons granulated sugar

18 tablespoons (2¼ sticks; 255 g) unsalted butter, frozen and cut into small cubes

6 to 8 tablespoons (90 to 120 ml) ice water

FOR THE FILLING

3 large firm-tart apples, (about 1½ pounds total; see Apple Notes), peeled, cored, and cut into very thin (about ⅛-inch-thick) slices

½ cup (105 g) granulated sugar

2 tablespoons fresh lemon juice

½ teaspoon freshly grated lemon zest

2 teaspoons ground cinnamon

FOR THE GLAZE

1 cup (120 g) confectioners' sugar

LEFT: Williamsburg Wrapples

1 • First, make the crust: In a medium bowl, whisk together the flour, salt, and sugar until well combined (for instructions on making crust in a food processor, see page 67). Sprinkle the butter cubes on top and use your fingers to work them in by rubbing your thumb against your fingertips, smearing the butter as you do. Stop when the mixture looks like wet sand with some pea-sized bits of butter remaining (try to work quickly so the butter doesn't melt). Sprinkle ¼ cup ice water on top and stir with a fork until the dough just begins to come together. If needed, add more ice water, one tablespoon at a time. Turn the dough out onto a lightly floured surface and knead just until smooth—three times should do it. Gather the dough into a ball, then divide in half and press each piece into a disk. Wrap in plastic wrap and refrigerate for at least 30 minutes.

2 • Meanwhile, in a medium bowl, combine apple slices, sugar, lemon juice and zest, and cinnamon. Stir well, then let sit at room temperature until the dough is chilled.

3 • Preheat the oven to 400°F and set a rack to the middle position. Remove the first disk of dough from the refrigerator. On a floured surface, roll out into a rectangle about 16 inches wide, 12 inches long, and ⅛ inch thick (if the dough becomes soft or sticky at any point during this process, put it in the freezer for 10 minutes). Cut the dough from top to bottom into four strips, each about 4 inches wide.

4 • Now, roll up the wrapples. You're basically making a jelly roll, only with apples as the filling. Lay four apple slices on the pastry about 4 inches from the bottom of the first strip. Overlap them like shingles. Use your bench scraper to help you fold the bottom 4 inches of dough up over the apples. Layer a few more apple slices just above the seam, then fold the dough over those slices, creating a roll. Repeat once more until you reach the top of the strip. Press the seam to seal the packet, then refrigerate uncovered. Repeat with remaining strips, then repeat with second disk of dough. You should have eight packets in all.

5 • Arrange the packets on an ungreased baking sheet, put them in the oven, and immediately reduce the heat to 350°F. Bake until golden brown, 30 to 35 minutes. Meanwhile, combine the confectioners' sugar with 2 tablespoons water and stir until smooth. Remove the wrapples from the oven, transfer to a wire cooling rack set over a baking sheet, cool to room temperature, and drizzle with the sugar glaze.

Apple Empanadas

This recipe is inspired by the fried apple pies, filled with reconstituted dried apples and spices, that hold a place of honor among Southern cooks, particularly in apple-growing regions of Appalachia, where people commonly dried their apples to store through the winter. Looking to lighten things up a bit, I tried baking the pies instead of frying them, and found that I liked the results just as well.

APPLE NOTES: Dried apple rings provide a wonderful concentrated apple flavor in this dish. Do go out of your way to find the unsulfured type sold at Whole Foods and other health food stores. The ivory-colored, mushier "dried" apple rings you'll find at most regular supermarkets tend to puff up during cooking into something nearly unrecognizable as an apple, both in flavor and appearance.

NOTE: The amount of cider you'll need for the filling depends on the texture of the dried apples you use. Some are simply drier than others. Use as much as you need to keep the filling moist and glossy.

EQUIPMENT: Large baking sheet

MAKES: *10 individual pies* • ACTIVE TIME: *1 hour, 30 minutes* • TOTAL TIME: *2 hours*

FOR THE CRUST

2½ cups (360 g) all-purpose flour

2 tablespoons granulated sugar

½ teaspoon baking powder

½ teaspoon table salt

16 tablespoons (2 sticks; 84 g) unsalted butter, chilled and cut into small cubes

1 large egg, lightly beaten

¼ cup (60 ml) ice water

FOR THE FILLING

6 ounces (170 g) dried apple rings, preferably unsulfured (see Apple Notes)

1 teaspoon ground cinnamon

1½ tablespoons firmly packed light brown sugar

2 to 2½ cups (475 to 590 ml) fresh apple cider (see Note)

½ teaspoon cider vinegar

⅛ teaspoon kosher salt

Confectioners' sugar for sprinkling

1 • First, make the crust: In a medium bowl, whisk together the flour, sugar, baking powder, and salt until well combined. Sprinkle the butter cubes on top and use your fingers to work them in (you want to rub your thumb against your fingertips, smearing the butter as you do). Stop when the mixture looks like cornmeal with some pea-sized bits of butter remaining. Whisk the egg with the ice water and drizzle evenly on top. Gently stir with a fork until combined. Continue adding water, one tablespoon at a time, until the dough comes together. Working in the bowl, knead the dough until smooth, no more than four times. Form into a ball, press into a disk, and wrap in plastic wrap. Refrigerate for at least 30 minutes.

2 • Meanwhile, make the filling: Combine the apple rings, cinnamon, brown sugar, and 2 cups apple cider in a large saucepan over high heat. Bring to a boil, then reduce the heat to medium-low, maintaining a gentle simmer. Cover and cook, occasionally stirring and mashing the apples with a wooden spoon, until they're very soft with the thickness of a chunky applesauce, 15 to 20 minutes. Add additional cider, ¼ cup at a time, as needed. Stir in the cider vinegar and salt. Remove from the heat and let cool.

3 • Preheat the oven to 400°F and set a rack to the middle position. To assemble the empanadas, unwrap the dough and put on a well-floured cutting board or countertop. Roll out, working from the center, to form a ⅛-inch-thick circle. Peel off the top sheet of parchment and, using a 5-inch circular cookie cutter (I use a cereal bowl), cut out ten rounds, re-rolling the dough as needed. Scoop 1 tablespoon filling into the center of each round and fold the dough over the filling. Lightly moisten the edges with water and crimp with a fork to seal.

4 • Transfer the empanadas to an ungreased baking sheet and bake for 10 minutes. Reduce the heat to 350°F and bake, rotating the pan 180 degrees halfway through cooking, until the crust is golden brown, 20 to 25 minutes more. Transfer the pies to a cooling rack for at least 30 minutes. Sprinkle with confectioners' sugar and serve warm or at room temperature.

Apple Pandowdy

Another old-fashioned charmer from New England, the pandowdy is, by definition, a cooked fruit dessert sweetened with maple syrup or molasses and topped with pie pastry. Food historians date it back to the nineteenth century; it was reportedly a favorite of President John Adams. The name refers to the act of "dowdying" the crust—that is, breaking it up with a knife and pressing it into the bubbling juices—midway through baking. Back in Adams's day, crusts weren't the buttery beauties they are today. They were flour and water "pastes," and they needed a good dunking to be truly flavorful. But even a nice flaky pastry can be improved by this technique, and what the dish lacks in streamlined good looks, it more than makes up for in rich flavor.

APPLE NOTES: If you can, use a mix of firm-tart apples (see page 30) for maximum flavor variety. The tartness is essential in balancing out the richness of the crust, but beyond that, this dish is a blank canvas that you can layer with different apple flavors.

NOTE: The filling for a dowdy should be wetter at the outset than that of a pie or a crisp. As the crust bakes, partially submerged in the filling, it has a thickening effect.

EQUIPMENT: 12-inch ovenproof skillet with sides at least 2 inches high (preferably cast iron)

MAKES: *6 servings* • ACTIVE TIME: *1 hour* • TOTAL TIME: *1 hour, 45 minutes*

FOR THE CRUST

1¼ cups (185 g) plus 2 tablespoons all-purpose flour

1 tablespoon granulated sugar

½ teaspoon kosher salt

9 tablespoons (126 g) cold unsalted butter, cut into small cubes

3 to 5 tablespoons (45 to 60 ml) ice water

FOR THE FILLING

8 large firm-tart apples (about 4 pounds total; see Apple Notes), peeled, cored, and sliced ¼-inch thick

2 tablespoons firmly packed light brown sugar

1 teaspoon ground cinnamon

1 teaspoon ground ginger

¼ teaspoon freshly ground nutmeg

⅛ teaspoon ground cloves

½ teaspoon kosher salt

⅓ cup (80 ml) maple syrup

1½ tablespoons granulated sugar for sprinkling

1 • First, make the crust: In a medium bowl, whisk together the flour, sugar, and salt until well combined (for instructions on making crust in a food processor, see page 67). Sprinkle the butter cubes on top and use your fingers to work them in (you want to rub your thumb against your fingertips, smearing the butter as you do). Do this until the mixture looks like cornmeal with some pea-sized bits of butter remaining. Sprinkle 3 tablespoons ice water on top and stir with a fork until the dough begins to come together. If needed, add another tablespoon ice water (you shouldn't need much more). Turn the dough out onto a lightly floured surface and knead three times. Gather the dough into a ball, then press into a disk and wrap in plastic wrap. Refrigerate for at least 30 minutes.

2 • Preheat the oven to 425°F and set a rack to the middle position. Arrange the apples in a skillet. Sprinkle with the brown sugar, cinnamon, ginger, nutmeg, cloves, and salt. In a small bowl, stir the maple syrup with ½ cup water and pour over the apples.

3 • On a lightly floured surface, roll the chilled dough out into a rectangle about 9 inches wide, 11 inches long, and ¼ inch thick. Using a knife or pizza cutter, cut into squares roughly 3 inches across. Arrange the squares over the apples, making a concentric pattern, then sprinkle with sugar. Bake the pandowdy until juices are bubbling and the pastry is golden brown, about 30 minutes. Remove from the oven and use a spatula to gently press the pastry down into the juices so it's mostly (about 80%) submerged. Return the pan to the oven and bake for an additional 10 to 15 minutes, until the pastry is nicely glazed and the sauce has thickened.

CHAPTER NINE

DUMPLINGS, BAKES, CAKES, AND PUDDINGS

Keepsake

The Preservation Orchards of Palermo, Maine

John Bunker was 21, a recent graduate of Colby College, when he fell in love with apples. It was 1972, and he and some friends had just purchased 100 acres of dirt-cheap land in Palermo, Maine, as a sort of back-to-the-land experiment. They named it Super Chilly Farm.

Walking around the forest and pastures of his new home, he encountered craggy old apple trees, most of them still bearing fruit. "I was looking for a free ride wherever I could get it," he says wryly. "And here was this free fruit dropping from trees."

From that inauspicious beginning, sitting in the crook of a tree like a modern-day Thoreau, came a life's work: An effort to keep Maine's once-prized apple varieties alive and to rescue the pomological history of a time when every town, if not every farm, had its own favorite breed of apple. Three decades into this project, Bunker is now a nationally recognized expert on antique apples, a partner in a successful fruit tree, berry, and ornamentals cooperative called Fedco Trees, and the founder of the country's first apple CSA (Community Supported Agriculture), called Out on a Limb, in which subscribers pay in advance to receive a biweekly selection of unusual and heirloom apples from several farms in central Maine— varieties such as Ashmead's Kernel, Wickson, Fameuse, and Blue Pearmain. He has become a sort of modern-day Johnny Appleseed, only rather than creating new apple varieties by scattering seeds willy-nilly over the country, he's leading us back to the best of those seedlings in order to preserve the old ways.

At the time when Bunker was first roaming the fields of Maine that heritage was fading. "Most of the old farmers were grandparents by then, living at home while their children were working in Augusta or Waterville," he says. "It wasn't a farming economy anymore. These trees were one hundred, one hundred fifty, two hundred years old, and they didn't know that the twentieth century had come and no one wanted to farm anymore. So they were happy to have me climb in them and pick their fruit."

When he speaks of the trees in this way, as if they are sentient beings, he can sound very much like the hippie homesteader he probably was back in 1972. Today, though, Bunker mostly has the air of a taciturn Mainer, slight of figure and almost professorial in appearance, but for his calloused hands and ruddy complexion. He is as rooted in this place as the trees around him.

In those early days, when he'd spend an afternoon merely walking and eating apples, he also began talking to the retired farmers he met. "They introduced me to the apple varieties they knew." he says. "In the nineteenth century, every farm had an orchard of fifteen, twenty trees. I could see there was an assortment of colors, shapes, sizes, and uses in these apples. And it dawned on me that I wanted to have something like that growing in my own yard."

To get started, he bought some young apple trees, Red and Golden Delicious and the like. But they floundered in Palermo's harsh climate, where the ground can stay frozen from November to mid-April and May frosts can wipe out an entire apple crop. "I couldn't get it out of my head that there were all these old trees all around me that were doing great," he says. Then a few chance encounters set his course: First, an elderly neighbor, an old farmer known as Papa Glidden, introduced him to the concept of grafting and encouraged him to learn the technique from other farmers. Not long after that, an old man came into the Belfast, Maine, food co-op that Bunker was managing at the time with a bushel of unusual apples: very dark purple, smaller in size, looking much like plums. The man said they were an old Maine variety called Black Oxford (see page 33 for a description), and he wanted to sell them on consignment. Bunker took a bite and promptly bought the whole bushel for himself. Later, he got some scion wood and grafted Black Oxford onto his own trees.

He suspected that there was a regional market for apples like this, rich in history and already adapted to the Down East climate. So as he launched his Fedco tree business, he began scouring rural Maine for apples that were "unusual, historic, and high quality," as he puts it. When he found ones he liked, he propagated them and sold them to other growers.

His reasons for resurrecting these old trees were partly practical—they were proven, a known quantity. But there were deeper reasons. He saw the apples as a sort of inheritance, a gift from earlier generations. And he wanted to endow future generations with that same gift.

"These apples connect us to our heritage," he says. "Whether we've lived here all our lives or for just a month, we're standing on the earth and that earth has a history. It's important to know it and be connected to it."

And so he became a fruit detective. "I began to discover varieties that were nearly lost," he says. As word spread of his efforts, other Mainers began to seek him out. *This apple grows on my land,* they'd say. *I don't know what it is. Can you help?* He'd begin by talking with locals, digging through old volumes of S. A. Beach's 1905 reference book *The Apples of New York*, looking at old catalogs. "It's extremely difficult to identify them," he says. "It takes decades. Sometimes I can identify them quickly, simply because the right person, who I determine can't possibly be wrong, says 'That's what it is.'"

But most of the time, he has to dig deeper. He began posting handmade "Wanted" posters around the state, describing the apple varieties he was seeking. He still does this. In one such case, he posted signs inquiring about Marlboro, a native Maine variety that he had heard references to, but never actually seen. He knew the apple came from Lamoine, a tiny town near Bar Harbor, and he had a rough visual description, but that was it.

Soon after the posters went up, a woman called him. "She said, 'I own the old Seneca Remick farm where this apple originated, but I'm not sure which tree it is. There are about twenty of them. I'll send you fruit from every one.'" Sure enough, a big box full of fruit arrived a few days later. Most of the apples were familiar and easily named. But one tree was a puzzle. It had produced two entirely different varieties, neither of which was readily identifiable to Bunker. He knew that it was likely a so-called "family tree," in which two or more varieties are grafted onto a single rootstock. But with no other identifying information, it was also a dead end.

He set that search aside for a time, but a year or two later, he gave the woman another call. She told him that they'd had a very good apple crop that year and invited him to come for a visit.

When he arrived, he went straight to the mystery tree. It was indeed a family tree, grafted with three different varieties. "I recognized the two apples she had sent me, and this time I was able to determine that one of them was an Alexander and the second was Tolman Sweet," he says. "But there was a third type, which was just a single branch on the tree, and it was clearly nothing I'd ever seen before. I had the description of the Marlboro with me, and I realized that this was it." In fact, this was the last known Marlboro branch in existence, and he had found it just in time. "Without that poster," he says, "I never would have." Since then, he has grafted several trees with Marlboro for the people of Lamoine, and they, in turn, have discovered that it makes a fine apple pie and stores well through the winter.

As with the Marlboro, Bunker finds that he's often working against time. Many of the original nineteenth-century trees are either gone or nearing the end of their lives. And as the old Maine farmers pass away, so does their knowledge.

In many ways, Bunker is also working against progress (which, like beauty, is in the eye of the beholder). The practice of apple growing has shifted almost exclusively in recent decades from standard-sized trees, which typically grow twenty or thirty feet high and can live for a century or two, to miniature rootstocks, which allow farmers to fit many more trees onto their existing acreage, but rarely survive for more than thirty years. Dwarf trees are tremendously efficient, but relatively short-lived.

"If our ancestors had planted only dwarfs or semi-dwarfs, there would be nothing left for us," he says. "Sometimes I'll find an old, standard tree with incredible fruit that hasn't been touched for decades. It's just been waiting behind a Walmart for someone to come along and discover it. These are incredibly patient beasts. The dwarfs would've been long gone."

The trees on Bunker's farm are standing fast, as is the wood-heated, solar-powered log cabin that he built for himself in the 1970s, complete with a nicely sited outhouse and a view of the surrounding woods. It's where we sit today, enjoying the wood stove and watching the thin afternoon light grow dim. Only now it's a house for the apprentices who travel from around the country to learn his trade. Bunker and his wife recently built a more conventional house on the property with creature comforts like standard plumbing, a wood-fired bread oven in the kitchen, and a large root cellar underneath. It's a comfortable place to settle into and, as Bunker enters his early sixties, contemplate something like retirement. But the work won't really stop. Too many people are invested in it now.

"I get invited into the homes of all these strangers," he says. People whose lives, politics, and religion may differ from his. "They didn't think anyone else cared about their old fruit. But they know that we have this thing in common—this love for these apples that have captured the imaginations of Americans in so many ways. What a wonderful position to be in."

Cider-Baked Apples

Finally, a virtuous, yet fully satisfying dessert! It's also incredibly simple—just whole, cored apples stuffed with dried cranberries, pecans, and a little brown sugar—and takes almost no time to prepare. Serve as a capper for rich meals (such as the Calvados braised pork on page 140) or as a side dish for brunch.

APPLE NOTES: Pink Lady and Jazz apples are ideal for baking because unlike the skin of most varieties, theirs retains its rosy hue, even after spending 45 minutes in a 350°F oven.

EQUIPMENT: 9- by 13-inch baking dish

MAKES: *6 servings* • ACTIVE TIME: *25 minutes* • TOTAL TIME: *60 minutes*

6 large Pink Lady or Jazz apples (about 3 pounds total; see Apple Notes)

¼ cup chopped pecans (35 g)

¼ cup chopped sweetened dried cranberries (33 g)

1 cup (240 ml) fresh apple cider

⅓ cup (75 g) packed light brown sugar

2 cinnamon sticks, each broken into 2 pieces

2 tablespoons fresh lemon juice

1 • Preheat the oven to 375°F and set a rack to the middle position. Prepare each apple by first slicing off the top ¾ inch, stem and all. Set aside the tops. Core the apples with an apple corer, then arrange in an ungreased baking dish. Divide the pecans and cranberries among the apples, stuffing them into the hollowed-out cores. Cover with the reserved tops.

2 • In a small bowl, stir together the cider and brown sugar. Pour around the apples, then add the cinnamon sticks to the pan.

3 • Cover the pan with foil and bake for 30 minutes. Remove the foil and continue to bake. Check the apples every 5 minutes to check for doneness. They will be done when tender (test by poking with a sharp knife), but not yet splitting their skins. They should need about 15 more minutes total. Transfer the apples to individual serving bowls and let cool for a few minutes.

4 • Remove the cinnamon sticks from the pan, and pour the cider sauce into a pitcher. Add lemon juice, then pour the sauce over the apples and serve warm or at room temperature.

Baked Apples with Frangipane Filling

These are not your usual baked apples! They're filled with frangipane (pronounced "frahn-jee-PAHN" or "FRAN-jih-pain," depending on how fancy you want to be), a sweet, almond-rich paste that dates back to seventeenth-century Italy. It commonly appears in the classic French pear tart, *tarte aux poires*, which made me think, "Well, why not apples?" And as I was mulling variations on baked apples, this seemed like a natural extension.

APPLE NOTES: As with the Cider-Baked Apples on page 228, I use Pink Lady and Jazz apples for baking because the skin retains its rosy hue and makes a prettier presentation.

NOTE: You can find almond paste in the baking aisle of most supermarkets.

EQUIPMENT: Melon baller; 9- by 13-inch baking dish

MAKES: *8 servings* • ACTIVE TIME: *35 minutes* • TOTAL TIME: *1 hour, 15 minutes*

1½ cups (360 ml) fresh apple cider

¼ cup (60 g) firmly packed light brown sugar

8 large Jazz or Pink Lady apples (about 5 pounds total; see Apple Notes)

1 (7-ounce or 200 g) tube almond paste (*not* marzipan, see Note)

4 tablespoons (½ stick; 57 g) salted butter

1 large egg

¼ cup (36 g) all-purpose flour

½ teaspoon kosher salt

¼ teaspoon almond extract

3 tablespoons chopped dried cherries

3 tablespoons slivered almonds

1 • Preheat the oven to 375°F and set a rack to the middle position. In a small bowl, whisk together the cider and brown sugar for the sauce. Set aside.

2 • Using a melon baller and working from the top (stem end) of the apple, scoop out the apple core and seeds down to about ¼ inch from the base. You want to create a cavity about 1¼ inches wide for the filling. Then, using a peeler, peel away a 1-inch band of skin from the top so that there's a nice ring of exposed flesh (this is just for appearance).

3 • In the bowl of a standing mixer (or in a large bowl if using a hand-held mixer), cream the almond paste with the butter. Add the egg, flour, salt, and almond extract. Gently stir in the cherries and almonds and mix until evenly distributed.

$4 \cdot$ Arrange the apples in an ungreased baking dish. Using a teaspoon and your fingers, stuff each apple with an equal portion of filling (depending on the size of your apples, you may have a little bit left over). Pour the cider mixture into the dish, cover with foil, and bake for 25 minutes. Remove the foil, baste the apples, and cook until tender but still intact, about 30 minutes more (check every 10 minutes to test for doneness by poking the apples with a sharp knife—it should slide in easily). Let the pan cool on a rack for 20 minutes, then serve in individual bowls, drizzled with the cider sauce.

Apple Dumplings with Cider-Rum Sauce

I love the look of an apple dumpling, the fruit so cozily bundled in its little four-point package. They have roots in Pennsylvania Dutch country, where the pastries emerged as a clever use for leftover pie dough on baking day. Served with a glossy cider sauce spiked with rum, they're very simple, and much more than the sum of their parts.

APPLE NOTES: Any firm-sweet apple (see page 30) will taste great with the sauce, but the apples need to be small to fit inside the pastry—about 3 inches tall. If you only have large apples on hand, just trim enough off the bottom to cut them down to the desired height.

MAKE-AHEAD TIP: You can prepare the dough through step 2 up to a day ahead, then assemble the dumplings just before baking.

EQUIPMENT: Parchment paper; 1- to 2-quart saucepan

MAKES: *6 dumplings* • ACTIVE TIME: *50 minutes* • TOTAL TIME: *1 hour, 30 minutes*

FOR THE DOUGH

2 cups (290 g) all-purpose flour

2 teaspoons baking powder

½ teaspoon table salt

1 tablespoon granulated sugar

6 tablespoons (85 g) cold unsalted butter, cut into small cubes

2 tablespoons cold vegetable shortening

½ cup (120 ml) cold milk

FOR THE SAUCE

1¾ cups (475 ml) fresh apple cider

⅓ cup (79 ml) dark rum, such as Gosling's brand

½ cup (115 g) packed light brown sugar

FOR THE APPLES

¼ cup (60 g) packed light brown sugar

½ teaspoon ground cinnamon

6 small (under 3 inches tall) firm-sweet apples (about 4 ounces each, or 1½ pounds total; see Apple Notes)

1 • Cut two pieces of parchment paper to a length of 16 inches. Set aside.

2 • Make the dough: In a medium bowl, whisk together the flour, baking powder, salt, and sugar. Sprinkle the butter cubes and shortening on top and use your fingers to work them in (you want to rub your thumb against your fingertips, smearing the butter as you do). Stop when the mixture looks like cornmeal with some pea-sized bits of butter remaining (try to work quickly so the butter doesn't melt). Add the milk and stir with a fork until the mixture

begins to hold together. Empty the dough onto one piece of parchment paper and knead three times until the dough feels cohesive. Shape into a rough rectangle, then cover with the second piece of parchment paper and roll out to a rough rectangle about 11 inches wide and 16 inches long. Chill in the refrigerator for at least 30 minutes.

3 • Meanwhile, preheat the oven to 425°F and set a rack to the middle position. Make the sauce: In a saucepan over high heat, stir together the cider, rum, and brown sugar. Simmer for 5 minutes, then remove from the heat and set aside.

4 • Prepare the apples: In a small bowl, stir together the brown sugar and cinnamon; set aside. Peel and core the apples and trim as needed (see Apple Notes).

5 • Remove the dough from the refrigerator and use a ruler and a knife to trim to an exact 10- by 15-inch rectangle. Cut into six 5-inch squares. Set one apple in the center of each square and fill the center with the brown sugar mixture. Bring the corners of the pastry up together around the apples to make four points, gently sealing at the top and along the seams so that the pastry fits snugly. Place each dumpling in an ungreased baking dish, pour the sauce around all, and bake, uncovered, for 10 minutes. Reduce the heat to 375°F and bake until the dumplings are golden brown and the sauce is bubbling, 25 to 30 minutes more. Serve warm, in a bowl, with extra sauce poured over the top.

Apple Bread Pudding with
Salted Caramel Sauce

Bread pudding is a crowd-pleaser, but it's unusual for this homey dessert to prove truly memorable. This version, studded with tangy apples and served with a crowning glory of homemade caramel sauce, breaks the mold. Prepare a half portion of the Caramelized Apples on page 247 for this recipe, using 2½ large firm-sweet apples.

APPLE NOTES: Firm-sweet apples (see page 30) have enough body to stand up to nearly an hour in the oven, and their sweetness pairs well with the caramel. Any variety will work well here.

EQUIPMENT: 11- by 7-inch baking pan; 2- to 3-quart saucepan

MAKES: *6 servings* • ACTIVE TIME: *45 minutes* •
TOTAL TIME: *1 hour, 15 minutes, plus at least 2 hours chilling time*

Butter for greasing pan

1 loaf (1 pound or 455 g) crusty white
    bread, such as Pullman style or Italian

½ portion of Caramelized Apples (about
    1½ cups; see page 247)

3 large eggs

2 cups (480 ml) half-and-half

¼ cup (51 g) granulated sugar

¼ cup (60 g) packed light brown sugar

1 tablespoon vanilla extract

½ teaspoon ground cinnamon

½ teaspoon kosher salt

FOR THE SALTED
CARAMEL SAUCE

1 cup (410 g) granulated sugar

1 cup (240 ml) heavy cream

¾ teaspoon kosher salt

1 • Butter a baking pan. Set aside. Trim the crusts off the sides and ends of the bread loaf, leaving the top and bottom intact. Cut the loaf into 1½-inch pieces. Arrange the pieces evenly in the prepared pan. Tuck the caramelized apples down among the bread pieces.

2 • In a large bowl, whisk together the eggs, half-and-half, sugars, vanilla, cinnamon, and salt. Pour over the bread, then cover and refrigerate for at least 2 hours and up to 8 hours.

3 • About 15 minutes before you're ready to bake the pudding, preheat the oven to 350°F and set a rack to the middle position. Toss the bread cubes and apples with your hands so that all

the pieces are moistened. Bake the pudding until the top is golden brown and the custard is set, about 50 minutes. Meanwhile, make the caramel: Pour ¾ cup water into the saucepan. Add the sugar in a mound in the center of the pot so that none of it touches the sides. Put the pot on high heat, cover, and cook until the sugar dissolves and the mixture begins to bubble and turn a pale amber, 12 to 15 minutes. Do not swirl or stir during this time. Reduce the heat to medium-low and cook until the caramel turns a darker amber color. Remove from the heat and carefully add cream—there will be a burst of steam, so be careful. Add salt and stir.

4 • Serve the pudding hot in individual bowls, with caramel poured over top.

Cinnamon Rice Pudding with Spiced Apple-Cranberry Compote

I like my rice pudding to be loaded with rich cinnamon. Using both sticks and powder creates lovely layers of flavor. It's comfort food at its best, and it's low in fat, too.

EQUIPMENT: 4-quart saucepan

MAKES: *6 servings* • ACTIVE TIME: *35 minutes* • TOTAL TIME: *50 minutes*

1 cup (200 g) short-grain rice such as Arborio or Canaroli

2 cinnamon sticks

4½ (1.1 L) cups milk

⅔ (140 g) cup sugar

½ teaspoon ground cinnamon

2 large egg yolks, lightly beaten

½ vanilla bean or 1½ teaspoons vanilla extract

1 teaspoon kosher salt

1 teaspoon fresh lemon zest

Spiced Apple-Cranberry Compote (page 236)

1 • Combine 3 cups water, the rice, and cinnamon sticks in a large saucepan over high heat. Bring to a boil, then reduce the heat to medium-low, cover, and gently simmer until the rice has absorbed almost all the water, about 20 minutes.

2 • Stir in the milk, sugar, and ground cinnamon. Increase the heat to medium-high and cook, stirring, until the mixture begins to bubble. Reduce the heat to low and continue to simmer, stirring often, until the rice absorbs about half the milk, 15 to 20 minutes.

3 • Spoon ½ cup pudding into a small bowl, then quickly stir in the egg yolks. Return the mixture to the pot. Stir in the vanilla and salt and continue cooking, stirring often, until the rice is very tender and the sauce is thickened and creamy, 10 to 15 minutes more. Serve warm in bowls, topped with Spiced Apple-Cranberry Compote.

Spiced Apple-Cranberry Compote

Compotes are like cooked fruit salads; the cooking allows you to produce a silky texture and to infuse the wonderful aromas of spices, herbs, citrus peel, and other flavorings. For best results, make this compote a day ahead to let the flavors intensify and blend. Then reheat and serve warm. Serve with the Cinnamon Rice Pudding (page 235) or Chestnut Soup (page 87). Or stir it into yogurt, spoon it over plain pound cake, or use it to accompany soft cheeses such as Brie and Camembert.

APPLE NOTES: The more apple varieties you use, the better. Just be sure to choose firm apples that hold their shape when cooked (see page 30).

EQUIPMENT: 3- to 4-quart saucepan

MAKES: *4 cups* • ACTIVE TIME: *30 minutes* • TOTAL TIME: *30 minutes*

2 large firm-tart apples (about 1 pound; see Apple Notes), peeled, cored, and cut into ½-inch cubes

2 large firm-sweet apples (about 1 pound), peeled, cored, and cut into ½-inch cubes

2 tablespoons packed light brown sugar

2 tablespoons apple brandy (Calvados) or applejack

Zest and juice from ½ lemon

1 cinnamon stick

½ teaspoon ground cinnamon

¼ teaspoon kosher salt

¼ teaspoon freshly ground black pepper

¼ dried vanilla bean

¼ cup (33 g) chopped dried cranberries

1 • In a saucepan over medium heat, stir together the apples, brown sugar, brandy, lemon zest, lemon juice, cinnamon stick, ground cinnamon, salt, and pepper. Add ½ cup water and stir. Using the tip of a small, sharp knife, slit the vanilla bean open, then use the blade to gently scrape the seeds out. Add the seeds and bean pod to the saucepan.

2 • Increase the heat to medium-high and bring the mixture to a low boil. Reduce the heat to a gentle simmer and cook, uncovered, for 10 minutes. Add the cranberries and cook for an additional 5 minutes until the apples are soft. Remove vanilla pod and serve warm.

Apple Clafoutis

As easy to make as a pancake, this classic French dessert from the
Limousin region involves making an egg-rich batter and pouring it over fresh fruit (typically
cherries). As the batter bakes, it puffs and turns golden brown, and cooks into a soft layer
whose texture falls somewhere between custard and cake.

APPLE NOTES: A firm-tart apple (see page 30) asserts itself nicely in the custardy batter of this
dessert. Any variety is good, but tart apples with lemony flavors, such as Granny Smith, Pink
Pearl, and Rhode Island Greening are particularly nice.

EQUIPMENT: 2-quart baking or gratin dish (a standard 8- by 8-inch baking dish works, too)

MAKES: *4 to 6 servings* • ACTIVE TIME: *15 minutes* • TOTAL TIME: *1 hour, 15 minutes*

FOR THE APPLES

1 large firm-tart apple (about 8 ounces;
  see Apple Notes), peeled, cored, and
  sliced into thin rings
Juice and zest of ½ lemon
1 tablespoon, plus ¼ cup (51 g)
  granulated sugar, divided

FOR THE CAKE

3 eggs
1 cup (240 ml) whole or 2% milk
⅔ cup (95 g) all-purpose flour
¼ cup (51 g) granulated sugar
1½ teaspoons vanilla extract
¼ teaspoon table salt
Confectioners' sugar for sprinkling

1 • Preheat the oven to 350°F and set a rack to the middle position. Generously grease a
baking dish. Prepare the apples: Toss the apple rings with the lemon juice, lemon zest, and
1 tablespoon sugar and let sit for at least 15 minutes and up to 3 hours, then arrange the slices
in the bottom of the dish and set aside.

2 • Make the cake: In a blender, whirl the eggs, milk, flour, ¼ cup granulated sugar, vanilla,
and salt until the mixture looks smooth and well combined, about 15 seconds. Pour the batter
over the apples.

3 • Bake until puffed, golden brown, and set in the center, 40 to 50 minutes. Sprinkle with
confectioners' sugar and serve warm.

Apple Brownies

This recipe, a favorite among my mom's circle of friends, gets its name from the fact that the cake is very moist, baked in a brownie pan, and made to be cut into bars. But the texture is much lighter than that of real brownies, and the flavor is all fruit and cinnamon. This is such an easy recipe to make: a great standby for those days when you want a sweet treat without a lot of fuss, or when you remember at 9 p.m. that you volunteered to make dessert for tomorrow's bake sale.

APPLE NOTES: I'm not kidding when I say that this recipe is easy. It's also extremely adaptable. Any firm-sweet apple variety (see page 30) will work beautifully.

EQUIPMENT: 11-by 7-inch baking dish

MAKES: *12 bars* • ACTIVE TIME: *15 minutes* • TOTAL TIME: *1 hour, 5 minutes*

1 cup (145 g) all-purpose flour

1 teaspoon ground cinnamon

½ teaspoon baking powder

½ teaspoon table salt

¼ teaspoon baking soda

8 tablespoons (1 stick; 113 g) salted butter, melted and cooled, plus more for greasing pan

1 cup (210 g) granulated sugar

1 large egg

½ cup (60 g) chopped walnuts

2 large firm-sweet apples (about 1 pound total; see Apple Notes), peeled, cored, and cut into ½-inch cubes

1 • Preheat the oven to 350°F and set a rack to the middle position. Generously grease the baking dish with butter and set aside.

2 • In a medium bowl, whisk together the flour, cinnamon, baking powder, salt, and baking soda. Set aside. In the bowl of a standing mixer at high speed or using a hand-held mixer, beat together the butter, sugar, and egg until pale, about 2 minutes. Add the walnuts and apples and stir by hand until evenly combined. Add the flour mixture and stir until combined, another 30 seconds.

3 • Spread the batter into the prepared pan and bake until golden brown and lightly firm to the touch, 40 to 50 minutes. Let cool on a rack for 30 minutes, then cut into 12 bars and transfer to a serving platter.

Simple Apple Nut Cake

My friend Jessica Battilana, a Vermont native, passed on the recipe for this single-layer cake, which was given to her by a family friend named Mrs. Stimets. It's a true dump-and-bake method, about as easy as cooking from a mix (aside from the chopping of apples and walnuts). It's also wonderfully tender and moist, and just dense enough to bring to mind a German apple torte. Serve with a dollop of whipped cream or crème fraîche.

APPLE NOTES: I've made this cake with many different firm-sweet apples (see page 30), and I haven't found any variety that I like more than another. All you need is a not-too-tart apple that won't dissolve when it's cooked.

EQUIPMENT: 8-inch round or square pan

MAKES: *8 servings* • ACTIVE TIME: *25 minutes* • TOTAL TIME: *44 minutes*

Butter for greasing pan

3 large firm-sweet apples (about 1½ pounds total; see Apple Notes), peeled, cored, and cut into ¼-inch cubes

1 cup (210 g) granulated sugar

1 cup (145 g) all-purpose flour

1 teaspoon ground cinnamon

1 teaspoon kosher salt

½ teaspoon baking soda

1 large egg, lightly beaten

⅓ cup (80 ml) vegetable oil, such as canola or corn

½ cup (60 g) roughly chopped walnuts

1 • Preheat the oven to 375°F and set a rack to the middle position. Generously grease the pan; set aside.

2 • In a medium bowl, stir the apples with the sugar and let sit until the sugar dissolves, about 15 minutes. Meanwhile, in a large bowl, whisk together the flour, cinnamon, salt, and baking soda. Add the apples with their juices and stir, then add the egg and oil and stir until combined. Add the nuts (at this point, the mixture will not look promising—as if there's not enough batter to coat the apple cubes. Don't worry—the recipe really does work).

3 • Pour the batter into the prepared pan and bake until nicely browned and a tester inserted in the center comes out clean, about 30 minutes. Let cool on a rack for 20 minutes.

Apple Tea Cake with Lemon Glaze

My favorite school roommate used to get regular care packages from home containing a rich lemon pound cake that was drizzled with tart glaze. It was incredible (she was good at sharing). Twenty years later, that cake inspired this variation, in which a buttermilk pound cake is layered with very thin slices of apple and topped with tangy lemon glaze. When you slice the cake, you see the pretty layers—a lovely presentation.

APPLE NOTES: Firm-sweet apples (see page 30) with pronounced lemon flavors are particularly good here. Try a Ginger Gold or Gravenstein if you can find one. Otherwise, a nice Pink Lady or Jazz would be great, too.

EQUIPMENT: 6-cup (8½- by 4½-inch) bread loaf pan; mandoline

MAKES: *1 cake; 8 servings* • ACTIVE TIME: *45 minutes* • TOTAL TIME: *1 hour, 15 minutes*

FOR THE CAKE

8 tablespoons (1 stick; 113 g) unsalted butter, at room temperature, plus more for greasing pan

1 cup (205 g) granulated sugar

1½ (215 g) cups all-purpose flour, plus more for dusting pan

1 teaspoon table salt

½ teaspoon baking powder

¼ teaspoon baking soda

2 large eggs plus 1 egg yolk, at room temperature

½ cup (80 ml) low-fat buttermilk

1 small (or ½ large) firm-sweet apple (about 4 ounces; see Apple Notes), unpeeled, cored, cut in half lengthwise, and very thinly sliced (about 3mm), preferably on a mandoline

½ teaspoon ground cinnamon

FOR THE GLAZE

2 tablespoons freshly squeezed lemon juice

1 cup confectioners' sugar

1 • Preheat the oven to 350°F and set a rack to the middle position. Butter and flour a loaf pan. Set aside.

RIGHT: Apple Tea Cake with Lemon Glaze

Apple Tea Cake with Lemon Glaze (page 240), ready to be served. Thinly sliced apples form a layer at the top and in the center of a tender lemon-scented pound cake.

2 • Combine the butter and sugar in a standing mixer, or, if using a hand-held mixer, in a large bowl. Using a whisk attachment, cream on high speed until pale, very fluffy, and almost mousselike. This will take between 6 and 8 minutes. Be patient, and be sure to scrape down the sides of the bowl periodically as you go. Meanwhile, in a medium bowl, whisk together the flour, salt, baking powder, and baking soda. Set aside.

3 • When the butter and sugar are fully whipped, add the eggs and egg yolk, one at a time, beating well after each. With the mixer on low speed, add a third of the flour mixture and mix until just incorporated. Add half the buttermilk and briefly mix. Repeat with another third of the flour mixture, then the remaining buttermilk, then the last of the flour mixture. Mix just until smooth—do not overmix.

4 • Pour a third of the batter into the prepared bread pan and smooth with an offset spatula. Top the batter with half the apples, overlapping the slices. Sprinkle the apples with half the cinnamon. Repeat with an additional third of the batter and the remaining apples. Top with the remaining batter and smooth with a spatula. Bake until the cake is golden brown and a cake tester or toothpick inserted into the center comes out clean, 45 to 55 minutes. Meanwhile, prepare the glaze: In a medium bowl, stir the lemon juice into the confectioners' sugar until smooth.

5 • Remove the cake from the oven and let sit for 5 minutes in the pan. While the cake is still warm, poke the top all over with a toothpick inserted all the way. Pour half the glaze on the cake and spread evenly with a spatula. Let sit for an additional 10 minutes to soak up the glaze, then remove from the pan and cool on a wire rack for 30 more minutes.

6 • When the cake is completely cool, drizzle generously with the remaining glaze, letting it run down the sides. Let the glaze dry for about 30 minutes, then serve.

Crêpes Filled with Caramelized Apples and Served with Maple Crème Fraîche

Crêpe batter is a busy cook's best friend. I like to make a batch (I use Julia Child's recipe) every few weeks and keep it in the refrigerator. Depending on our mood, that batter can be the basis of dinner (filled with savory treats like cheese, sausage, and vegetables), breakfast, or dessert, which is how I use it in this dish. The delicate pancakes are filled with caramelized apples and a sprinkling of brown sugar, then topped with maple-sweetened cream.

MAKE-AHEAD TIP: You can prepare the batter up to two days ahead of cooking.

EQUIPMENT: Blender; 6- to 7-inch skillet or crêpe pan

MAKES: *12 crêpes; about 6 servings* • ACTIVE TIME: *35 minutes* •
TOTAL TIME: *35 minutes, plus at least 30 minutes chilling time*

FOR THE CRÊPES

1 cup (240 ml) cold water

1 cup (240 ml) cold milk (whole, 2%, or 1%)

4 large eggs

½ teaspoon salt

2 cups (280 g) all-purpose flour

4 tablespoons (½ stick; 57 g) salted butter, melted and cooled

2 to 3 tablespoons vegetable oil for cooking

FOR THE MAPLE CRÈME FRAÎCHE

6 ounces (¾ cup, or 170 g) crème fraîche (I like Vermont Butter & Cheese Creamery brand)

3 tablespoons maple syrup

FOR THE FILLING

3 cups Caramelized Apples (page 247)

2 tablespoons brown sugar, divided

1 • Put all the crêpe batter ingredients (water, milk, eggs, salt, flour, and butter) in your blender jar. Cover and blend at high speed for 1 minute, stopping several times to scrape down the sides and bottom of the jar to loosen any bits of flour that may have stuck to the glass. Cover and refrigerate for at least 30 minutes and up to 2 days.

LEFT: Crêpes Filled with Caramelized Apples and Served with Maple Crème Fraîche

2 • Meanwhile, in a small bowl, stir together the crème fraîche and maple syrup. Cover and refrigerate until ready to use.

3 • Preheat the oven to 200°F and set a rack to the middle position. Put a skillet or crêpe pan over medium-high heat and brush with a thin layer of oil. Remove the pan from the heat and hold it in one hand while using the other to scoop out ¼ cup of batter and pour it into the pan. Quickly tilt the pan in all directions to get the batter to spread out in a very thin 6-inch-wide circle. Return the pan to the heat just until the crêpe is golden brown on the bottom, about a minute. Use a spatula to loosen the crêpe and use your hands to gently flip it over. Cook just until the crêpe is no longer raw on that side, about 30 seconds. Slide it out onto a large plate and cover with foil. Put it in the oven to keep warm as you cook the rest of the crêpes using the same method.

4 • To assemble the crêpes, fill each with ¼ cup Caramelized Apples and a sprinkling of brown sugar. Fold the sides up over the filling, turn the crêpe seam side down, transfer to a serving plate, and top with a dollop of Maple Crème Fraîche.

Caramelized Apples

This dish serves as a filling for the apple crêpes on page 245, but it also makes a wonderful side dish for breakfast and brunch. Pair it with sausages, bacon, and pancakes, or with ham and biscuits.

APPLE NOTES: As long as the apples are sweet and hold their shape when cooked, they'll work beautifully, so any firm-sweet variety (see page 30) is good.

MAKE-AHEAD TIP: The apples will keep, covered, for several days in the refrigerator.

EQUIPMENT: 12- to 14-inch skillet or sauté pan

MAKES: *About 3 cups* • ACTIVE TIME: *30 minutes* • TOTAL TIME: *30 minutes*

3 tablespoons (42 g) salted butter

2½ pounds (about 5, or 1.13 kg) firm-sweet apples (see Apple Notes), peeled, cored, and cut into ½-inch cubes

¼ teaspoon ground cinnamon

¼ teaspoon ground nutmeg

¼ teaspoon ground ginger

½ cup (120 ml) fresh apple cider, divided

½ cup maple syrup

2 tablespoons granulated sugar

Melt the butter in a skillet over medium-high heat. Add the apples and spices and cook, stirring occasionally, until the apples are softened and lightly browned in spots, 8 to 10 minutes. Stir in the apple cider and cook, stirring often, until the cider reduces to a glaze, about 3 minutes. Add half the maple syrup and the sugar and cook, stirring often, until the sauce is thickened and glossy and the apples are tender, 4 to 6 minutes. Finish with the remaining maple syrup, stir, and serve.

Kentucky Apple Stack Cake—Modern Version

The inspiration for this cake comes from Appalachia, where stack cakes were traditionally made by layering thin, biscuity layers with apple butter, which served as the "icing." Left to sit overnight, the biscuits would soften as they absorbed moisture from the apple butter, melding all into a luscious special-occasion dessert. You can find a recipe for that cake on page 251. This version features layers of spice cake stacked with a chunky sauce made from dried apples cooked in cider. It's delicious, unexpected, and faster to make, not to mention striking.

APPLE NOTES: When it's time to shop for the dried apple rings, do go out of your way to find the unsulfured type sold at Whole Foods and other health food stores. The ivory-colored, mushier "dried" apple rings you'll find at most regular supermarkets tend to puff up during cooking into something nearly unrecognizable as an apple, both in flavor and appearance.

MAKE-AHEAD TIP: You can make the filling up to three days in advance, but you may need to add a few tablespoons of water to thin it out before using.

EQUIPMENT: Two 9-inch cake pans; offset spatula

MAKES: *12 servings* • ACTIVE TIME: *45 minutes* • TOTAL TIME: *1 hour, 30 minutes*

FOR THE CAKE

3 cups (435 g) all-purpose flour, plus more for dusting pans

1½ teaspoons baking powder

½ teaspoon baking soda

1 teaspoon ground ginger

1 teaspoon ground cinnamon

1 teaspoon table salt

16 tablespoons (2 sticks; 227 g) unsalted butter, at room temperature, plus more for greasing pans

1½ cups (345 g) firmly packed light brown sugar

2 large eggs, at room temperature

1¼ cups (295 ml) buttermilk, at room temperature

FOR THE FILLING

1 pound (455 g) dried apple rings, preferably unsulfured (see Apple Notes)

5 cups (1.2 L) fresh apple cider

Confectioners' sugar for garnish

1 • Preheat the oven to 350°F and set a rack to the middle position. Butter and flour the cake pans; set aside.

2 • Make the cake: In a medium bowl, sift together the flour, baking powder, baking soda, ginger, cinnamon, and salt. In a large bowl, using a hand-held mixer or a standing mixer with a whisk attachment, beat the butter and sugar together, stopping occasionally to scrape down the sides of the bowl, until very light and fluffy and almost mousselike; 6 to 8 minutes. Add the eggs one at a time, beating well after each. Add a third of the flour mixture and stir just to combine. Add half the buttermilk and stir to combine. Repeat, alternating another third of the flour mixture with half the buttermilk and finishing with the remaining third of the flour mixture. Divide the batter between the prepared pans and bake until a cake tester comes out clean, 30 to 35 minutes. Set the pans on a wire rack to cool for 15 minutes, then turn the cakes out onto the rack (keep them top side up) to cool completely.

3 • Meanwhile, make the filling: Combine the dried apple rings, cider, and 2 cups water in a large saucepan over high heat. Bring to a boil, then reduce the heat to medium-low, maintaining a gentle simmer. Cook, occasionally stirring and mashing the apples with a wooden spoon, until they're very soft and have the texture of chunky applesauce, 30 to 40 minutes. Let cool.

4 • When the cakes are completely cool, use a sharp serrated knife to carefully halve them crosswise so that you now have four layers. The best technique is to turn the cake as you cut, rather than sawing your way through from one direction.

5 • Assemble the cake: Choose your prettiest, smoothest "top" layer and set aside. Choose your bottom layer and top it with a third of the filling. Smooth out with an offset spatula, then top with another cake layer and more filling. Repeat once more, then top the cake with the layer you set aside. Just before serving, sprinkle the whole production with confectioners' sugar. The cake will keep for a day or so after baking, but in this case, fresh is best.

Kentucky Apple Stack Cake—Traditional Version

I can't say enough about the deliciousness and simple beauty of this historic cake, which has its roots in nineteenth-century Appalachia. In those days, it served as a sort of potluck wedding cake: Members of the community would contribute layers, which were held together with a spread of mashed dried apples, applesauce, or apple butter.

The dish is extremely easy to make, since the dough resembles that of giant sugar cookies, baked in pans and stacked. Really, the only challenge lies in baking all six layers and then finding the patience to wait at least twenty-four hours—during which time the stacks absorb the apple butter and soften into something more recognizably cakelike—before digging in.

APPLE NOTES: You can use store-bought or homemade apple butter in this cake, though naturally I prefer the Overnight Apple Butter on page 275. For store-bought, I recommend Eden brand, which is sold in most Whole Foods stores.

MAKE-AHEAD TIP: You can prep the cake through step 3 up to a day before baking.

NOTE: This cake has six layers, each baked individually. If you have a large oven and a large pan collection, you can bake them all at once. Otherwise, I've written the recipe based on the assumption that you'll be using three pans and baking the layers in two phases (you can also use two pans and bake in three phases).

EQUIPMENT: At least 2 standard 9-inch cake pans, preferably 3 (see Note); offset spatula

MAKES: *12 servings* • ACTIVE TIME: *50 minutes* •
TOTAL TIME: *2 hours, plus at least 24 hours resting time*

1 cup (210 g) granulated sugar

¾ cup (175 g) firmly packed light brown sugar

16 tablespoons (2 sticks; 227 g) unsalted butter, at room temperature, plus more for greasing pan

5½ cups (780 g) all-purpose flour, plus more for dusting pan

2 teaspoons baking powder

1½ teaspoons baking soda

1 teaspoon table salt

1 teaspoon ground cinnamon

⅔ cup (160 ml) buttermilk

2 extra-large eggs

1 tablespoon vanilla extract

2½ cups (600 ml) apple butter (see Apple Notes)

Confectioners' sugar for garnish

LEFT: Traditional Kentucky Apple Stack Cake layers apple butter between tender rounds of biscuit-like cake.

1 • Preheat the oven to 400°F and set a rack to the middle position. Butter and flour the cake pans (see Note). In the bowl of a standing mixer (or using a hand-held mixer), cream the sugar, brown sugar, and butter together at medium speed until quite fluffy, 3 to 5 minutes. In a medium bowl, sift together the flour, baking powder, baking soda, salt, and cinnamon. Set aside. In a small bowl, whisk together the buttermilk, eggs, and vanilla.

2 • Add a third of the flour mixture to the butter-sugar mixture and mix just to combine at medium-low speed. Add half of the buttermilk mixture and mix just to combine. Repeat, adding another third of the flour mixture, then the remaining buttermilk mixture, then the remaining flour mixture.

3 • Turn the dough out onto a lightly floured surface, knead four times to bring it all together, then roll into an even cylinder about 18 inches long. Cut the cylinder into six equal parts (each 3 inches long), then press each part into a disk, wrap in plastic wrap, and refrigerate for at least 30 minutes and up to a day.

4 • On a lightly floured surface, roll out one disk of dough to a 10-inch circle (use a light sprinkling of flour if it begins to stick). Using a cake pan as your guide, trim the dough into a perfect 9-inch circle, then lay it in a pan to bake. Repeat with two more pieces of dough. Bake all three, rotating the pans halfway through, until the layers are lightly golden and just beginning to pull away from the sides, 10 to 12 minutes. Remove from the oven and cool the pans on wire racks for 10 minutes. Remove the layers and set aside. When the pans are cool, butter and flour them once more and repeat the rolling, cutting, and baking with the other three dough rounds.

5 • Assemble the cake: Choose your prettiest, smoothest "top" layer and set it aside. Choose your bottom layer and use an offset spatula to spread ½ cup apple butter over the top, all the way to the edges. Top with another cake layer and another ½ cup topping. Repeat three more times, then top with the prettiest layer. Cover with plastic wrap and refrigerate for 24 to 48 hours, then sprinkle the top with confectioners' sugar, cut into thin slices, and serve.

Apple Gingerbread Upside-Down Cake

Here's a recipe with some history: Gingerbread in one form or another dates all the way back to the Middle Ages, and emerged in the fifteenth century as a spiced cake. Apple and gingerbread have long been a favorite combination in Britain. Meanwhile, upside-down cakes became popular standards in the United States in the 1920s and 1930s (though early versions were typically made with pineapple). All three streams flow together in this tender, flavorful treat. Serve with whipped cream.

APPLE NOTES: Choose any tart apples that hold their shape when cooked (see page 30).

EQUIPMENT: 9-inch round cake pan

MAKES: *12 servings* • ACTIVE TIME: *30 minutes* • TOTAL TIME: *1 hour, 5 minutes*

FOR THE CAKE

6 tablespoons (85 g) salted butter

½ cup (115 g) firmly packed light brown sugar

2 large eggs, at room temperature

¼ cup (60 ml) molasses

1½ cups (220 g) all-purpose flour

1 teaspoon baking soda

1 teaspoon ground ginger

1 teaspoon ground cinnamon

½ teaspoon table salt

½ cup (120 ml) buttermilk, at room temperature

FOR THE TOPPING

⅓ cup (70 g) granulated sugar

1 teaspoon ground cinnamon

¼ teaspoon freshly grated nutmeg

2 large firm-tart apples, (about 1 pound total; see Apple Notes), peeled, cored, and sliced into ⅛-inch-thick rings

1 • Preheat the oven to 350°F and set a rack to the middle position. Generously grease a cake pan. First, make the cake: With a standing or hand-held mixer, cream the butter and sugar until pale and fluffy, 5 to 7 minutes. Add the eggs one at a time, mixing well after each. Beat in the molasses.

2 • In a medium bowl, sift together the flour, baking soda, ginger, cinnamon, and salt. Add one-third of the flour mixture to the butter-sugar mixture. Stir to combine, then stir in half of the buttermilk. Repeat, adding another third of the flour mixture, then the remaining buttermilk, then the remaining flour mixture. Do not overmix.

3 • Make the topping: In a small bowl, stir together the sugar, cinnamon, and nutmeg. Toss the apple slices in half the sugar mixture, then arrange in the prepared pan, making overlapping concentric circles. Sprinkle the remaining sugar mixture over the apples. Pour the cake batter over the apples and bake until a tester comes out clean, 35 to 40 minutes. Let the cake cool on a rack for 10 minutes, then run a knife between the cake and the pan sides to loosen. Lay a serving plate face down over the cake pan, then flip to unmold the cake. Serve warm or at room temperature.

Applesauce-Pistachio Bundt Cake with Cider Glaze

This cake was a star player in my Aunt Madeline's repertoire, though she didn't make it with the glaze. I added that after deciding it needed just a little something to jazz it up. As a dessert, this is pretty cozy stuff, perfect for a casual dinner or potluck.

APPLE NOTES: In the applesauce hierarchy, homemade is king. However, it's not worth making a fresh batch of sauce for baking. Feel free to use any store-bought variety, as long as it has plenty of real fruit and isn't loaded with too much sweetener.

EQUIPMENT: 10-inch Bundt pan

MAKES: *12 servings* • ACTIVE TIME: *30 minutes* • TOTAL TIME: *1 hour, 30 minutes*

FOR THE CAKE

2 cups (290 g) all-purpose flour, plus more for dusting pan

1 teaspoon baking powder

1 teaspoon ground cinnamon

½ teaspoon baking soda

½ teaspoon table salt

½ teaspoon ground cloves

10 tablespoons (1¼ sticks; 142 g) salted butter, at room temperature, plus more for greasing pan

1 cup (210 g) granulated sugar

1 large egg plus 1 large egg yolk, at room temperature

1½ cups (360 ml) applesauce (see Apple Notes), at room temperature

⅓ cup (160 g) roughly chopped unsalted pistachios

FOR THE CIDER GLAZE

1 cup (120 g) confectioners' sugar

2 tablespoons fresh apple cider

Pinch of table salt

1 • Preheat the oven to 350°F. Grease the pan with butter, then sprinkle with flour. Shake the pan to distribute evenly, then dump out any excess. Set aside.

2 • In a medium bowl, whisk together the flour, baking powder, cinnamon, baking soda, salt, and cloves. Set aside. In a standing mixer (or in a large bowl if using a hand-held mixer), cream together the butter and sugar with a whisk attachment for 3 minutes, scraping down the bowl halfway through. Add the egg and egg yolk and beat to combine.

3 • Set a rack to the middle position. Add one third of the flour mixture to the butter-sugar mixture and briefly stir to combine. Add half of the applesauce, then stir again. Repeat, adding another third of the flour mixture, the remaining applesauce, then the remaining flour mixture. Fold in pistachios. Pour the batter into the prepared pan and bake until the middle of the cake is firm to the touch and a cake tester comes out clean, about 1 hour.

4 • Meanwhile, make the glaze: Stir together the sugar, cider, and salt until smooth. When the cake is done baking, cool in the pan on a wire rack for 15 minutes, then carefully turn the pan over to remove the cake. Cool completely, then drizzle the glaze over the cake.

Lowfat Gingerbread Applesauce Cake

This cake contains no dairy products and is relatively low in fat, but has all the flavor of traditional gingerbread. The secret is in the applesauce, which adds flavor and moistness without adding many calories.

EQUIPMENT: 2- to 3-quart saucepan; 8- by 8-inch square baking pan

MAKES: *8 servings* • ACTIVE TIME: *30 minutes* • TOTAL TIME: *60 minutes*

Grease (butter or vegetable shortening) for the pan

1 cup (237 ml) unsweetened or lightly sweetened applesauce

½ cup (120 ml) light or medium molasses

1½ cups (215 g) all-purpose flour, plus more for dusting pan

1 teaspoon baking soda

1 teaspoon ground ginger

1 teaspoon ground cinnamon

¼ teaspoon ground cloves

½ teaspoon table salt

2 large eggs

⅔ cup granulated sugar

⅓ cup (80 ml) vegetable oil, such as corn or canola

Confectioners' sugar for dusting

1 • Preheat the oven to 325°F and set a rack to the middle position. Grease the baking pan with the butter or shortening, then dust with a couple tablespoons of flour. Shake pan around to distribute an even coating of flour, then dump out any extra. Set aside.

2 • In a saucepan over medium-high heat, bring the applesauce to a simmer. Remove the pan from the heat, then stir in the molasses and the baking soda. The mixture will foam up and bubble. Let this mixture sit and cool a bit.

3 • Meanwhile, in a medium bowl, whisk together the flour, baking soda, ginger, cinnamon, cloves, and salt. In a standing mixer with the whisk attachment (or using a hand-held mixer), beat together the eggs and sugar on high speed until the mixture is thick and pale yellow, about 4 minutes. Drizzle in the oil in a thin stream, continuing to mix as you do.

4 • Add about a third of the flour mixture to the egg-sugar-oil mixture and whisk just to blend. Add half the applesauce-molasses mixture. Mix again to blend and use a spatula to scrape down the sides of your bowl, making sure the batter is evenly mixed. Add another third of the flour mixture and mix, then add the remaining applesauce-molasses mixture. Mix, then scrape the bowl down once more with a spatula. Finally, add the last of the flour mixture and mix until smooth.

5 • Pour this batter into the prepared pan and bake until the cake is firm in the center and a tester inserted into the middle comes out clean, 40 to 45 minutes. Set the cake on a rack and let cool in the pan for about 10 minutes, then use a thin knife to loosen the cake around the edges and carefully turn it out onto the rack. Let the cake cool to room temperature (about 30 minutes), then dust with confectioners' sugar and serve.

Spiced Apple Cupcakes with Cinnamon Cream Cheese Frosting

It took several attempts to create a cupcake that was full of apple flavor without being mistaken for a breakfast muffin. Among the experiments: a liquid apple butter center, a scattering of finely diced apples. Finally, I considered adding boiled cider, which is just very concentrated apple juice. It did the trick, adding rich flavor to the batter while also producing a very tender, identifiably cakelike product. Spiced cream cheese frosting was the perfect finish. Honestly, I can't think of any cake that wouldn't be improved by cream cheese frosting. And it's so much easier to make than buttercream.

NOTE: This recipe has a large yield, 24 cakes. I think this is a sensible amount for most birthday parties—plenty of people will eat two cakes each. However, you can cut the recipe in half fairly easily—most everything divides into two, except for the eggs and the boiled cider. In that case, use 2 eggs plus 1 egg yolk and 3½ tablespoons boiled cider. (You can order boiled cider from the King Arthur Flour catalog or from Wood's Cider Mill at woodscidermill.com.) The frosting divides neatly in half.

MAKE-AHEAD TIP: You can bake the cupcakes up to a week in advance. When cool, arrange them on a cookie sheet and put in the freezer. When frozen, transfer them to zip-top bags. You can make the frosting up to four days in advance. Bring everything to room temperature before frosting.

EQUIPMENT: 2 standard (2½-inch) muffin pans; paper liners

MAKES: *2 dozen cupcakes* • ACTIVE TIME: *1 hour* • TOTAL TIME: *1 hour, 45 minutes*

16 tablespoons (2 sticks; 227 g) unsalted butter, at room temperature

2 cups (420 g) granulated sugar

3½ cups (510 g) all-purpose flour

1 tablespoon baking powder

1 teaspoon table salt

1½ teaspoons ground cinnamon

1 teaspoon ground ginger

5 large eggs, at room temperature

1 teaspoon vanilla extract

⅓ cup (80 ml) boiled cider (see Note)

1 cup (240 ml) whole or 2% milk, at room temperature

FOR THE FROSTING

2 (8 ounce) packages (455 g total) cream cheese, at room temperature

8 tablespoons (1 stick; 113 g) salted butter, at room temperature

2 cups (240 g) confectioners' sugar

2 teaspoons ground cinnamon

1 teaspoon vanilla extract

1 • Preheat the oven to 325°F and set a rack to the middle position.

2 • Using a standing mixer fitted with a whisk attachment or a hand-held mixer, combine the butter and sugar at medium-high speed until pale, very fluffy, and mousselike, 7 to 10 minutes (I usually average about 8 minutes). Stop every few minutes to scrape down the sides of your bowl with a spatula—you want everything evenly mixed, with no clumps of butter.

3 • While you're waiting for the butter and sugar to whip, combine the flour, baking powder, salt, cinnamon, and ginger in a medium bowl. Whisk together and set aside.

4 • When the butter-sugar mixture is fully whipped, add 1 egg and continue mixing at medium-high speed until fully combined. Repeat with the remaining 4 eggs. Add the vanilla.

5 • In a small bowl, stir the boiled cider into the milk. It may look a bit curdled—that's fine. Add about a third of the flour mixture to the butter-egg-sugar mixture and mix on low speed just until combined. Do not overmix. Add about a half of the milk mixture and mix just until combined. Repeat with the flour, then the milk, then the flour.

6 • Using a ⅓ cup measuring cup or large spoon, fill each muffin cup two-thirds of the way. Bake until the tops of the cakes are firm but still pale and a cake tester comes out clean, 25 to 30 minutes.

7 • While the cupcakes are baking, make the frosting: Using your standing mixer fitted with a whisk or paddle attachment or a hand-held mixer, combine the cream cheese, butter, confectioners' sugar, cinnamon, and vanilla. Beat well, scraping down the sides once or twice, until evenly combined. Set aside.

8 • When the cakes are done, remove from the oven and let cool in the pan on a rack for 10 minutes before removing, then let cool for at least 30 minutes before frosting. Frost generously.

RIGHT: Spiced Apple Cupcakes with Cinnamon Cream Cheese Frosting (page 259)

Salted Caramel Apples with Cinnamon Graham Cracker Crumbs

These apples, dipped in salted homemade caramel and then crowned with a dusting of crushed graham crackers, are just pure fun. Feel free to play with the toppings, substituting crushed almonds or M&Ms for the graham crackers as desired. Crushed gingersnaps are another good choice.

APPLE NOTES: Maybe it's a result of all the carnival food I've eaten over the years, but I'm awfully fond of caramel apples made with the Granny Smith. Nevertheless, any firm-tart variety (see page 30) will be delicious here.

NOTE: Store-bought apples are coated with food-grade wax to make them shiny, which can make it difficult for the caramel to stick to the fruit. You can remove the wax if you like by briefly dunking the apples in boiling water and then wiping them off with a dish towel. I've found that this step is unnecessary when I use organic apples, which seem to have less wax. Even better, buy your apples directly from a farm, in which case they'll be wax free.

EQUIPMENT: 4- to 5-quart heavy-bottomed pot; instant-read thermometer; popsicle sticks; parchment paper or wax paper

MAKES: *8 servings* • ACTIVE TIME: *1 hour, 5 minutes* • TOTAL TIME: *1 hour, 5 minutes*

8 medium firm-tart apples (about 6 ounces each, or 3 pounds total; see Apple Notes), unpeeled, stems removed and chilled in refrigerator for at least an hour before using (see Note)

2 tablespoons (28 g) salted butter

1 cup (235 g) packed light brown sugar

½ cup (120 ml) sweetened condensed milk

½ cup (120 ml) light corn syrup

½ cup (120 ml) whole milk

¼ cup (60 ml) heavy cream

¼ teaspoon sea salt or table salt

1½ teaspoons vanilla extract

4 whole cinnamon graham crackers, crushed

1 • Insert a popsicle stick into each apple, then set aside. Line a baking sheet with parchment paper or wax paper. Put the crushed graham crackers in a bowl and keep near the stove.

2 • In a large pot over medium heat, combine the butter, sugar, condensed milk, corn syrup, milk, cream, and salt. Cook, stirring gently, until the mixture begins to bubble. It will foam up quite a bit as it cooks, which is why a large pot is essential. Begin using your instant-read thermometer at this stage to track the caramel's temperature. You want to bring it up to between 238°F and 240°F, which can take up to 20 minutes. Don't be tempted to raise the temperature—too high and the mixture will scald. Patience is essential! Gently stir and check the temperature every minute or so. The caramel will thicken and turn a toffee color as it reaches 238°F. When this happens, stir in the vanilla and remove from the heat.

3 • Working quickly, wipe the apples with a paper towel to remove any condensation, then dip, one at a time, into the caramel, swirling to coat evenly. Turn the apple up, scrape off any excess caramel, and dunk the apple in graham crackers about halfway, so the pieces stick to the caramel. Set the apple on a baking sheet, then repeat with the remaining apples. Refrigerate all until the caramel is firm.

Apple-Gingersnap Ice Cream

The only difficult thing about this scrumptious ice cream is planning ahead to allow for plenty of chilling time (at least 4 hours). Your efforts will be rewarded, though, with incredibly smooth and creamy ice cream jazzed up with apples and gingersnap cookies.

APPLE NOTES: Here's the perfect recipe for using Fuji or Gala apples. They have just the right flavor and tenderness and are easy to find.

EQUIPMENT: 3- to 4-quart saucepan; 8- to 10-inch skillet; ice cream maker

MAKES: *About 5 cups* • ACTIVE TIME: *30 minutes* •
TOTAL TIME: *60 minutes, plus at least 4 hours chilling time*

1 cup (237 ml) 2% or whole milk

2 cups (474 ml) light cream

Yolks of 5 large eggs, at room temperature

1 cup (205 g) granulated sugar

¼ teaspoon kosher salt

1 tablespoon vanilla extract

2 medium tender-sweet apples (about 12 ounces total; see Apple Notes), peeled, cored, and cut into ¼-inch cubes

1 teaspoon ground cinnamon

25 gingersnap cookies, roughly crushed, with some cookie dust and some larger pieces

1 • In a saucepan over medium-high heat, bring the milk and cream to a simmer, then remove from the heat. Meanwhile, in a standing mixer fitted with a whisk attachment or using a hand-held mixer, beat the egg yolks with the sugar on high speed until pale and fluffy, about 3 minutes. Reduce the speed to low and add ½ cup of the hot cream-milk mixture into the egg mixture. This will slowly bring up the temperature of the eggs so they won't curdle when you mix them with the rest of the hot cream.

2 • Pour the egg mixture back into the saucepan with the cream-milk mixture and stir to combine. Cook over medium heat, stirring constantly, until the mixture reaches 175°F on an instant-read thermometer (this is the point at which it will thicken noticably), about 10 minutes. Remove from the heat, add the salt and vanilla extract, and pour through a strainer into a bowl. Cover and refrigerate for at least 4 hours and up to overnight.

3 • Meanwhile, prepare the apples: In a skillet, stir the apples with 3 tablespoons water and the cinnamon over medium heat. Cook until the apples are tender and translucent, and the water has evaporated, 8 to 10 minutes. Use a fork to mash the apples to the consistency of chunky applesauce. Transfer to a bowl and refrigerate, covered, until you're ready to freeze the ice cream.

4 • Once chilled, your ice cream base should register between 35°F and 40°F on an instant-read thermometer. If it doesn't, you can set the bowl over some ice and stir to quickly cool it. Stir the apples and gingersnaps into the ice cream base. Pour the mixture into an ice-cream maker, leaving an inch at the top to allow for expansion, and prepare according to the manufacturer's instructions. Eat immediately or pour into an airtight plastic container and freeze for up to 1 week.

Green Apple Sauvignon Blanc Sorbet

If you've ever attended a Sauvignon Blanc tasting, you've probably heard some reference to the wine's green apple "notes." I even remember one fellow taster who described a Napa Sauvignon Blanc as tasting like "a tart green apple sliced with a cold steel knife." Specific! And, in that case, oddly fitting. The metaphor stayed with me and inspired this sorbet, which isn't the least bit metallic, but is most certainly cold.

APPLE NOTES: Only green apples really work here, so don't cheat. Fortunately, Granny Smith is easy to find.

EQUIPMENT: Ice cream maker

MAKES: *3½ cups* • ACTIVE TIME: *25 minutes* • TOTAL TIME: *1 hour, 10 minutes*

1 cup (210 g) granulated sugar

1¼ pounds (566 g; about 2½ large) green apples, such as Granny Smith or Rhode Island Greening (see Apple Notes), unpeeled, cored and cut into 1-inch chunks

¾ cup (180 ml) chilled Sauvignon Blanc wine

¼ teaspoon kosher salt

1 • In a medium saucepan over medium-high heat, bring 1 cup water, the sugar, and apples to a low boil, then reduce the heat to low, partially cover the pan, and gently simmer until the apples are very tender, 10 to 15 minutes. Remove from the heat and stir in the wine and salt. Process the mixture through a sieve or food mill to remove the skins.

2 • Pour the puree into a shallow baking dish and put in the freezer for 20 minutes to cool. Freeze in the ice cream maker according to the manufacturer's instructions. For a firmer texture, chill in the freezer for an additional 8 hours before serving.

CHAPTER TEN

CONDIMENTS AND COCKTAILS

Ginger Gold

Classic Applesauce

Applesauce is so simple that a recipe seems a little redundant. But there is a right way to make it. First, leave the peels on. They add flavor, vitamins, and a little color—you'll remove them later when you run the sauce through the food mill. Second, do use the food mill—it creates the best velvety texture. Third, the amount of sugar you add depends on the apples you choose, so start with a tablespoon and keep adding and tasting until you get it right. (See page 116 for a photograph of the finished applesauce.)

APPLE NOTES: The more apple varieties you use, the better your sauce will be. Ideally, you want to taste the full range of apple flavor notes, from lemon to raspberry to spice. For a list of tender-sweet and tender-tart apples, see page 30.

NOTE: Adding 3 tablespoons of water to the pot creates just enough steam to break down the apples quickly. If you like a looser sauce, add another tablespoon or two of water after you put the apples through the food mill.

EQUIPMENT: 3- to 4-quart Dutch oven or other heavy-bottomed pot; food mill

MAKES: *3 cups* • ACTIVE TIME: *30 minutes* • TOTAL TIME: *30 minutes*

3-pounds (1.4 kg; about 6 large) tender-sweet and tender-tart apples (see Apple Notes)

¼ cup (60 ml) water
1 tablespoon granulated sugar, plus more to taste

1 • Core the apples (do not peel), then cut into large chunks (about 2 inches). Put the apples and water in a pot over medium-high heat and cover. When the water begins producing vigorous steam, reduce the heat to medium-low and cook, stirring occasionally, until the apples become quite tender and can be smashed with the back of a wooden spoon, 15 to 20 minutes.

2 • Process the apples through a food mill. Add sugar, taste, and add another tablespoon or two as desired. Thin with additional water, if needed. Serve cold or at room temperature.

Orange-Scented Spiced Applesauce

This variation on regular applesauce has the same rich apple flavors and velvety texture, but with the added punch of orange and spice.

APPLE NOTES: As with the regular sauce, the more apple varieties you use, the better the sauce will taste. (For a list of tender apple varieties, see page 30.)

EQUIPMENT: 3- to 4-quart Dutch oven or other heavy-bottomed pot; food mill

MAKES: *3 cups* • ACTIVE TIME: *35 minutes* • TOTAL TIME: *35 minutes*

3-pounds (1.4 kg; 3 large) tender-sweet and tender-tart apples (see Apple Notes)

1 teaspoon freshly grated orange zest

1 teaspoon ground cinnamon

¼ teaspoon ground cloves

1 tablespoon firmly packed light brown sugar, plus more to taste

½ cup (120 ml) freshly squeezed orange juice

1 • Core apples (do not peel), then cut into large chunks (about 2 inches). Put the apples, orange zest, cinnamon, cloves, and 3 tablespoons water into a large pot over medium-high heat and cover. When the liquid begins to simmer, reduce the heat to medium-low and cook, stirring occasionally, until the apples become quite tender and can be smashed with the back of a wooden spoon, 15 to 20 minutes.

2 • Process the apples through the food mill. Add the brown sugar and orange juice, taste, and add another tablespoon or two of orange juice as desired.

Quick Bread-and-Butter Apple Pickles

Okay, this relish is actually a bit different from the bread-and-butter pickles you may know from childhood. It's also much simpler. It does have a similar flavor profile, though: sweet and bright, with warm spices.

It's a quick pickle in every sense—just a thirty-minute bath in the vinegar before it's ready to serve, and I simply keep it in the refrigerator for up to two weeks, rather than canning it. It never lasts long enough to put up, anyway. Serve as a side salad, or on sandwiches and burgers, or chop up and mix into potato salad. Pairs well with the Apple and Mustard Grilled Cheese Sandwiches on page 107.

APPLE NOTES: Red-skinned apples look prettiest here, so consult the apple portraits on pages 31–60 to find some red firm-sweet apple varieties. I often use Jazz, Baldwin, and Melrose here.

NOTE: To make this pickle truly pretty (and easy), the mandoline and biscuit cutter are essential. The mandoline because you want paper-thin slices, and the biscuit cutter so you can create apple slices that are the same size as the cukes. You don't need anything fancy, though. See my recommendations for affordable tools on pages 71–72.

EQUIPMENT: Mandoline; 1½-inch biscuit cutter (see Note)

MAKES: *About 4 cups* • ACTIVE TIME: *25 minutes* • TOTAL TIME: *60 minutes*

1 large seedless (English) cucumber (about 14 ounces or 400 g), unpeeled

1 tablespoon kosher salt

2 large firm-sweet apples (about 1 pound total; see Apple Notes), unpeeled and cut in half lengthwise

2 medium shallots

1 cup (240 ml) rice vinegar

½ cup (120 ml) water

½ cup (120 ml) honey

1 tablespoon granulated sugar

1 cinnamon stick

1 sprig fresh tarragon, cut into 4 pieces

1 • First, prep your cucumbers: Cut off the ends and discard, then slice on a mandoline. Put in a colander and toss with the salt. Let sit for at least 20 minutes.

RIGHT: Quick Bread-and-Butter Apple Pickles

2 • Meanwhile, prep the apples: Trim the seeds and core from each apple half, then set, cut side down, on a cutting board. Use a biscuit cutter to push down into the flesh, extracting two little cylinders from each apple half. Because the apples are round, the cylinders won't be perfectly level. That's fine. Thinly slice each cylinder on the mandoline (again, don't worry if some slices are not perfect circles). Slice the shallots on the mandoline as well, then put in a medium bowl with the apples.

3 • In a small bowl, whisk together the vinegar, water, honey, and sugar until the sugar dissolves. Add the cinnamon stick and tarragon, and pour the mixture over the apples and shallots.

4 • Rinse the cucumbers well and lightly blot dry (still in the colander) with paper towels. Add the cucumber slices to the bowl with the apples and stir well. Let sit for at least 30 minutes before serving. Refrigerate for up to two weeks.

Apple, Date, and Almond Charoset

Charoset is a ritual food, a sweet relish served during the Passover seder to represent the mortar used by enslaved Israelite laborers in Egypt. Jews of Eastern European descent typically base their *charoset* on apples, while many Mediterranean Jews use dates or dried fruits. I decided to combine the two traditions, adding apples, dates, and toasted almonds to the mix, along with cinnamon, sweet red wine, and lemon. Only after I developed the recipe did I learn of a traditional Turkish *charoset* with a very similar list of ingredients.

APPLE NOTES: I especially like newer varieties like Jazz and Piñata here because they have a little more acidity to balance the sweetness. For more firm-sweet varieties, see page 30.

EQUPMENT: 8- to 12-inch heavy-bottomed skillet

MAKES: *About 4 cups* • ACTIVE TIME: *25 minutes* • TOTAL TIME: *25 minutes*

½ cup (58 g) slivered almonds

3 large firm-sweet apples (about 1½ pounds total; see Apple Notes), unpeeled and cored

7 ounces (200 g) dates, preferably Medjool

6 tablespoons (90 ml) sweet red wine, such as Manischewitz brand

3 tablespoons fresh lemon juice

¾ teaspoon ground cinnamon

½ teaspoon freshly grated lemon zest

1 • In a skillet over medium-low heat, toast the almonds, stirring often, until golden brown, about 10 minutes. Chop well, then set aside until ready to serve. Meanwhile, in a food processor or chopping bowl, very finely chop the apples and dates—to about the size of corn kernels. Stir in the wine, lemon juice, cinnamon, and lemon zest and let sit for 30 minutes, or cover and refrigerate for up to 2 days.

2 • Just before serving, add the almonds. Stir and serve immediately.

Apple, Cucumber, Lime, and Mint Salsa

I love the green, slightly vegetal quality of the Granny Smith apple, and how its flavors echo other green foods, such as cucumbers, bell peppers, and even herbs such as mint and basil. On a hot spring afternoon, it occurred to me that if they echo each other, they'd probably taste good together in a cooling salsa. Jalapeños inject just the right dose of heat, and honey ties it all together. This recipe always gets the same reaction: first, a scratching of the head, then a smile.

APPLE NOTES: This is one time where only one variety of apple will do, so no substitutions please.

NOTE: With plenty of acid to prevent the apples from browning, this salsa keeps for up to five days in the refrigerator.

MAKES: *About 4 cups* • ACTIVE TIME: *20 minutes* • TOTAL TIME: *20 minutes*

¼ cup (60 ml) lime juice

2 tablespoons honey

½ teaspoon kosher salt

2 large Granny Smith apples (about 1 pound total; see Apple Notes), unpeeled and diced

1¼ cups (182 g) diced English (seedless) cucumber (about half a standard cucumber)

½ cup (75 g) finely diced red bell pepper

1 tablespoon minced jalapeño

1 tablespoon thinly sliced mint leaves

In a small bowl, stir together the lime juice, honey, and salt. In a medium bowl, toss together the apples, cucumber, bell pepper, jalapeño, and mint. Pour the dressing over the apple mixture and toss. Serve cold.

Overnight Apple Butter

I'm not one to spend my late summer days at the stove canning pickles and preserves for hours on end. Maybe I should be, but I'm not. This apple butter, however, lets me satisfy that primal urge to put up and store away without demanding that I sacrifice the nicest days of the year. Using a slow cooker, I can make the preserves while I sleep. And the result—bright, with just a hint of complex spice—is a terrific reward.

NOTE: For more information on home preservation safety, visit the National Center for Home Food Preservation at www.uga.edu/nchfp.

EQUIPMENT: 5- to 7-quart slow cooker; twelve 8-ounce canning jars, lids, and bands; tongs; large stock pot or canner

MAKES: *Twelve 8-ounce jars* • ACTIVE TIME: *1 hour;* • TOTAL TIME: *9 to 11 hours*

5 pounds (2.25 kg; about 10 large) apples, any type (preferably a mix of types), peeled, cored, and cut into medium chunks

1¾ cups (365 g) granulated sugar

1 whole star anise pod

½ teaspoon ground cinnamon

½ teaspoon kosher salt

¼ teaspoon freshly ground nutmeg

¼ teaspoon ground ginger

2 cups (480 ml) fresh apple cider

¼ cup (60 ml) fresh lemon juice

1 • Turn the slow cooker on high and add all the ingredients. Cover and cook for 1½ hours, stirring occasionally. The mixture should be bubbling vigorously. Reduce the heat to low, cook for another hour, then remove the star anise pod. Set the lid slightly ajar, then cook for an additional 7 to 9 hours, until the apple butter is dark brown and thick. Stir well, and, if needed, pass through a food mill or strainer to remove any lumps.

2 • Sterilize the canning jars by boiling in the large stock pot for 10 minutes (do not boil the lids or bands). Turn off the heat and leave the jars in the water until ready to use. Wash the lids and bands in hot, soapy water, then dry with clean paper towels. Use tongs to remove the jars from the water and divide the apple butter among them, leaving ¼ inch of headspace at the top of each jar (see Note). Use tongs to put the lids on top of the jars, then use your hands to screw on the bands. Bring the water in a large stock pot or canner back to a boil and submerge the filled jars for 10 minutes to seal. Let cool to room temperature.

Mulled Apple Cider

There's a good reason why real estate agents love to brew up a pot of mulled cider at their open houses. It fills the house with the most appealing scent and tastes like home and autumn and everything cozy and warm. If you're looking to feel even warmer, add an ounce or two of rum or apple brandy to each serving. (See page 154 for a photograph of Mulled Apple Cider.)

NOTE: If you're serving a crowd, simply double the recipe.

EQUIPMENT: 4- to 5-quart Dutch oven or stock pot

MAKES: *8 cups* • TOTAL TIME: *30 minutes*

8 cups (½ gallon or 1.9 L) fresh apple cider

¼ cup (55 g) firmly packed light brown sugar

8 whole cloves

8 whole allspice berries

4 whole black peppercorns

4 slices fresh, peeled ginger, each about ⅛ inch thick

3 cinnamon sticks

½ orange, cut crosswise into ¼-inch-thick slices

Pour the cider into a pot and set over medium-high heat. Add the brown sugar and stir. Put the cloves, allspice, and peppercorns into a tea infuser, a tea bag, or a piece of cheesecloth tied up in a sack. Add to the cider, along with the ginger, cinnamon sticks, and orange slices. Bring to a boil, then reduce the heat to medium-low and simmer for 10 minutes. Remove the pot from the heat and steep for an additional 10 minutes. Remove the spice pack and cinnamon sticks (leave the oranges) and serve. You can set the pot over low heat and let it sit for 2 or so hours—a great option if you're hosting brunch or a party.

Jack Rose

Here's a cocktail with a literary pedigree: the blend of lime juice (sometimes lemon, but I prefer the former), grenadine, and applejack earned a mention in Ernest Hemingway's 1926 classic *The Sun Also Rises* (the narrator, Jake Barnes, drinks one in a Paris hotel bar). The exact origins of the drink are uncertain, but pre-Prohibition New York is the most likely candidate.

NOTES: If you can't find applejack, you can substitute Calvados (French apple brandy). Use the best grenadine you can find. I like Sonoma Syrup Co. and Stirrings brands.

EQUIPMENT: Cocktail shaker

MAKES: *1 drink* • TOTAL TIME: *5 minutes*

2 ounces Laird's Applejack (see page 284)

½ ounce grenadine (pomegranate syrup)

Juice of ½ lime

Combine the ingredients in a shaker and fill with ice. Shake vigorously for 10 seconds, then strain into a cocktail glass.

Coming-in-from-the-Cold Cocktail

On a cool and cloudy early October day in 2004, my husband and I were married under the apple trees at Arrows Restaurant in Ogunquit, Maine. Arrows is an extraordinary place, where owners Clark Frasier and Mark Gaier maintain a do-it-yourself ethos in everything from the gardens where they grow the bulk of their vegetables and flowers in season, to the house-made breads and charcuterie, to the apple cider they pressed on-site and served to our guests as they were arriving for the ceremony. To keep everyone warm, the cider was offered with a shot of brandy, which may be why no one seemed to mind too much when the skies opened up during the reception and pounded our tent with a biblical deluge. When the power went out, everyone assumed we'd arranged for a candlelit main course. At least, that's what they told us.

NOTE: You can double, triple, or quadruple this recipe as needed to serve a crowd.

EQUIPMENT: 1- to 2-quart saucepan

MAKES: *1 drink* • TOTAL TIME: *10 minutes*

5 ounces (148 ml) sweet apple cider
Cinnamon stick
Pinch of granulated sugar

2 ounces (60 ml) brandy (I like Germain-Robin Fine Alambic Brandy from California)

In a small saucepan over medium-high heat, warm the cider with the cinnamon stick and sugar until just barely steaming, about 8 minutes. Pour the cider into an 8-ounce Irish coffee–style glass and stir in the brandy. Serve warm.

CHAPTER ELEVEN

BEYOND BAKING: APPLE FESTIVALS, PRODUCTS, AND PAIRINGS

Pink Pearl

A Select List of American Apple Festivals

Each fall, hundreds of growers, regions, and booster organizations all over the country host apple festivals of varying stripes and sizes. Add to that a long list of spring apple blossom celebrations, and you have an apple bonanza (not to mention a major distribution channel for cider donuts and scented candles).

Most every festival is worth a visit, and there are far too many to list here (for a longer list, visit www.allaboutapples.com/festivals or www.pickyourown.org/applefestivals.php). The following are my favorites, organized by region. Please note that dates are approximate, and can change from year to year.

CENTRAL/MIDWEST

Charlevoix Apple Festival: It's hard to imagine a prettier spot for an apple festival than downtown Charlevoix on the shores of Lake Michigan, in the heart of Michigan's northwest apple country. This 3-day event features more than 30 varieties of apples, assorted local produce, crafts, and a petting zoo.

Early October, downtown Charlevoix, MI
charlevoix.org

Johnny Appleseed Festival: In the latter part of his life, John Chapman, a.k.a. Johnny Appleseed, roamed the lands around Fort Wayne, planting orchards and preaching the Gospel. This festival pays homage to America's first apple ambassador, turning the city over for two full days of historic reenactments, farmers' markets, live music, and a food court in which all the food is prepared according to nineteenth-century methods.

Third week of September, downtown Fort Wayne, IN
johnnyappleseedfest.com

NORTHEAST

Franklin Applefest: How's this for a draw: in addition to the usual sweet treats, crafts, and contests, there's an "Apple Ever After" contest in which one lucky couple wins an all-expenses-paid wedding ceremony and reception in the midst of the festival.

First weekend in October, downtown Franklin, PA
franklinapplefest.com

Franklin County Ciderdays: My personal favorite: a weekend-long celebration of New England apple culture, with orchard tours, a grand cider tasting, free fruit samples, cooking demos, cider-making workshops, an apple pancake breakfast, a harvest supper, and a class on cider and cheese pairing.

Early November, multiple locations in Franklin County, MA
ciderday.org

Goold Orchard Apple Festival: An apple festival that actually takes place in an orchard! This charming celebration features local produce *and* local wine (made from assorted fruit and traditional *vinifera* grapes), along with arts and crafts vendors.

Second weekend in October, Rte. 150, Shodack, NY
goold.com

Great Maine Apple Day: The Maine Organic Farmers and Growers Association sponsors this jam-packed, single-day festival, with rare and heirloom apple tastings, cider pressing, fruit tree pruning workshops, cooking demonstrations, and artisan products.

Late October, 294 Crosby Brook Road, Unity, ME
mofga.org

National Apple Harvest Festival: Come for the food: There are fried apples, apple fritters, apple syrup, and an entire patio devoted to apple pancakes.

First two weekends in October, South Mountain Fairgrounds, Route 234, near Arendtsville, PA
appleharvest.com

Queen's County Farm Museum Apple Festival: This is a charming, if modest festival, with apple samplings, cider-pressing demonstrations, hay rides, and the "nation's largest apple cobbler." And because it's held on New York City's (well, Queens's) largest tract of undisturbed farmland, this is one ag fest you can travel to by subway.

Early October, 73-50 Little Neck Pkwy, Floral Park, NY
queensfarm.org

SOUTHEAST

Casey County Apple Festival: Home of the "World's Largest Apple Pie." Or so they say. At "just" 10 feet in diameter, it's not actually the world's biggest pie, but it is made from scratch every year and given out free to the public on Saturday.

Late September, downtown Liberty, KY
caseycountyapplefestival.org

Vintage Virginia Apple Harvest Festival: At Abermarle Cider Works, just a few miles from Monticello, the festival features apple and artisan cheese tastings led by renowned heirloom apple expert Tom Burford, plus ample opportunity to sample local cider and wine.

Early November, Rural Ridge Farm, 2550 Rural Ridge Lane, North Garden, VA
vintagevirginiaapples.com

WEST

Gravenstein Apple Fair: An old-time country fair, California style. Chef demos, beekeeping and goat milking demos, caramel apple eating contests, live music, farm animals, and a wine and beer garden.

Mid-August, Ragle Ranch Park, Sebastopol, CA
gravensteinapplefair.com

Hood River County Heirloom Apple Celebration: The Hood River Fruit Loop is a 35-mile drive through the valley's orchards, and every October, these farms host a weekend of tours, tastings, apple-butter-making demonstrations, cider pressings, and a corn maze.

Late October, Hood River County, OR
hoodriverfruitloop.com

Malibu Pie Festival: It's not strictly an apple festival, but there are plenty of apple pies on offer at this surprisingly homespun event. And where else can you spot so many celebrities while digging into some deep dish?

Early October, 3835 Cross Creek Road, Malibu, CA, 310-457-7505

Washington State Apple Blossom Festival: It's only fitting that the country's biggest apple-producing region would host the country's biggest apple festival. This 11-day extravaganza takes over the city of Wenatchee each spring with two parades, a carnival, a three-day arts and crafts fair, a food fest, a car show, and live music.

Late April, downtown Wenatchee, WA
appleblossom.org

Where to Buy Fresh Apples by Mail

If you can't find heirloom and heritage apple varieties in your region, the following farms will ship directly to you.

ALYSON'S ORCHARD, WALPOLE, NH

Varieties: 26 in all, from Ginger Gold to Gala to Esopus Spitzenburg and Black Gilliflower. And manager Fran Imhoff says that any of the other 24 varieties they grow can be shipped via special order.

Price: $35 for 18 apples, plus shipping; $49 for 32 apples, plus shipping

Contact: 603-756-9800, *alysonsorchard.com*

DOUD'S ORCHARD, DENVER, IN

Varieties: This large, family-run orchard ships up to 75 different varieties. The Antique Apple Sampler box includes rarities like Moyer's Prize, Rhode Island Greening, and Winter Banana.

Price: Approximately $22 for 12 apples of one variety, plus shipping; $26 for 12 apples in sampler, plus shipping

Contact: 765-985-3937, *doudsorchard.com*

GRAY WOLF PLANTATION, NEW OXFORD, PA

Varieties: Gray Wolf specializes in varieties that were popular before the Civil War. Their "Vintage Varieties" gift box includes York, Smokehouse, Paradise, Summer Rambo, Northwestern Greening, and Jonathan.

Price: $19.50 for 12 apples, plus shipping

Contact: 717-624-7204, *graywolfplantation.com*

KIYOKAWA FAMILY ORCHARDS, PARKDALE, OR

Varieties: 73 apple varieties, from Sonata to Valstar, to the most exciting, Pink Pearl, a rose-fleshed variety that tastes like raspberries.

Price: $28 to $32 for 12 to 15 pounds of fruit, plus shipping

Contact: 541-352-7115, *mthoodfruit.com*

TREE-MENDUS FRUIT, EAU CLAIRE, MI

Varieties: Choose from nearly 200 varieties of apples, including the superlative Calville Blanc d'Hiver (see page 35).

Price: Heirloom apples start at $40 for 20 apples, plus shipping; standard apples are $25 for 20, plus shipping

Contact: 877-863-3276, *treemendus-fruit.com*

Favorite Apple Products, from Cider Donuts to Vinegar

While researching this book, I sampled an incredible number of apple food products around the country. The following emerged as favorites, each capturing the beauty of the fruit, or reflecting the local apple culture, or ingeniously preserving fresh fruit for long keeping, or simply presenting a delicious way to enjoy apples.

APLETS

Liberty Orchards: A Washington State apple country signature, aplets are little apple fruit jellies studded with walnuts. They were first invented in 1918 in Cashmere, Washington, by two Armenian-born fruit growers, Armen Tertsgian and Mark Balaban, who cleverly made use of their surplus fruit by adapting a traditional recipe for Turkish Delight. They cooked the fruit down with some sugar and gelatin, stirred in walnuts, let the mixture set, then cut the slabs into cubes and rolled them in sugar. If you don't like very sweet things, best avoid these. But they're a sentimental favorite of many Northwesterners—the kind of retro treat your grandmother always had on hand.
aplets.com

APPLE BALSAMIC VINEGAR

Philo Apple Farm Apple Balsamic Vinegar: This family-run farm in Anderson Valley, CA, not only grows exceptional apples (including my all-time favorite apple variety, the Pink Pearl), but turns the fruit into a line of wonderful products, most notably this vinegar, which combines aged cider vinegar and cider syrup. Use in place of regular balsamic in vinaigrettes and sauces, or drizzled over fruits and cheeses.
philoapplefarm.com

APPLE BUTTER, COMMERCIAL

Eden Organic Apple Butter: Among all the store-bought brands I've sampled, this simple spread has the freshest apple flavor, with just enough apple juice concentrate to balance the tartness. I especially like that it's organic, given how concentrated apple butter is, and that it's usually made with the skins left on and then strained out after cooking.
edenfoods.com

APPLE BUTTER, GOURMET

June Taylor Sierra Beauty and Ginger Apple Butter: The Sierra Beauty apple, grown mostly in Northern California, boasts a rich sweetness and warm spicy notes. Paired with fresh ginger, it really sings. If you haven't tried June's products before, you're in for a revelation. They taste like the most intense, fragrant distillation of the fruit, and they're organic, too.
junetaylorjams.com

APPLE CHIPS

Bare Fruit Granny Smith Apple Chips: Crunchy like a potato chip, but fat-free and made without added sugar—this is my idea of a miracle snack. Kids love them, too. Made in Washington, from organic apples.
barefruitsnacks.com

APPLE CIDER DONUTS

Atkins Farm: Praised by *Saveur* as some of the best donuts in the country, these moist little cakes from a now-famous Amherst, Massachusetts, orchard and farmstand have rich apple flavor that comes from a combination of house-made cider plus the farm's own apples. An optional dusting of cinnamon sugar adds crunch and sweet spice flavor—opt for it! I used to eat these gems regularly when I was a student at Smith College, and still try to get out there every fall to buy a bag or two. You can order them by mail, too, but fresh is always best.

atkinsfarm.com

APPLE COFFEE CAKE

Harvest Apple Cake, Jennifer's Kitchen: If you don't have time to make your own, this is a very good substitute. Made in Indiana by Jennifer Korb, a home baker turned entrepreneur, it's quite sweet and exceedingly moist, stuffed with apples, and topped with a generous crown of streusel.

cookingbyjennifer.com

APPLEJACK

Laird's Applejack Brandy: The first spirit-drinking colonists learned to produce potent liquors by leaving homemade hard cider outside in the winter and disposing of the frozen water on top. Using more sophisticated methods, the Laird family of New Jersey has been producing a similar spirit for twelve generations, since patriarch William Laird, a Scotsman by birth, first began distilling his own cider in 1698. Six decades later, President George Washington, an apple grower himself, wrote to secure a copy of the Laird recipe for his own home distilling. In deference to contemporary tastes, Laird's most popular brandy is now blended with neutral spirits and apple wine to give it a smoother taste. It's spunkier than Calvados and adds a terrific kick to cocktails like the Jack Rose on page 277.

lairdandcompany.com

APPLE JELLY

Cold Hollow Farm Apple Cider Jelly: Made simply from apple cider, boiled down until the apple pectin turns to jelly, this is the ultimate glaze for country ham. It's also great on scones, muffins, and toast.

coldhollow.com

APPLE MUSTARD

Ingrid Oswald Apple and Calvados Mustard: Given how well apples and mustard go together, it's no surprise

that this Calvados and apple-enriched mustard from Germany is so delicious. Try it on sausages or in a grilled Cheddar cheese with some thinly sliced tart apples (see recipe on page 107).

formaggiokitchen.com

APPLE PASTE

June Taylor Gravenstein Apple Paste: Thicker than apple butter, this sweet-tart organic apple paste from one of the country's most celebrated confectioners can be used much like quince paste (*membrillo*): baked into sweet empanadas; served with cheeses or pâtés; served alongside ham, pork, or duck dishes.

junetaylorjams.com

APPLESAUCE

Bauman's Cider Applesauce: Straight from Pennsylvania Dutch country comes this no-sugar-added blend, made in small batches by three generations of the Bauman family. Homemade may be best, but this is a great substitute if you're short on time.

baumanfamily.com

APPLE SORBET

Ciao Bella Green Apple Sorbet: If you're not inclined to make your own apple sorbet (see page 266), this bright, pleasingly tart blend is certainly the next best thing. It tastes just like a fresh Granny Smith right off the tree, only cold and somehow creamy (it's fat free and dairy free).

ciaobellagelato.com

APPLE SYRUP

Wood's Cider Mill Boiled Cider: Vermont might be maple syrup country, but Vermont-made Wood's boiled cider is my other favorite choice for drizzling over pancakes or yogurt. Made by evaporating sweet cider, it's thick, tart, and delicious, and keeps forever in the refrigerator. If you love to cook with apples, it's well worth going to the trouble of securing a bottle. I use it to give my cider donuts and apple cupcakes their rich fruity flavor.

woodscidermill.com or *kingarthurflour.com*

APPLE TEA

Elma Meyve Çayı: Apple tea is the national soft drink of Turkey, and this brand, flavored with blackberry leaves, hibiscus, lemon, and cinnamon, is a delight. It also makes a wonderful iced tea.
formaggiokitchen.com

APPLEWOOD BACON

Zingerman's Applewood Smoked Bacon: The late R. W. Apple of the *New York Times* called this "the Beluga of Bacon, the Rolls Royce of rashers," and I have to agree. Made by the Nueske family of Hillcrest, WI, it has slightly sweet, fruity notes from being smoked in applewood, and there's no better companion to the Dutch Baby recipe on page 159 or the Baked Apple French Toast on page 156.
zingermans.com

CIDER VINEGAR

Katz Gravenstein Apple Cider Vinegar: This vinegar, made in Napa, California, is barrel-aged long enough to develop rich vanilla flavors, but true to the apple variety it's made from, retains a hint of sweetness. The result is so mild that you could almost sip it straight up, but it still has enough acidity to brighten stews or work brilliantly in vinaigrettes.
katzandco.com

FROZEN APPLE PIE

Vermont Mystic Pie Company: The only frozen pie I know that you could bake up and pass off as your own. Vermont Mystic was founded by a Ben & Jerry's alum named Dave Barash and funded by Ben himself, and like the ice cream behemoth, the company has a mission to use Vermont ingredients in its products. Hence, you'll find local apples (Northern Spy, Empire, and Cortland), King Arthur flour, and Cabot butter in every pie—the same stuff I use at home. As a result, each bite is flaky, buttery, sweet-tart, and fresh.
vermontmysticpie.com

SPICED APPLES

Robert Lambert Spiced Crab Apples: I know many people have a soft spot for the beet-red apples that come in a can and taste primarily of sugar and cinnamon oil, but if you want to know spiced apples as they used to taste back when they were made with native crab apples, try these. Robert Lambert makes his preserves in Marin County, California, using a mix of apple juice, cider vinegar, sugar, and spices. The result is tart, but not vinegary, delicately spiced, and simply much more interesting than that red stuff. Serve it as an accompaniment to cheeses or meats.
robertlambert.com

Cider: Twenty Favorite Labels, with Tasting Notes

This is just a small sampling of the hundreds of ciders that are produced commercially all over the world, but I've tried to provide a range of styles and geographic areas, in the hope that you'll be inspired to explore cider drinking as a worthy pursuit, much in the way of tasting fine wine. The noble grape may sit at the top of the oenological pyramid, but apples can produces wines and ciders with tremendous complexity, variability, and plain deliciousness. And since ciders are generally made to be drunk fresh, there's no need to invest in a wine cellar and wait for them to age.

Another reason I love cider is that it's a fully local product in many regions where grapes simply don't thrive. I'd love to see a more vibrant New England or Michigan or British Columbia cider culture, complete with "cider trails" for tourists (who, incidentally, would be safer in their travels than their wine-drinking friends, since cider typically has 5 to 7 percent alcohol, as opposed to wine's average in the low teens). I've seen so many people express delighted surprise at their first taste of a good hard cider—why not host a tasting party of your own and help support the modern cider renaissance?

ÆPPELTREOW WINERY, BURLINGTON, WI

Appely Brut Sparkling Cider: This cider, fermented in the bottle according to the traditional Champagne method, is much drier than most of the others listed here, with sweet flowers and yeast in the nose. Tannins are more pronounced, but they're lightened by ripe pear flavors. All in all, an intriguing sipper, and a natural partner to sharp Cheddar cheeses, roast chicken, or Thanksgiving turkey.
aeppeltreow.com

ALMAR ORCHARDS, FLUSHING, MI

J.K.'s Scrumpy Hard Cider: This is one of my favorite ciders to serve with dessert or with a cheese course. It is tongue-coatingly sweet, with an apple blossom nose and lots of ripe nectarines in the mouth. Even better,

it's a true farmstead cider, which means it's made with juice from apples that are grown on-site, in this case by the Koan family, who have been in the apple business for four generations.
organicscrumpy.com

ERIC BORDELET, CHARCHIGNE, NORMANDY, FRANCE

Sydre Argelette: This cider strikes me as particularly French: lean and complex, with identifiable caramel and fruit flavors, but also hints of smoke, wood, toast, and a nearly medicinal quality that somehow manages to balance out the flavors and lend interest. This is a cider to contemplate, not to guzzle with picnic food. Instead, try it with with creamy soups or sauces or mild creamy cheeses.
http://bordelet.ifrance.com

DOMAINE CHRISTIAN DROUIN, COUDRAY-RABUT, NORMANDY, FRANCE

Cidre Pays d'Auge: This velvety cider from Domaine Drouin—a respected Calvados maker—has the most wonderful smokiness, which plays off the caramelized apple flavors in a way that makes me think of eating tarte tatin in front of a roaring fire. The blend of 70% bitter apples, 20% sweet, and 10% acidic fruit results in a brew that is rich and complex, and yet entirely accessible.
calvados-drouin.com

ÉTIENNE DUPONT, VICTOT-PONTFOL, NORMANDY, FRANCE

Cidre Bouché: The nose is all leather and minerals, but the flavor is surprisingly sweet and fruity, with fresh apple, some spice, and an overlay of peach. Tannins round up the finish without overriding the fruit. If you're new to cider drinking or hoping to convert a wine snob, start with this truly lovely example.
calvados-dupont.com

EDEN ICE CIDER COMPANY, WEST CHARLESTON, VT

Calville Blend Ice Cider: Much like ice wine made from grapes, ice cider (or apple icewine, as it's sometimes called) is made from juice that is concentrated by freezing. There are different ways to do this, but here the juice is extracted from the apples and then frozen, at which point some of the water separates out and is removed. The concentrated juice is then fermented and aged. This wine is so rich, you could really serve it for dessert, but it's never cloying, thanks to the perfectly balanced acidity. It's ambrosia in a glass.
edenicecider.com

FARNUM HILL CIDERS, LEBANON, NH

Semi-Dry Cider: Light and lovely, with lots of delicate bubbles, plenty of crisp, tart apple and subtle tannins, it has a long dried fruit finish. Lovers of sweet cider may find that this is a dry type that they can embrace, particularly chilled and served with cheeses, pork, and egg dishes.
povertylaneorchards.com

FOGGY RIDGE CIDER, DUGSPUR, VA

First Fruit: This mildly sweet cider from the Blue Ridge mountains is made from a blend of American heirlooms like Harrison, Graniwinkle, and Roxbury Russet, along with traditional English and French cider varieties. It's an easy drinker—lightly effervescent, with ripe apple, peach, and strawberry flavors.
foggyridgecider.com

FURNACE BROOK WINERY, RICHMOND, MA

French Cidre: Some aging time in French oak barrels gives this cider its deep wood and vanilla flavors, but there's also a wonderful tartness and a hit of lemon in the nose. This is a sweeter cider, and would hold up to a wide range of cheeses (try Comté) and fruit desserts.
furnacebrookwinery.com

HENNEY'S CIDER COMPANY, BISHOPS FROME, HEREFORDSHIRE, ENGLAND

Frome Valley Dry Cider: Smooth as silk, with abundant tropical fruit (mostly guava and mango) flavors that give the cider an almost-sweet finish, even though there is very little residual sugar. The nose is very subtle, with the slightest hint of tobacco. A nice backbone of tannins balances the fruitiness, and tiny bubbles lend a festive air.
henneys.co.uk

OLIVER WINERY, BLOOMINGTON, IN

Beanblossom Hard Cider: This semi-sweet, easy-drinking cider is made from a combination of antique apple varieties, such as Cox's Orange Pippin, and relative newcomers, like Goldrush. It's crisp and just barely carbonated, and has the nicest fresh apple aromas and flavors. It's another great starter cider for the newcomer, and I can't think of a nicer drink to have on a picnic.
oliverwinery.com

OLIVER'S CIDER & PERRY, OCLE PYCHARD, HEREFORDSHIRE, ENGLAND

Herefordshire Dry Cider: Herefordshire is an ancient apple-growing region, and the orchards at Oliver's boast such colorfully named varieties as Broxwood Foxwhelp, Slack ma Girdle, Chisel Jersey, and Hangy Down. The Dry Cider here is still (that is, no bubbles), and with its assertive tannins, green apple tartness, and dry finish, it's great example of a much leaner and earthier style of cider-making.

theolivers.org.uk

ORIGINAL SIN, NEW YORK, NY

Hard Cider: The *New York Times* gave this cider a rave back in 2003, and it's one of the better widely available American varieties. In appearance, it brings to mind a prosecco, with pale color and ample delicate bubbles. The nose is of green apple skins (fitting, as it's made entirely from domestic Granny Smith apples). The flavor is very ripe and round, with a bit of pear, forward tannins, and a buttery middle. It's great with salmon, butternut squash, popcorn, and nutty cheeses, such as Gruyère.

origsin.com

SEA CIDER FARM & CIDERHOUSE, VICTORIA, BC, CANADA

Rumrunner: Talk about noble origins: This extraordinary cult favorite is made from organic heirloom apples grown in an ocean-view orchard in northeast Victoria Island. Varieties like Winter Banana and Winesap are pressed and then aged in rum barrels (hence the name), which contribute incredible flavors of toffee and brown sugar and play off the tartness of the juice.

seacider.ca

SLYBORO CIDER HOUSE, GRANVILLE, NY

Hidden Star: A semi-dry cider made from Northern Spy and Liberty apples, this Hudson River Valley star boasts gentle bubbles, the slightest hint of sweetness, and clean tropical fruit flavors.

slyboro.com

SAMUEL SMITH OLD BREWERY, TADCASTER, NORTH YORKSHIRE, ENGLAND

Organic Cider: This is a simple and inexpensive cider (about $4 for a pint), and it presents a good value for a new cider drinker, with nice fresh apple and green grape flavors and enough acidity to stand up to the sweetness. There aren't any notable tannins to lend complexity, and the finish is short, but I like that it's made from organic apple juice and is light enough to be fully refreshing on a hot summer's day.

merchantduvin.com

WANDERING AENGUS CIDERWORKS, SALEM, OR

Semi-Dry Cider: The hint of sweetness in this semi-dry cider boosts the wonderful fruit flavors without dulling the complexity that the "serious" cider crowd demands. I taste green apple peel, citrus, pear, and even some ginger. Consider it a natural accompaniment for barbecue.

wanderingaengus.com

WARWICK VALLEY WINERY AND DISTILLERY, WARWICK, NY

Doc's Draft: The nose is a curious blend of lemon and petrol, and the flavor tends more toward the funky/"farmyard" end of the spectrum that I usually like. That's not a criticism, though. Farmyard flavors are common in cider. And there's a nice liveliness here, from the vigorous bubbles to the hint of sweetness, to the warm spice flavor that coats the middle of your tongue. It's made from local New York apples, and it simply tastes like fall. Try it with pork dishes, the Braised Brisket with Apples and Hard Cider on page 126, or spiced apple desserts.

wvwinery.com/cider

WEST COUNTY CIDER, COLRAIN, MA

Heritage Apple: Vibrant with acidity, spice, and abundant fizz and anchored by forward tannins and minerality, this cider blends Baldwin, Roxbury Russet, and various European cider apples for a nice balance of flavor and structure. I love the mix of native Massachusetts apples (the Baldwin and Roxbury) with proven Old World varieties. The late Terry Maloney, who founded West County with his wife, Judith, was a driving force in the American cider revival, and his family still produces beautiful ciders, many made from single apple varieties. This blend is my favorite, and it's terrific with a cup of traditional New England clam chowder.

westcountycider.com

WOODCHUCK DRAFT CIDER, MIDDLEBURY, VT

Hard Cider: Woodchuck's ciders are known for being accessible crowd-pleasers, sweeter than most, with simple ripe fruit flavors. In other words, they're the wine coolers of the cider world. Serious drinkers may turn their nose up at this, but I include this one because it's tasty and, in a world where cider is still trying to catch on, widely available. If you're looking for an easy pairing for barbecue and haven't tried cider before, this is a good entry point.

woodchuck.com

PAIRING CIDER AND CHEESE

Apples complement such a wide variety of cheeses, it's no surprise that cider should also pair well, too. In fact, I find that the average cider is better-suited to cheese than the average wine, for two reasons: Cider boasts more prominent yeast flavors, which tend to echo the nutty and tangy flavors in cheese. In addition, most widely available ciders are carbonated to some degree, and bubbles have a wonderful way of cutting through the butter in your Brie.

A few guidelines will help you get started:

1 Pair region with region. Ciders from Normandy tend to go beautifully with local soft-rind cheeses like Camembert and Pont l'Évêque. Somerset ciders are lovely with mild to medium-sharp Cheddars. The parallels aren't quite as clear in the U.S., where cider-making and cheese-making haven't evolved together over hundreds of years. But I've certainly enjoyed a buttery Vermont-made Tarantaise from Thistle Hill Farm with Summer Cider from nearby Farnum Hill. Likewise, Jasper Hill Farm in Greensboro, VT, makes a Bayley Hazen Blue that can dance a tango with local Eden Ice Cider.

2 Moo. Baa. Broadly considered, sheep and cow's milk cheeses tend to pair with cider better than goat's milk varieties. But very strong cheeses such as certain blues and very sharp Cheddar or Grana Padano will overwhelm many ciders. Proceed with caution, and ask your cheesemonger or cider-maker.

3 Think nuts, caramel, and fruit. If your cheese has a profile that fits any of those descriptions (think Manchego, Basque, Abbaye de Belloc, Tarantaise), it'll pair well with a wider variety of ciders.

4 Accessorize. Even if your pairing isn't perfect, adding classic cheese accompaniments like almonds, honey, quince paste, and fig cakes can create a flavor bridge between stronger cheeses and drier ciders.

5 When in doubt, go sweet. Even blue cheeses and the other difficult-to-pair types mentioned above may do just fine if your cider is sweet enough to smooth their rough edges. The floral notes in, say, Gorgonzola dolce, would bring out the best in an ice cider. A sweet and easy drinker with strong apple flavor, like J.K.'s Scrumpy, would be fine with a sharper Cheddar or an aged goat cheese that had lost some of its lemony tang.

BIBLIOGRAPHY

S. A. Beach. *The Apples of New York*, vol I and II. Albany, New York: State of New York Department of Agriculture, 1903.

Frank Browning. *Apples: The Story of the Fruit of Temptation*. New York: North Point Press, 1999.

Beth Hanson, ed. *The Best Apples to Buy and Grow*. New York: Brooklyn Botanic Garden, 1995.

Barrie E. Juniper and David J. Mabberly. *The Story of the Apple*. Portland, Oregon: Timber Press, 2006.

Joan Morgan and Alison Richards. *The New Book of Apples: The Definitive Guide to Over 2,000 Varieties*. London: Ebury Press, 2003.

Michael Pollan. *The Botany of Desire: A Plant's-Eye View of the World*. New York: Random House, 2001.

Annie Proulx and Lew Nichols. *Cider: Making, Using & Enjoying Sweet & Hard Cider*. North Adams, Massachusetts: Storey Publishing, 2003.

Mark Rosenstein. *In Praise of Apples: A Harvest of History, Horticulture & Recipes*. Asheville, North Carolina: Lark Books, 1996.

Roger Yepsen. *Apples*. New York: W. W. Norton & Company, 1994.

Pink Lady

INDEX

Page numbers in **boldface** type refer to recipes themselves; page numbers in *italic* type refer to photographs.

acorn squash
    Acorn Squash Stuffed with Kasha and Apple, **112–13**
    Squash Stuffed with Apples, Pancetta, and Walnuts, **114–15**
Adam and Eve story, 18–19
Adams, John, 221
Aerlie Red Fleshed apple. *See* Hidden Rose apple
Albany Horticultural Society, 46
Albemarle Pippin apple. *See* Newtown Pippin apple
Alexander apple, 226
almond paste
    Baked Apples with Frangipane Filling, **229–30**
almonds
    Apple, Date, and Almond Charoset, **273**
    Baked Apples with Frangipane Filling, **229–30**
Ambrosia apple, 30, 31, *31*
Aomori Experiment Station, 49
aplets, about and source for, 283
appetizers. *See* starters
Apple, Cheddar, and Caramelized Onion Pastry Puffs, **83**
Apple, Cucumber, Lime, and Mint Salsa, 26, 28, **274**
Apple, Date, and Almond Charoset, **273**
Apple, Pistachio, Persimmon, and Pomegranate Salad, *94*, **95**
Apple and Chestnut–Stuffed Pork Loin with Cider Sauce, 99, *144*, **145–47**, *146*
Apple and Mustard Grilled Cheese Sandwiches, *106*, **107–8**, 284
Apple-Apricot Kuchen, **171–72**
apple balsamic vinegar, about and source for, 283
apple brandy/applejack
    Applejack-Sage Gravy, 123, **125**
    Chicken Liver Pâté with Apple, *80*, **81–82**
    Cider-Braised Pork with Calvados and Prunes, **140–41**, 228
    Jack Rose, **277**, 284
    about and source for, 284
    Spiced Apple-Cranberry Compote, 57, 87, 235, **236**
Apple Bread Pudding with Salted Caramel Sauce, **233–34**
apple breeding programs
    Department of Agriculture and Food of western Australia, 52
    New York State Agricultural Experiment Station (NYSAES), 36, 37, 46, 48, 57, 74–77
    Ohio Agricultural Experiment Station, 49

    Purdue University Horticultural Research Farm, 41
    Rutgers University Horticultural Research Farm, 58
    Tohoku Research Station, 39
    University of Idaho Agricultural Experiment Station, 45
    University of Minnesota Horticultural Research Center, 44, 47, 58, 76–77
Apple Brownies, 40, **238**
apple butter
    Kentucky Apple Stack Cake—Traditional Version, 248, *250*, **251–52**
    Overnight Apple Butter, 251, **275**
    Pumpkin and Apple Custard, **111**
    about and source for, 283
apple chips
    Apple Chips with Spiced Yogurt Dip, **84**
    about and source for, 283
apple cider. *See* boiled cider; cider; cider, fresh; cider, hard
Apple Cider–Brined Turkey with Applejack-Sage Gravy, **123–24**
apple cider donuts
    about and source for, 283–84
    Vermont Apple Cider Donuts, 71, **153–55**, *154*
Apple Clafoutis, 53, **237**
apple coffee cake, 284
apple corer, 71
Apple Cranberry Scones, **167**
apple crisp
    Grandma's Apple Crisp, 14, **185–86**, 187, 189
    Oatmeal-Topped Apple Crisp, **187–88**, 197
Apple Dumplings with Cider-Rum Sauce, **231–32**
Apple Empanadas, **219–20**
apple festivals, 280–81
Apple Gingerbread Upside-Down Cake, **253–54**
Apple-Gingersnap Ice Cream, **264–65**
apple industry, globalization of, 22, 184
applejack. *See* apple brandy/applejack
Applejack-Sage Gravy, 123, **125**
apple jelly, about and source for, 284
apple mustard, about and source for, 284
Apple Pandowdy, **221–22**
apple paste, about and source for, 284
Apple-Pear Cobbler with Lemon-Cornmeal Biscuits, **212–13**

apple peeler, 71

apple peeler/corer, 71

Apple Pie with Crumb Topping, **197–98**

Apple Pumpkin Walnut Muffins, **173**

Apple Risotto (Risotto alle Melle), **104–5**

applesauce

    Applesauce-Pistachio Bundt Cake with Cider Glaze, **255–56**

    Classic Applesauce, *116*, *117*, **268**

    Lowfat Gingerbread Applesauce Cake, **257–58**

    Orange-Scented Spiced Applesauce, **269**

    about and source for, 284

Appleseed, Johnny (John Chapman), 20, 43, 280

apple size, weight, and yield, 69, 70

apple slicer, 71

apple sorbet, about and source for, 284

Apple-Studded Brown Butter Streusel Coffee Cake, *168*, **169–70**

Apple-Stuffed Biscuit Buns, **164–66**, *165*

apple syrup, about and source for, 284

apple tea, about and source for, 285

Apple Tea Cake with Lemon Glaze, **240–43**, *241*, *242*

apple varieties. *See* varieties of apple

applewood bacon, about and source for, 285

apricot jam

    Apple-Apricot Kuchen, **171–72**

apricots, dried

    Baked Apple Oatmeal Pudding, **163**

Arkansas Black apple, 30, 31, *31*, 196

arugula

    Apple, Pistachio, Persimmon, and Pomegranate Salad, *94*, **95**

    Duck Panzanella with Apples and Thyme, 51, **138–39**

Ashmead's Kernel apple, 30, 32, *32*, 224

Ashton Bitter apple, 150

Atkins Farm, 153, 283–84

Autumn "Coleslaw" with Dates, Apples, and Pecans, **93**

bacon

    Apple Cider–Brined Turkey with Applejack-Sage Gravy, **123–24**

    applewood, about and source for, 285

    Bacon-Wrapped Dates with Curried Apple Hash, 26, **78–79**

    Braised Brisket with Apples and Hard Cider, **126–27**

    Chestnut Soup with Bacon, **88**

    Spinach, Apple, Pickled Onion, and Bacon Salad with Cider Vinaigrette, **98**

    Squash Stuffed with Apples, Pancetta, and Walnuts, **114–15**

Bacon-Wrapped Dates with Curried Apple Hash, 26, **78–79**

Bailsford, Mary Anne, 35

Baked Apple French Toast with Hazelnut Crumb Topping, 36, **156–57**, 285

Baked Apple Oatmeal Pudding, **163**

baked apples

    Baked Apples with Frangipane Filling, **229–30**

    Cider-Baked Apples, **228**, 229

Baldwin, Loammi, 32

Baldwin apple, 30, 32, *32*, *63*

Ball, John, 32

Battilana, Jessica, 239

Beach, S. A., 36, 226

Bedfordshire Clanger, 129

beef

    Braised Brisket with Apples and Hard Cider, **126–27**

bell peppers

    Apple, Cucumber, Lime, and Mint Salsa, 26, 28, **274**

Ben Davis apple, 20

biscuit cutter, 71

Bittman, Mark, 114

Black Oxford apple, *23*, 30, 33, *33*, 225

Black Twig apple, 30, 33, *33*

Blaxton, William, 19

Blaxton's Yellow Sweeting apple, 19

Blue Pearmain apple, 20, 30, 34, *34*, 224

Blue Ribbon Deep-Dish Apple Pie, *192*, **193–96**, *195*

boiled cider

    about, 153, 259

    Spiced Apple Cupcakes with Cinnamon Cream Cheese Frosting, **259–60**, *261*

    Vermont Apple Cider Donuts, 71, **153–55**, *154*

Braeburn apple, *27*, 28, 30, 34, *34*, 183

Braeburn Orchard, 34

Braised Brisket with Apples and Hard Cider, **126–27**

Bramley, Matthew, 35

Bramley's Seedling apple, 30, 35, *35*

brandy

    apple. *See* apple brandy/applejack

    Coming-in-from-the-Cold Cocktail, **278**

bread. *See also* buns; cornbread; muffins; sandwiches; scones

    Apple and Chestnut–Stuffed Pork Loin with Cider Sauce, 99, *144*, **145–47**, *146*

    Apple Bread Pudding with Salted Caramel Sauce, **233–34**

    Baked Apple French Toast with Hazelnut Crumb Topping, 36, **156–57**, 285

    Duck Panzanella with Apples and Thyme, 51, **138–39**

    Holiday Apple-Raisin Challah, *178*, **179–80**

    Irish Soda Bread with Apples and Currants, **177**

    Rustic Apple Brown Betty, 42, **211**

    Sausage, Apple, and Cheddar Strata, **175–76**

    Squash and Apple Gratin, *100*, **101–2**

    Welsh Rarebit with Apples, **109–10**

bread pudding

    Apple Bread Pudding with Salted Caramel Sauce, **233–34**

    Sausage, Apple, and Cheddar Strata, **175–76**

breeding apples, 76. *See also* horticulture

breeding programs. *See* apple breeding programs

brined dishes

    Apple Cider–Brined Turkey with Applejack-Sage Gravy, **123–24**

    Cider-Brined Pork Chops with Mustard Pan Sauce, 99, **142–43**

brioche
    Baked Apple French Toast with Hazelnut Crumb Topping, 36, **156–57**, 285
British Columbia Experimental Station, 56
brix, 75
Brown, Susan, 24, 74–76, 77
brown betty
    Rustic Apple Brown Betty, 42, **211**
browning
    apples resistant to, 30
    preventing, 65
buckle
    Buttermilk Apple Buckle, **214–15**
buckwheat groats. *See* kasha
budding, 90
Buel, J., 46
Bunker, John, *23*, 224–27
buns
    Apple-Stuffed Biscuit Buns, **164–66**, *165*
butter, about, 70
buttermilk
    about, 70
    Apple Cranberry Scones, **167**
    Apple Gingerbread Upside-Down Cake, **253–54**
    Apple-Studded Brown Butter Streusel Coffee Cake, *168*, **169–70**
    Apple-Stuffed Biscuit Buns, **164–66**, *165*
    Apple Tea Cake with Lemon Glaze, **240–43**, *241*, *242*
    Buttermilk Apple Buckle, **214–15**
    Irish Soda Bread with Apples and Currants, **177**
    Kentucky Apple Stack Cake—Modern Version, **248–49**
    Kentucky Apple Stack Cake—Traditional Version, 248, *250*, **251–52**
    Oatmeal-Apple Pancakes, 39, **161–62**
    Southern-Style Cornbread, 132, **134**
    substitute for, 70
    Vermont Apple Cider Donuts, 71, **153–55**, *154*
Buttermilk Apple Buckle, **214–15**
butternut squash
    Cider-Glazed Root Vegetables, **99**, *144*, *146*
    Squash and Apple Gratin, *100*, **101–2**

cabbage. *See* red cabbage
cakes. *See also* coffee cake; cupcakes
    Apple-Apricot Kuchen, **171–72**
    Apple Brownies, 40, **238**
    Apple Gingerbread Upside-Down Cake, **253–54**
    Applesauce-Pistachio Bundt Cake with Cider Glaze, **255–56**
    Apple Tea Cake with Lemon Glaze, **240–43**, *241*, *242*
    Kentucky Apple Stack Cake—Modern Version, **248–49**
    Kentucky Apple Stack Cake—Traditional Version, 248, *250*, **251–52**
    Lowfat Gingerbread Applesauce Cake, **257–58**
    mixing, 68
    Simple Apple Nut Cake, **239**

Calvados. *See* apple brandy/applejack
Calville Blanc d'Hiver apple, *13*, 19, 30, 35, *35*, 152, 196
Cameo apple, 30, 36, *36*, 183
caramel apples
    Salted Caramel Apples with Cinnamon Graham Cracker Crumbs, **262–63**
Caramelized Apples, 233, 245, **247**
carrots
    Cider-Glazed Root Vegetables, **99**, *144*, *146*
    Morning Glory Muffins, 40, **174**
    Sweet Potato, Apple, and Ginger Soup, 26, **85–86**
cashews
    Acorn Squash Stuffed with Kasha and Apple, **112–13**
celery
    Chicken Waldorf Salad, **96–97**
challah
    Baked Apple French Toast with Hazelnut Crumb Topping, 36, **156–57**, 285
    Holiday Apple-Raisin Challah, *178*, **179–80**
Champagne apple, 120, 122
Chapman, John (Johnny Appleseed), 20, 43, 280
Cheddar cheese
    Acorn Squash Stuffed with Kasha and Apple, **112–13**
    Apple and Mustard Grilled Cheese Sandwiches, *106*, **107–8**, 284
    Apple, Cheddar, and Caramelized Onion Pastry Puffs, **83**
    Pork and Apple Pie with Cheddar-Sage Crust, *2*, 51, *128*, **129–31**, *130*
    Sausage, Apple, and Cheddar Strata, **175–76**
    Welsh Rarebit with Apples, **109–10**
cheese. *See also specific types of cheese*
    pairing with cider, 290
cherries, dried
    Baked Apples with Frangipane Filling, **229–30**
chestnuts
    Apple and Chestnut–Stuffed Pork Loin with Cider Sauce, 99, *144*, **145–47**, *146*
    Chestnut Soup with Bacon, **88**
    Chestnut Soup with Spiced Apple-Cranberry Compote, **87–88**, 236
Chicken Liver Pâté with Apple, *80*, **81–82**
Chicken Waldorf Salad, **96–97**
China, apple production of, 22, 184
Chisel Jersey apple, 150
cider
    about, 19, 20, 21, 286–89
    boiled. *See* boiled cider
    pairing with cheese, 290
    production of, 152
    sources for, 286–89
cider, fresh
    Apple and Chestnut–Stuffed Pork Loin with Cider Sauce, 99, *144*, **145–47**, *146*
    Apple, Cheddar, and Caramelized Onion Pastry Puffs, **83**

cider, fresh (*continued*)

Apple Cider–Brined Turkey with Applejack-Sage Gravy, **123–24**

Apple Dumplings with Cider-Rum Sauce, **231–32**

Apple Empanadas, **219–20**

Applesauce-Pistachio Bundt Cake with Cider Glaze, **255–56**

Baked Apples with Frangipane Filling, **229–30**

Caramelized Apples, 233, 245, **247**

Cider-Baked Apples, **228**, 229

Cider-Brined Pork Chops with Mustard Pan Sauce, 99, **142–43**

Cider-Glazed Root Vegetables, **99**, *144, 146*

Coming-in-from-the-Cold Cocktail, **278**

Kentucky Apple Stack Cake—Modern Version, **248–49**

Mulled Apple Cider, *154*, **276**

Overnight Apple Butter, 251, **275**

Pan-Seared Salmon with Cider-Glazed Onions, **148**

Sausage with Braised Cabbage and Apples, 36, **137**

Skillet Apple Pie, **199–200**

Sweet Potato, Apple, and Ginger Soup, 26, **85–86**

cider, hard

Acorn Squash Stuffed with Kasha and Apple, **112–13**

Apple Cider–Brined Turkey with Applejack-Sage Gravy, **123–24**

Braised Brisket with Apples and Hard Cider, **126–27**

Cider-Braised Pork with Calvados and Prunes, **140–41**, 228

Tennessee Cornbread Dressing with Sausage and Apple, 56, **132–33**

Cider-Baked Apples, **228**, 229

Cider-Braised Pork with Calvados and Prunes, **140–41**, 228

Cider-Brined Pork Chops with Mustard Pan Sauce, 99, **142–43**

cider donuts

about and source for, 283–84

Vermont Apple Cider Donuts, 71, **153–55**, *154*

Cider-Glazed Root Vegetables, **99**, *144, 146*

ciderjack, 19

cider vinegar, source for, 285

Cinnamon Rice Pudding with Spiced Apple-Cranberry Compote, **235**, 236

clafoutis

Apple Clafoutis, 53, **237**

Classic Applesauce, *116*, 117, **268**

coatings on apples, 61

cobbler

Apple-Pear Cobbler with Lemon-Cornmeal Biscuits, **212–13**

cocktails

Coming-in-from-the-Cold Cocktail, **278**

Jack Rose, **277**, 284

coconut

Morning Glory Muffins, 40, **174**

coffee cake, apple

about and source for, 284

Apple-Apricot Kuchen, **171–72**

Apple-Studded Brown Butter Streusel Coffee Cake, *168*, **169–70**

Cohen, Aaron, 189

Cohen, Kathy, 179

Cold Hollow Cider Mill, 153

coleslaw

Autumn "Coleslaw" with Dates, Apples, and Pecans, **93**

columnar apples, 76. *See also* horticulture

Coming-in-from-the-Cold Cocktail, **278**

compote

Spiced Apple-Cranberry Compote, 57, 87, 235, **236**

controlled atmosphere storage (CA), 61

cooking times, 68

coring apples, 64, *64*

cornbread

Southern-Style Cornbread, 132, **134**

Tennessee Cornbread Dressing with Sausage and Apple, 56, **132–33**

cornmeal

Apple-Pear Cobbler with Lemon-Cornmeal Biscuits, **212–13**

Southern-Style Cornbread, 132, **134**

Cortland apple, 28, 30, 36, *36*, *73*, 75

Costard apple, 19

Cox, Richard, 37

Cox's Orange Pippin apple, 30, 37, *37*, 184

cranberries

dried. *See* dried cranberries

Free-Form Apple-Pear-Cranberry Tart, **208–10**, *209*

cream

Apple Bread Pudding with Salted Caramel Sauce, **233–34**

Apple-Gingersnap Ice Cream, **264–65**

Salted Caramel Apples with Cinnamon Graham Cracker Crumbs, **262–63**

cream cheese

Spiced Apple Cupcakes with Cinnamon Cream Cheese Frosting, **259–60**, *261*

Crêpes Filled with Caramelized Apples and Served with Maple Crème Fraîche, 38, *244*, **245–46**, *247*

Cripps, John, 52

Cripps Pink apple. *See* Pink Lady apple

Crispin apple. *See* Mutsu apple

crust, pie. *See* pie crust

cucumbers

Apple, Cucumber, Lime, and Mint Salsa, 26, 28, **274**

Quick Bread-and-Butter Apple Pickles, *106*, **270–72**, *271*

cupcakes

Spiced Apple Cupcakes with Cinnamon Cream Cheese Frosting, **259–60**, *261*

currants

Irish Soda Bread with Apples and Currants, **177**

curry

Bacon-Wrapped Dates with Curried Apple Hash, 26, **78–79**

custard

Pumpkin and Apple Custard, **111**

dates

Acorn Squash Stuffed with Kasha and Apple, **112–13**

Apple, Date, and Almond Charoset, **273**

Autumn "Coleslaw" with Dates, Apples, and Pecans, **93**
Bacon-Wrapped Dates with Curried Apple Hash, 26, **78–79**
Deerfield Pie, 201
Department of Agriculture and Food of western Australia, 52
dicing apples, 65
dip
    Apple Chips with Spiced Yogurt Dip, **84**
Dixon, Fred, 120, 121–22
Dixon's Apple Farm, 120–22
donuts, cider
    about and source for, 283–84
    Vermont Apple Cider Donuts, 71, **153–55**, *154*
dormant wood grafting, 90–91
Double-Crust Apple Pie, **190–91**
dressing
    Tennessee Cornbread Dressing with Sausage and Apple, 56,
      132–33
dried apples
    Apple Cranberry Scones, **167**
    Apple Empanadas, **219–20**
    Kentucky Apple Stack Cake—Modern Version, **248–49**
dried apricots
    Baked Apple Oatmeal Pudding, **163**
dried cherries
    Baked Apples with Frangipane Filling, **229–30**
dried cranberries
    Acorn Squash Stuffed with Kasha and Apple, **112–13**
    Apple Cranberry Scones, **167**
    Baked Apple Oatmeal Pudding, **163**
    Cider-Baked Apples, **228**, 229
    Spiced Apple-Cranberry Compote, 57, 87, 235, **236**
Duchess of Oldenburg apple, 184
Duck Panzanella with Apples and Thyme, 51, **138–39**
dumplings
    Apple Dumplings with Cider-Rum Sauce, **231–32**
Dutch Baby, 38, *158*, **159–61**, *160*, 285

eggs
    Apple Bread Pudding with Salted Caramel Sauce, **233–34**
    Apple Clafoutis, 53, **237**
    Baked Apple French Toast with Hazelnut Crumb Topping, 36, **156–57**,
      285
    Baked Apple Oatmeal Pudding, **163**
    Cinnamon Rice Pudding with Spiced Apple-Cranberry Compote, **235**,
      236
    Dutch Baby, 38, *158*, **159–61**, *160*, 285
    Holiday Apple-Raisin Challah, *178*, **179–80**
    Pumpkin and Apple Custard, **111**
    Sausage, Apple, and Cheddar Strata, **175–76**
    Spiced Apple Cupcakes with Cinnamon Cream Cheese Frosting,
      259–60, *261*
    Sweet Potato–Apple Latkes, *116*, **117–18**

Tennessee Cornbread Dressing with Sausage and Apple, 56, **132–33**
egg yolks
    Apple-Gingersnap Ice Cream, **264–65**
empanadas
    Apple Empanadas, **219–20**
Empire apple, 30, 37, *37*, 75
Endive Salad with Apples, Walnuts, and Gorgonzola, **92**
equipment, 71–72
Esopus Spitzenburg apple, 30, 38, *38*
Etter, Albert, 52
evaporated milk
    Pumpkin and Apple Custard, **111**

Fameuse apple, 30, 38, *38*, 224
Fedco Trees, 224
festivals, apple, 280–81
Field, Michael, 81
firm-sweet apples, 26, 28, 30, 196
    Baldwin, 30, 32, *32*, 63
    Black Oxford, *23*, 30, 33, *33*, 225
    Blue Pearmain, 20, 30, 34, *34*, 224
    Braeburn, *27*, 28, 30, 34, *34*, 183
    Cameo, 30, 36, *36*, 183
    Ginger Gold, 28, 30, 40, *40*, 267
    Golden Delicious, 28, 30, 40, *40*, 183, 184, 225
    Golden Russet, 30, 41, *41*
    Gravenstein, 30, 42, *42*, 62, 196
    Grimes Golden, 20, 30, 43, *43*
    Honeycrisp, 30, 44, *44*, 62, 183
    Jazz, 22, 25, 29, 30, 45, *45*, 184
    Jonagold, 30, 46, *46*, 75, 183, 196
    Keepsake, 30, 47, *47*, 223
    Melrose, 30, 49, *49*, 149
    Mutsu, 30, 49, *49*
    Opalescent, 30, 51, *51*
    Piñata, 30, 51, *51*, 184
    Pink Lady, 22, 28, 29, 30, 52, *52*, 183, 184, *292*
    Reine des Reinette, 30, 53, *53*
    Spigold, 30, 57, *57*
    SweeTango, 25, 30, 58, *58*
    Winter Banana, 15, 30, 59, *59*
    Zabergau Reinette, 30, 60, *60*, *89*
firm-tart apples, 26, 28, 30, 196
    Arkansas Black, 30, 31, *31*, 196
    Ashmead's Kernel, 30, 32, *32*, 224
    Bramley's Seedling, 30, 35, *35*
    Calville Blanc d'Hiver, *13*, 19, 30, 35, *35*, 152, 196
    Esopus Spitzenburg, 30, 38, *38*
    Goldrush, 30, 41, *41*
    Granny Smith, 28, 30, 42, *42*, 68, 183
    Hidden Rose, 30, 43, *43*, 119
    Idared, 30, 45, *45*, 68

firm-tart apples (*continued*)

    Newtown Pippin, 15, 30, 50, *50*, 68, 196

    Northern Spy, 15, 28, 30, 50, *50*, 68, 196

    Pink Pearl, 30, 52, *52*, 279

    Rhode Island Greening, 28, 30, 54, *54*, 68, 196

    Ribston Pippin, 30, 54, *54*

    Rome, 30, 55, *55*

    Roxbury Russet, 15, 19, 28, 30, 55, *55*, 196

    Sierra Beauty, 30, 56, *56*, 196, 283

    Stayman Winesap, 30, 57, *57*, 196

    Suncrisp, 30, 58, *58*

fish

    Pan-Seared Salmon with Cider-Glazed Onions, **148**

flavor of apples

    storage and, 61

    terroir and, 62

Flory, David, 59

flour, about, 70

food mill, 72

food processor, making pie crust in, 67

Foxwhelp apple, 150

Franklin, Benjamin, 50

Frasier, Clark, 278

Free-Form Apple-Pear-Cranberry Tart, **208–10**, *209*

French toast

    Baked Apple French Toast with Hazelnut Crumb Topping, 36, **156–57**, 285

freshness of apples, 61

frozen apple pie, about and source for, 285

frozen desserts. *See* ice cream; sorbet

Fuji apple, 28, 30, 39, *39*, 183, 184

Gaier, Mark, 278

Gala apple, 25, 28, 30, 39, *39*, 183, 184

genetic engineering, 25, 75. *See also* horticulture

genetics of apples, 24–25. *See also* horticulture

Gilson, Will, 78

ginger

    Apple Cider–Brined Turkey with Applejack-Sage Gravy, **123–24**

    Mulled Apple Cider, *154*, **276**

    Sweet Potato, Apple, and Ginger Soup, 26, **85–86**

Ginger Gold apple, 28, 30, 40, *40*, 267

gingersnaps

    Apple-Gingersnap Ice Cream, **264–65**

goat cheese

    Bacon-Wrapped Dates with Curried Apple Hash, 26, **78–79**

Golden Delicious apple, 28, 30, 40, *40*, 183, 184, 225

Golden Russet apple, 30, 41, *41*

Goldrush apple, 30, 41, *41*

Goodricke, Henry, 54

Gorgonzola cheese

    Squash Stuffed with Apples, Pancetta, and Walnuts, **114–15**

Gorgonzola dolce

    about, 92

    Endive Salad with Apples, Walnuts, and Gorgonzola, **92**

Gouda cheese

    Apple and Mustard Grilled Cheese Sandwiches, *106*, **107–8**, 284

grafting. *See* horticulture

graham crackers

    Salted Caramel Apples with Cinnamon Graham Cracker Crumbs, **262–63**

Grandma's Apple Crisp, 14, **185–86**, 187, 189

Granny Smith apple, 28, 30, 42, *42*, 68, 183

grapes

    Chicken Waldorf Salad, **96–97**

gratin

    Squash and Apple Gratin, *100*, **101–2**

Gravenstein Apple-Raspberry Tart, 28, 42, 43, 52, **205–7**, *206*

Gravenstein apple, 30, 42, *42*, 62, 196

gravy

    Applejack-Sage Gravy, 123, **125**

Green Apple Sauvignon Blanc Sorbet, **266**, 284

grenadine syrup

    Jack Rose, **277**, 284

Grimes, Thomas, 43

Grimes Golden apple, 20, 30, 43, *43*

Gruyère cheese

    Acorn Squash Stuffed with Kasha and Apple, **112–13**

    Apple and Mustard Grilled Cheese Sandwiches, *106*, **107–8**, 284

    Squash and Apple Gratin, *100*, **101–2**

Haedrich, Ken, 205

half-and-half

    Apple Bread Pudding with Salted Caramel Sauce, **233–34**

hard cider. *See* cider, hard

Harvey, Frances "Ginger" and Clyde, 40

Hasbrouck, Jonathan, 46

Havarti cheese

    Apple and Mustard Grilled Cheese Sandwiches, *106*, **107–8**, 284

hazelnuts

    Baked Apple French Toast with Hazelnut Crumb Topping, 36, **156–57**, 285

heirloom apples, 76, 150–52, 224

Hemingway, Ernest, 277

Hensley, Tim, 21

Hidden Rose apple, 30, 43, *43*, 119

history of the apple, 17–22

Holiday Apple-Raisin Challah, *178*, **179–80**

honey

    Apple, Cucumber, Lime, and Mint Salsa, 26, 28, **274**

    Apple, Pistachio, Persimmon, and Pomegranate Salad, *94*, **95**

    Apple Chips with Spiced Yogurt Dip, **84**

    Autumn "Coleslaw" with Dates, Apples, and Pecans, **93**

    Chicken Waldorf Salad, **96–97**

Endive Salad with Apples, Walnuts, and Gorgonzola, **92**
Holiday Apple-Raisin Challah, *178*, **179–80**
Spinach, Apple, Pickled Onion, and Bacon Salad with Cider Vinaigrette, **98**
Quick Bread-and-Butter Apple Pickles, *106*, **270–72**, *271*
Honeycrisp apple, 30, 44, *44*, 62, 183
hors d'oeuvres. *See* starters
horticulture
  breeding apples, 76
  columnar apples, 76
  genetic engineering, 25, 75
  genetics of apples, 24–25
  grafting, 18, 20, 25, 74–75, 90–91
  hybridization of apples, 17–18, 20–21, 24–25
  terroir, 62
Hough, Fred, 58
Howlett, Freeman, 49
Hubbell, Sue, 24
Hudson's Golden Gem apple, 30, 44, *44*
Hudson Wholesale Nurseries, 44
hybridization of apples. *See* horticulture

ice cream
  Apple-Gingersnap Ice Cream, **264–65**
Idared apple, 30, 45, *45*, 68
ingredients. *See also specific ingredients*
  about, 69–70
  measuring, 65–66
Irish Soda Bread with Apples and Currants, **177**

Jack Rose, **277**, 284
Jackson, Andrew, 33
jalapeños
  Apple, Cucumber, Lime, and Mint Salsa, 26, 28, **274**
  Braised Brisket with Apples and Hard Cider, **126–27**
Jazz apple, 22, 25, 29, 30, 45, *45*, 184
Jefferson, Thomas, 38
Johnny Appleseed (John Chapman), 20, 43, 280
Jonagold apple, 30, 46, *46*, 75, 183, 196
Jonamac apple, 75
Jonathan apple, 30, 46, *46*

kasha
  Acorn Squash Stuffed with Kasha and Apple, **112–13**
Keepsake apple, 30, 47, *47*, *223*
Kentucky Apple Stack Cake—Modern Version, **248–49**
Kentucky Apple Stack Cake—Traditional Version, 248, *250*, **251–52**
Kidd, J. H., 39
Kimzey, Louis, 43
King David apple, 20
King of the Pippins apple. *See* Reine des Reinette apple
Kingston Black apple, 150

kosher salt, about, 70

Lady Apple apple, 30, 47, *47*
large apples, size, weight, and yield of, 69, 70
latkes
  Sweet Potato–Apple Latkes, *116*, **117–18**
lemon
  Apple-Pear Cobbler with Lemon-Cornmeal Biscuits, **212–13**
  Apple Tea Cake with Lemon Glaze, **240–43**, *241*, *242*
lime juice
  Apple, Cucumber, Lime, and Mint Salsa, 26, 28, **274**
  Jack Rose, **277**, 284
live wood grafting, 90
Lowfat Gingerbread Applesauce Cake, **257–58**

Macoun, W. T., 48
Macoun apple, 28, 30, 48, *48*, 75
Maiden Blush apple, 20
Mammoth Blacktwig apple. *See* Black Twig apple
mandoline slicer, 72
maple syrup
  Apple Pandowdy, **221–22**
  Crêpes Filled with Caramelized Apples and Served with Maple Crème Fraîche, 38, *244*, **245–46**, 247
  Caramelized Apples, 233, 245, **247**
  Rustic Apple Brown Betty, 42, **211**
Marlboro apple, 226–27
Marlborough Pie, 41, **201–2**
matzo meal
  Sweet Potato–Apple Latkes, *116*, **117–18**
May, Robert, 201
McDonald's, 76
McIntosh, Alan, 48
McIntosh, John, 48
McIntosh apple, 28, 30, 48, *48*, 76
McKinstry, Pam, 174
McNary and Gaines Company, 51
measuring ingredients, 65–66
Medaille d'Or apple, 150
medium apples, size, weight, and yield of, 69, 70
melon baller, 72
Melrose apple, 30, 49, *49*, *149*
Mennell, Wilfried and Sally, 31
Michigan Hard Cider Club, 152
microplane, 72
milk. *See also* evaporated milk; sweetened condensed milk
  Apple Clafoutis, 53, **237**
  Apple-Gingersnap Ice Cream, **264–65**
  Baked Apple French Toast with Hazelnut Crumb Topping, 36, **156–57**, 285
  Baked Apple Oatmeal Pudding, **163**
  Cinnamon Rice Pudding with Spiced Apple-Cranberry Compote, **235**, 236

milk (*continued*)

    Crêpes Filled with Caramelized Apples and Served with Maple Crème Fraîche, 38, *244*, **245–46**, 247

    Dutch Baby, 38, *158*, **159–61**, *160*, 285

    Salted Caramel Apples with Cinnamon Graham Cracker Crumbs, **262–63**

    Sausage, Apple, and Cheddar Strata, **175–76**

mint

    Apple, Cucumber, Lime, and Mint Salsa, 26, 28, **274**

mixing cakes, 68

molasses

    Apple Gingerbread Upside-Down Cake, **253–54**

    Lowfat Gingerbread Applesauce Cake, **257–58**

Moran, O., 34

Morning Glory Muffins, 40, **174**

muffins

    Apple Pumpkin Walnut Muffins, **173**

    Morning Glory Muffins, 40, **174**

Mullane, Becky and Jim, 120–21

Mulled Apple Cider, *154*, **276**

Mullins, Andrew, 40

Mullins' Yellow Seedling apple. *See* Golden Delicious apple

mushrooms

    Acorn Squash Stuffed with Kasha and Apple, **112–13**

mustard

    apple, about and source for, 284

    Apple and Mustard Grilled Cheese Sandwiches, *106*, **107–8**, 284

    Cider-Brined Pork Chops with Mustard Pan Sauce, 99, **142–43**

Mutsu apple, 30, 49, *49*

natural wax coating, 61

Newell, Lucky and Audrey, 43

Newtown Pippin apple, 15, 30, 50, *50*, 68, 196

New York State Agricultural Experiment Station (NYSAES), 36, 37, 46, 48, 57, 74–77

non-browning apples, 30

Northern Spy apple, 15, 28, 30, 50, *50*, 68, 196

Northwest Cider Society, 152

nuts. *See specific types of nut*

oats

    Baked Apple Oatmeal Pudding, **163**

    Oatmeal-Apple Pancakes, 39, **161–62**

    Oatmeal-Topped Apple Crisp, **187–88**, 197

Ohio Agricultural Experiment Station, 49

oldtimecider.com, 152

onions. *See also* red onions

    Apple, Cheddar, and Caramelized Onion Pastry Puffs, **83**

    Braised Brisket with Apples and Hard Cider, **126–27**

    Sausage, Apple, and Cheddar Strata, **175–76**

Opalescent apple, 30, 51, *51*

oranges

Mulled Apple Cider, *154*, **276**

    Orange-Scented Spiced Applesauce, **269**

Out on a Limb, 224

Overnight Apple Butter, 251, **275**

pancakes

    Dutch Baby, 38, *158*, **159–61**, *160*, 285

    Oatmeal-Apple Pancakes, 39, **161–62**

    Sweet Potato–Apple Latkes, *116*, **117–18**

pancetta

    Squash Stuffed with Apples, Pancetta, and Walnuts, **114–15**

pandowdy

    Apple Pandowdy, **221–22**

Pan-Seared Salmon with Cider-Glazed Onions, **148**

Parmesan cheese

    Apple Risotto (Risotto alle Melle), **104–5**

parsnips

    Cider-Glazed Root Vegetables, **99**, *144*, *146*

    Parsnip-Apple Puree, **103**

pastry puffs

    Apple, Cheddar, and Caramelized Onion Pastry Puffs, **83**

pastry rolls

    Williamsburg Wrapples, *216*, **217–18**

Pearmain apple, 19

pears

    Apple-Pear Cobbler with Lemon-Cornmeal Biscuits, **212–13**

    Free-Form Apple-Pear-Cranberry Tart, **208–10**, *209*

pecans

    Apple Pie with Crumb Topping, **197–98**

    Autumn "Coleslaw" with Dates, Apples, and Pecans, **93**

    Baked Apple Oatmeal Pudding, **163**

    Buttermilk Apple Buckle, **214–15**

    Cider-Baked Apples, **228**, 229

    Oatmeal-Topped Apple Crisp, **187–88**, 197

    Tennessee Cornbread Dressing with Sausage and Apple, 56, **132–33**

peeling apples, 64, *64*

Pepperl, Roger, 183, 184

persimmons

    Apple, Pistachio, Persimmon, and Pomegranate Salad, *94*, **95**

pickles

    Quick Bread-and-Butter Apple Pickles, *106*, **270–72**, *271*

pie

    Apple Pie with Crumb Topping, **197–98**

    best apples for, 196

    Blue Ribbon Deep-Dish Apple Pie, *192*, **193–96**, *195*

    Deerfield Pie, 201

    Double-Crust Apple Pie, **190–91**

    frozen, about and source for, 285

    Marlborough Pie, 41, **201–2**

    Pork and Apple Pie with Cheddar-Sage Crust, *2*, 51, *128*, **129–31**, *130*

    Skillet Apple Pie, **199–200**

Swedish Apple Pie, 38, **189**

pie crust

making by hand, 66–67

making in food processor, 67

rolling out, 67

pie crust bag, 67

Piñata apple, 30, 51, *51*, 184

pineapple

Morning Glory Muffins, 40, **174**

Pink Lady apple, 22, 28, 29, 30, 52, *52*, 183, 184, *292*

Pink Pearl apple, 30, 52, *52*, *279*

Pinova apple. *See* Piñata apple

Pippin apple, 19

pistachios

Apple, Pistachio, Persimmon, and Pomegranate Salad, *94*, **95**

Applesauce-Pistachio Bundt Cake with Cider Glaze, **255–56**

pomegranate seeds

Apple, Pistachio, Persimmon, and Pomegranate Salad, *94*, **95**

Pomme d'Api, 19. *See also* Lady Apple apple

Pomme Gris (Pomme Grise) apple, 30, 53, *53*

pork. *See also* bacon; pancetta; sausage

Apple and Chestnut–Stuffed Pork Loin with Cider Sauce, 99, *144*, **145–47**, *146*

Cider-Braised Pork with Calvados and Prunes, **140–41**, 228

Cider-Brined Pork Chops with Mustard Pan Sauce, 99, **142–43**

Pork and Apple Pie with Cheddar-Sage Crust, *2*, 51, *128*, **129–31**, *130*

potato pancakes

Sweet Potato–Apple Latkes, *116*, **117–18**

poultry. *See specific types of poultry*

Poverty Lane Orchards, 35, 150–52

Preservation Orchards, 224–27

protective coatings, 61

prunes

Cider-Braised Pork with Calvados and Prunes, **140–41**, 228

pudding. *See also* bread pudding

Baked Apple Oatmeal Pudding, **163**

Cinnamon Rice Pudding with Spiced Apple-Cranberry Compote, **235**, 236

puff pastry

Apple, Cheddar, and Caramelized Onion Pastry Puffs, **83**

Tarte Tatin, **203–4**

pumpkin

Apple Pumpkin Walnut Muffins, **173**

Pumpkin and Apple Custard, **111**

Purdue University Horticultural Research Farm, 41

puree

Parsnip-Apple Puree, **103**

Quagliaroli, Mary, 185

quercetin, 75

Quick Bread-and-Butter Apple Pickles, *106*, **270–72**, *271*

raisins

Baked Apple Oatmeal Pudding, **163**

Holiday Apple-Raisin Challah, *178*, **179–80**

raspberries

Gravenstein Apple-Raspberry Tart, 28, 42, 43, 52, **205–7**, *206*

Red Apple Farm, 90–91

red cabbage

Autumn "Coleslaw" with Dates, Apples, and Pecans, **93**

Sausage with Braised Cabbage and Apples, 36, **137**

Red Delicious apple, 29, 183–84, 225

red grapes

Chicken Waldorf Salad, **96–97**

red onions

Pan-Seared Salmon with Cider-Glazed Onions, **148**

Sausage and Red Onion Sandwich, **135–36**

Sausage with Braised Cabbage and Apples, 36, **137**

Spinach, Apple, Pickled Onion, and Bacon Salad with Cider Vinaigrette, **98**

red wine

Apple, Date, and Almond Charoset, **273**

Reine des Reinette apple, 30, 53, *53*

relish

Apple, Date, and Almond Charoset, **273**

Quick Bread-and-Butter Apple Pickles, *106*, **270–72**, *271*

Rennet apple, 19

Rhode Island Greening apple, 28, 30, 54, *54*, 68, 196

Ribston Pippin apple, 30, 54, *54*

rice

Apple Risotto (Risotto alle Melle), **104–5**

Cinnamon Rice Pudding with Spiced Apple-Cranberry Compote, **235**, 236

Rick, Phillip, 46

Reinette apple, 19

risotto

Apple Risotto (Risotto alle Melle), **104–5**

rolling out pie crust, 67

Rome apple, 30, 55, *55*

Rome Beauty apple. *See* Rome apple

root vegetables

Cider-Glazed Root Vegetables, 99, *144*, *146*

Rose, Al, 90, 91

Roxbury Russet apple, 15, 19, 28, 30, 55, *55*, 196

rum

Apple Dumplings with Cider-Rum Sauce, **231–32**

Rustic Apple Brown Betty, 42, **211**

Rutgers University Horticultural Research Farm, 58

salads

Apple, Pistachio, Persimmon, and Pomegranate Salad, *94*, **95**

apple varieties for, 30

Autumn "Coleslaw" with Dates, Apples, and Pecans, **93**

Chicken Waldorf Salad, **96–97**

salads (*continued*)

Duck Panzanella with Apples and Thyme, 51, **138–39**

Endive Salad with Apples, Walnuts, and Gorgonzola, **92**

Spinach, Apple, Pickled Onion, and Bacon Salad with Cider Vinaigrette, **98**

salmon

Pan-Seared Salmon with Cider-Glazed Onions, **148**

salsa

Apple, Cucumber, Lime, and Mint Salsa, 26, 28, **274**

salt, about, 70

Salted Caramel Apples with Cinnamon Graham Cracker Crumbs, **262–63**

sandwiches

Apple and Mustard Grilled Cheese Sandwiches, *106*, **107–8**, 284

Sausage and Red Onion Sandwich, **135–36**

sausage

Sausage and Red Onion Sandwich, **135–36**

Sausage, Apple, and Cheddar Strata, **175–76**

Sausage with Braised Cabbage and Apples, 36, **137**

Tennessee Cornbread Dressing with Sausage and Apple, 56, **132–33**

savory pie

Pork and Apple Pie with Cheddar-Sage Crust, *2*, 51, *128*, **129–31**, *130*

scones

Apple Cranberry Scones, **167**

Scott Farm, 60

Seek-No-Further apple. *See* Westfield Seek-No-Further apple

Seneca Remick farm, 226

shallots

Cider-Braised Pork with Calvados and Prunes, **140–41**, 228

Sweet Potato–Apple Latkes, *116*, **117–18**

shellac coating, 61

shiny versus cloudy apples, 61

Sierra Beauty apple, 30, 56, *56*, 196, 283

Simple Apple Nut Cake, **239**

Simpson, Aemilius, 21

sizes of apples, 69–70

Skillet Apple Pie, **199–200**

slicing apples, 65

small apples, size, weight, and yield of, 69, 70

SmartFresh technology (1-methylcyclopropene), 61

Smith, John, 19

Snow Apple apple. *See* Fameuse apple

Somerset Redstreak apple, 150

Sonata apple. *See* Piñata apple

sorbet, apple

about and source for, 284

Green Apple Sauvignon Blanc Sorbet, **266**, 284

soups

Chestnut Soup with Bacon, **88**

Chestnut Soup with Spiced Apple-Cranberry Compote, **87–88**, 236

Sweet Potato, Apple, and Ginger Soup, 26, **85–86**

sources

for apples, 282

for apple cider, 286–89

for apple products, 283–85

Southern-Style Cornbread, 132, **134**

Sparkling Burgundy apple, 120, 122

species of apples, 17

Spencer apple, 30, 56, *56*, *181*

Spiced Apple-Cranberry Compote, 57, 87, 235, **236**

Spiced Apple Cupcakes with Cinnamon Cream Cheese Frosting, **259–60**, *261*

spiced apples, about and source for, 285

Spigold apple, 30, 57, *57*

spinach

Sausage and Red Onion Sandwich, **135–36**

Spinach, Apple, Pickled Onion, and Bacon Salad with Cider Vinaigrette, **98**

Spitzenburg apple, 25

squash. *See* acorn squash; butternut squash

Squash and Apple Gratin, 100, **101–2**

Squash Stuffed with Apples, Pancetta, and Walnuts, **114–15**

Stark Bro's Nurseries, 40

starters

Apple, Cheddar, and Caramelized Onion Pastry Puffs, 83

Apple Chips with Spiced Yogurt Dip, 84

Bacon-Wrapped Dates with Curried Apple Hash, 26, **78–79**

Chicken Liver Pâté with Apple, *80*, **81–82**

Stayman, J., 57

Stayman apple. *See* Stayman Winesap apple

Stayman Winesap apple, 30, 57, *57*, 196

Stemilt Growers, 51, 183, 184

storing apples, 15, 68

controlled atmosphere storage (CA) for, 61

SmartFresh technology (1-methylcyclopropene) for, 61

stout

Welsh Rarebit with Apples, **109–10**

strata

Sausage, Apple, and Cheddar Strata, **175–76**

sugar concentration, 75

Suncrisp apple, 30, 58, *58*

Super Chilly Farm, 224

Sussman, Adeena, 135, 171

Swedish Apple Pie, 38, **189**

SweeTango apple, 25, 30, 58, *58*

sweetened condensed milk

Salted Caramel Apples with Cinnamon Graham Cracker Crumbs, **262–63**

sweet pie

Apple Pie with Crumb Topping, **197–98**

Blue Ribbon Deep-Dish Apple Pie, *192*, **193–96**, *195*

Deerfield Pie, 201

Double-Crust Apple Pie, **190–91**

Marlborough Pie, 41, **201–2**

Skillet Apple Pie, **199–200**

Swedish Apple Pie, 38, **189**
Sweet Potato, Apple, and Ginger Soup, 26, **85–86**
Sweet Potato–Apple Latkes, *116*, **117–18**

table salt, about, 70
tarts
    Free-Form Apple-Pear-Cranberry Tart, **208–10**, *209*
    Gravenstein Apple-Raspberry Tart, 28, 42, 43, 52, **205–7**, *206*
    Tarte Tatin, **203–4**
Temperance Movement and cider, 21
tender-sweet apples, 26, 28, 30
    Ambrosia, 30, 31, *31*
    Cox's Orange Pippin, 30, 37, *37*, 184
    Fameuse, 30, 38, *38*, 224
    Fuji, 28, 30, 39, *39*, 183, 184
    Gala, 25, 28, 30, 39, *39*, 183, 184
    Hudson's Golden Gem, 30, 44, *44*
    Pomme Gris, 30, 53, *53*
    Spencer, 30, 56, *56*, *181*
tender-tart apples, 26, 28, 30
    Black Twig, 30, 33, *33*
    Cortland, 28, 30, 36, *36*, *73*, 75
    Empire, 30, 37, *37*, 75
    Jonathan, 30, 46, *46*
    Lady Apple, 30, 47, *47*
    Macoun, 28, 30, 48, *48*, 75
    McIntosh, 28, 30, 48, *48*, 76
    Westfield Seek-No-Further, 30, 59, *59*
Tennessee Cornbread Dressing with Sausage and Apple, 56, **132–33**
terroir, 62. *See also* horticulture
Thomas, Anna, 161
Thoreau, Henry David, 21
Tohoku Research Station, 39
Tolman Sweet apple, 226
Toole, Rankin, 33
tools, 71–72
Tropic Sweet apple, 14
Tschirsky, Oscar, 96
turkey
    Apple Cider–Brined Turkey with Applejack-Sage Gravy, **123–24**

University of Idaho Agricultural Experiment Station, 45
University of Minnesota Horticultural Research Center, 44, 47, 58, 76–77

Valentine farm, 33
van der Goes, Hugo, 19
varieties of apple, 27–60. *See also* firm-sweet apples; firm-tart apples;
    tender-sweet apples; tender-tart apples; *specific varieties of apple*
    cheat sheet, 30
    finding, 69

firm-sweet, 26, 28, 30, 196
firm-tart, 26, 28, 30, 196
heirloom, 76, 150–52, 224
in-depth guide, 31–60
substituting, 69
tender-sweet, 26, 28, 30
tender-tart, 26, 28, 30
Vermont Apple Cider Donuts, 71, **153–55**, *154*
vinaigrette
    for Endive Salad with Apples, Walnuts, and Gorgonzola, **92**
    for Spinach, Apple, Pickled Onion, and Bacon Salad with Cider
        Vinaigrette, **98**
Vintage Virginia Apples, 60
volume measurement, 65–66

walnuts
    Apple Brownies, 40, **238**
    Apple Pumpkin Walnut Muffins, **173**
    Chicken Waldorf Salad, **96–97**
    Endive Salad with Apples, Walnuts, and Gorgonzola, **92**
    Morning Glory Muffins, 40, **174**
    Rustic Apple Brown Betty, 42, **211**
    Simple Apple Nut Cake, **239**
    Squash Stuffed with Apples, Pancetta, and Walnuts, **114–15**
    Tennessee Cornbread Dressing with Sausage and Apple, 56, **132–33**
Washington Apple Commission, 182, 184
Washington state apples, 22, 182–84
Watson, Ben, 62
wax coatings, 61
weight measurement, 66
weight of apples, 69, 70
Welsh Rarebit with Apples, **109–10**
Westfield Seek-No-Further apple, 30, 59, *59*
white wine
    Apple Risotto (Risotto alle Melle), **104–5**
    Green Apple Sauvignon Blanc Sorbet, **266**, 284
Wickson apple, 224
Williamsburg Wrapples, *216*, **217–18**
wine. *See* red wine; white wine
Winter Banana apple, 15, 30, 59, *59*
Wood, Stephen, 150, 151–52
Woodpecker apple. *See* Baldwin apple
Wood's Cider Mill, 153

yogurt
    Apple Chips with Spiced Yogurt Dip, **84**
    Chicken Waldorf Salad, **96–97**
Young, James Webb, 122

Zabergau Reinette apple, 30, 60, *60*, *89*

A NOTE ABOUT THE AUTHOR

Amy Traverso grew up picking apples and eating apple crisp in northern Connecticut. A graduate of Smith College, Amy has lived in California, New Mexico, and around New England, and wherever she has gone, she has been a student of the local apple culture. Formerly a food editor at *Boston* and *Sunset* magazines, she is now a senior food and home editor at *Yankee* magazine. She lives in Brookline, Massachusetts, with her husband, Scott, and son, Max. Her favorite apples are Calville Blanc d'Hiver and Pink Pearl.